T0338291

Hedge Fund Modelling and Analysis

Hedge Fund Modelling and Analysis

An Object Oriented Approach Using C++

PAUL DARBYSHIRE
DAVID HAMPTON

WILEY

Library of Congress Cataloging-in-Publication Data is available

A catalogue record for this book is available from the British Library.

ISBN 978-1-118-87957-3 (hbk) ISBN 978-1-118-87955-9 (ebk)
ISBN 978-1-118-87956-6 (ebk) ISBN 978-1-118-87954-2 (ebk)

Cover Design: Wiley
Cover Images: Top Image: ©iStock.com/agsandrew
            Bottom Image: ©iStock.com/Storman

Set in 11/13pt Times by Aptara Inc., New Delhi, India
Printed in Great Britain by TJ International Ltd, Padstow, Cornwall, UK

Mum and Dad,

Whose love and support encourages me to achieve success.
– P.D.

For Marie-Christine, Juliette and Antoine.
– D.H.

Contents

Preface

This book is a practical introduction to modelling and analysing hedge funds using the C++ programming language. The structure of the book is as follows. Chapter 1 gives an overview of the C++ syntax in enough detail to approach the material covered in the technical chapters. Chapter 1 also introduces the concept of object oriented programming which allow us to build large and complex programs that can be broken down into smaller self-contained reusable code units known as classes. We will develop a series of classes throughout the book to tackle many of the problems encountered. Please note that this book is not intended to be an exhaustive exploration of C++ to solve problems in modelling and analysing hedge fund data. In addition, C++ is used to facilitate the solution of such problems through object oriented programming methods and various details highlighted as and when necessary.

Chapters 2 and 3 give an update of the current state of the global hedge fund industry and a detailed look at the primary data sources available to hedge fund managers and analysts. With this fundamental knowledge in place, Chapters 4–7 cover the more quantitative and theoretical material needed to effectively analyse a series of hedge fund returns and extract the relevant information required in order to make critical investment decisions.

C++ SOURCE CODE

Throughout the book there are numerous C++ source boxes (e.g., Source 2.4) typically listing the `AClass.h`, `AClass.cpp`, and `main.cpp` files and a console window showing the results of the class implementation. For example, an extract from the `Optimise` class is shown in Source P.1.

SOURCE P.1: A SAMPLE C++ SOURCE CODE

```
// Optimise.h
#pragma once;
```

```cpp
#include "Matrix.h"
#include "Stats.h"

class Optimise: public Stats
{
   public:
    Optimise() {}
    virtual ~Optimise() {}

    // Member function declarations
    Matrix PRet(const V2DD& v); // PRet()
    Matrix PVar(const V2DD& v); // PVar()
   private:
    // Member variable declarations
    Matrix m_matrix; // An instance of the Matrix class
};

// Optimise.cpp
#include "Optimise.h"

Matrix Optimise::PRet(const V2DD& v)
{
UINT n = v[0].size()-1;

   // Declare wT and R matrices
Matrix wT = Matrix(1, n);
Matrix R = Matrix(n, 1);

// Transpose weights
for (UINT i=1; i<=n; i++)
   wT(1, i) = 1 / (DBL)n; // Equal weights

// Mean returns
V1DD r = Mean(v, 12);

// R matrix
   for (UINT i=1; i<=n; i++)
   R(i, 1) = r[i-1];

   return wT * R;
}

Matrix Optimise::PVar(const V2DD& v)
{
```

```
UINT n = v[0].size()-1;

// Declare w, wT and VCV matrices
Matrix w = Matrix(n, 1);
Matrix wT = Matrix(1, n);
Matrix VCV = Matrix(n, n);

   // Initialise portfolio weights
for (int i=1; i<=n; i++)
   w(i, 1) = 1 / (DBL)n; // Equal weights

// Transpose weights
   for (int i=1; i<=n; i++)
   wT(1, i) = 1 / (DBL)n; // Equal weights

// Covariance matrix
V1DD cov = Cov(v);

// VCV matrix
int k = 0; // Covariance offset
for (UINT i=1; i<=n; i++)
{
  for (UINT j=1; j<=n; j++)
  {
     VCV(i, j) = cov[j+k-1];
      if(i == j)
         VCV(i, j) *= 12; // Annualise variance
  }
  k+=10;
}

return wT * VCV * w;
}

// ...
// main.cpp
// ...

// Create class instances
Import thfs;
Optimise optimise;

// Declare and call GetData()
V2DD data = thfs.GetData("./data/10_hedge_funds.dat");
```

```
// Declare and call PRet() and PVar() member function
Matrix pret = optimise.PRet(data);
Matrix pvar = optimise.PVar(data);

// Output results
cout << "\n Port. Ret. (%) = ";
pret.Print();
cout << " Port. Var. (%) = ";
pvar.Print();

// ...
```

```
Console Output                                    _  □  ×

File:./data/10_hedge_funds.dat
Imported 720 values successfully!

Port. Ret. (%) = 8.552
Port. Var. (%) = 10.725
```

Comment blocks, such as:

```
// ...
// main.cpp
// ...
```

are used to omit parts of the source code (above and below) when new code is added to existing definitions or implementations. As we progress through the book we will gradually reduce unnecessary overuse of comments (//) within source listings once we feel confident we have clearly defined such routines and concepts in previous listings.

Please note that we do not give any warranty for completeness, nor do we guarantee that the code is error free. Any damage or loss incurred in the application of the C++ source code, algorithms and classes discussed in the book are entirely the

TABLE P.1 10 Hypothetical Hedge Funds

Hedge Fund	Abbreviation
Commodity Trading Advisor	CTA1, CTA2, CTA3
Long Short Equity	LS1, LS2, LS3
Global Macro	GM1, GM2
Market Neutral	MN1, MN2

reader's responsibility. If you notice any errors in the C++ source code, algorithms or classes, or you wish to submit some new method as a C++ function, algorithm, class, model or some improvement of the method illustrated in the book, you are very welcome.

HYPOTHETICAL HEDGE FUND DATA

Throughout the book there is constant reference to many monthly hedge fund return series. The 10 hedge funds are all *hypothetical* and have been simulated by the authors as a unique data set for demonstration purposes only. The techniques and models used in the book can therefore be tested on the hypothetical data before being applied to real-life situations by the reader. The hypothetical data is nonetheless close to what would be expected in reality. The 10 funds are a mixture of several major hedge fund strategies i.e. *Commodity Trading Advisor* (CTA), *Long/Short Equity* (LS), *Global Macro* (GM) and *Market Neutral* (MN) strategies as described in Table P.1.

All data files used throughout the book are identified in italics e.g. *10_hedge_funds.dat*.

BOOK WEBSITE

The official website for the book is located at: www.darbyshirehampton.com

The website provides free downloads to all of the hypothetical data, C++ programs and classes, as well as many other useful resources.

The authors can be contacted on any matter relating to the book, or in a professional capacity, at the following email addresses:

Paul Darbyshire: pd@darbyshirehampton.com
David Hampton: dh@darbyshirehampton.com

CHAPTER 1

Essential C++

T his chapter covers the fundamental requirements necessary to allow the reader to get up and running building quantitative models using the C++ programming language. This introduction is in no way intended to be an in-depth treatment of the C++ programming language but more an overview of the basics required to build your own efficient and adaptable programs. Once the key concepts have been developed, object-oriented principles are introduced and many of the advantages of building quantitative systems using such programming approaches are outlined. It is assumed that the reader will have some prerequisite knowledge of a low-level programming language and the necessary computation skills to effectively grasp and apply the material presented here.

1.1 A BRIEF HISTORY OF C AND C++

C is a *procedural*[1] programming language developed at Bell Laboratories between 1969 and 1973 for the UNIX operating system. Early versions of C were known as K&R C after the publication of the book *The C Programming Language* written by Brian Kernighan and Dennis Ritchie in 1978. However, as the language developed and became more standardised, a version known as ANSI[2] C became more prominent. Although C is no longer the choice of many developers, there is still a huge amount of *legacy* software coded in it that is actively maintained. Indeed, C has greatly influenced other programming languages, in particular C++ which began purely as an extension of C.

---

[1] *Procedural* programming is a form of *imperative programming* in which a program is built from one or more procedures i.e. subroutines or functions.

[2] Founded in 1918, the *American National Standards Institute* (ANSI) is a private, non-profit membership organisation that facilitates the development of *American National Standards* (ANS) by accrediting the procedures of the *Standards Developing Organizations* (SDOs). These groups work cooperatively to develop voluntary national consensus standards.

Often described as a *superset* of the C language, C++ uses an entirely different set of programming concepts designed around the *Object-Oriented Programming* (OOP) paradigm. Solving a computer problem with OOP involves the design of so-called *classes* that are abstractions of physical objects containing the state, members, capabilities and methods of the object. C++ was initially developed by Bjarne Stroustrup in 1979 whilst at Bell Laboratories as an enhancement to C; originally known as C with Classes. The language was renamed C++ in the early 80s and by 1998, C++ was standardised as ANSI/ISO[3] C++. During this time several new features were added to the language, including virtual functions, operator overloading, multiple inheritance and exception handling. The ANSI/ISO standard is based on two main components: the *core language* and the *C++ Standard Library* that incorporates the C Standard Library with a number of modifications optimised for use with the C++ language. The C++ Standard Library also includes most of the *Standard Template Library* (STL); a set of tools, such as *containers* and *iterators* that provide array-like functionality, as well as *algorithms* designed specifically for sorting and searching tasks. C++11 is the most recent *complete* overhaul of the C++ programming language approved by ANSI/ISO on 12 August 2011, replacing C++03, and superseded by C++14 on 18 August 2014. The naming convention follows the tradition of naming language versions by the year of the specification's publication, although it was formerly known as C++0x to take into account many publication delays. C++14 is the informal name for the most recent revision of the C++ ANSI/ISO standard, intended to be a small extension over C++11, featuring mainly bug fixes and small syntax improvements.

1.2 A BASIC C++ PROGRAM

Without doubt the best method of learning a programming language is to actually start by writing and analysing programs. Source 1.1 implements a basic C++ program that simply outputs a string of text, once the program has been compiled and executed, to the console window. Although the program looks very simple it nevertheless contains many of the fundamental components that every C++ program generally requires.

SOURCE 1.1: A BASIC C++ PROGRAM

```
// main.cpp
 #include <windows.h>
 #include <iostream>
```

---

[3] The *International Organisation for Standardisation* (ISO) is an international standard-setting body made up of representatives from a range of *National Standards Organisations* (NSOs).

```
using std::cout;
using std::cin;

int main()
{
    SetConsoleTitle(L"Console Output"); // Set title of console
    window

    cout << "\n " << "Hedge Fund Modelling and Analysis: An Object
    Oriented Approach Using C++";

    cin.get(); // Pause console window
    return 0; // Return null integer and exit
}
```

Console Output	— □ ×

Hedge Fund Modelling and Analysis: An Object Oriented Approach Using C++

Statements beginning with a hash symbol (#) indicate *directives* to the *preprocessor* that initialise when the compiler is first invoked, in this case, to inform the compiler that certain functions from the C++ Standard Library must be included. #include <windows.h> gives the program access to certain functions in the library, such as SetConsoleTitle() whilst #include <iostream> enables console input and output (I/O). Typical objects in the iostream library include cin and cout which are explicitly included through the using statement at the top of the program. Writing using std::cout at the top of the program avoids the need to keep retyping std through the *scope resolution operator* (::) every time cout is used. For example, if we had not specified using std::cout we would have to explicitly write std in front of each usage throughout the program, that is:

```
std::cout << "\n " << "Hedge Fund Modelling and Analysis: An Object
Oriented Approach Using C++";
std::cin.get();
```

Although in this case there are only two occasions where we need `std`, you can imagine how this could quickly clog up code for very large programs. Note also that all C++ statements must end with a semi-colon (;).

A commonly identified problem with the C language is the issue of running out of names for definitions and functions when programs reach very large sizes eventually resulting in name clashes. Standard C++ has a mechanism to prevent such a clash through the use of the `namespace` keyword. Each set of C++ definitions in a library or program is *wrapped* into a namespace, and if some other definition has an identical name, but is in a different namespace, then there is *no* conflict. All Standard C++ libraries are wrapped in a single namespace called `std` and invoked with the `using` keyword:

```
using namespace std;
```

Whether to use `using namespace std` or explicitly state their use through `using std::cout`, for example, is purely a preference of programming style. The main reason we do not invoke `using namespace std` in our programs is that this leaves us the opportunity of defining our own namespaces if we wish and it is generally good practice to have only one namespace invocation in each program.

The `main()` function is the point at which all C++ programs start their execution even if there are several other functions declared in the same program. For this reason, it is an essential requirement that all C++ programs have a `main()` function within the body at some point in the program. Once the text is output to the console window, `cin.get()` is used to cause the program to pause so that the user can read the output and then close and exit the window by pressing any key. Technically, in C or C++ the `main()` function must return a value because it is declared as `int` i.e. the main function should return an integer data type. The `int` value that `main()` returns is usually the value that will be passed back to the operating system; in this case it is 0 i.e. `return 0` which indicates that the program ran successfully. It is not necessary to state `return 0` explicitly, because the compiler invokes this automatically when `main()` terminates, but it is good practice to include a return type for all functions (including `main()`).

1.3 VARIABLES

A variable is a name associated with a portion of memory used to *store* and *manipulate* the data associated with that variable. The compiler sets aside a specific amount of memory space to store the data *assigned* to the variable and associates the variable name with that memory *address*. As the name implies, variables can be changed within a program as and when required. When new data is assigned to the same variable, the old data is *overwritten* and restored in the same memory address. The data stored in a

TABLE 1.1   Reserved C++ keywords

```
asm, auto, bool, break, case, catch, char, class, const,
const_cast, continue, default, delete, do, double,
dynamic_cast, else, enum, explicit, export, extern, false,
float, for, friend, goto, if, inline, int, long, mutable,
namespace, new, operator, private, protected, public,
register, reinterpret_cast, return, short, signed, sizeof,
static, static_cast, struct, switch, template, this,
throw, true, try, typedef, typeid, typename, union,
unsigned, using, virtual, void, volatile, wchar_t, while
```

variable is only *temporary* and only exists as long as the variable itself exists (defined by the *scope* of the variable). If the data stored in a variable is required beyond its existence then it must be written to a *permanent* storage device, such as a disk or file.

A variable name can be any length and composed of lower and upper case letters, numbers and the underscore (_) character, but keep in mind that variables are *case-sensitive*. In practice, a programmer will usually develop their own variable naming convention but bear in mind that C++ reserves certain keywords for variable names so try not to clash with these. Table 1.1 shows a list of reserved C++ keywords.

There are sevenal built-in *data types* provided by C++ along with specific *type modifiers* to further quantify the data. A complete list of all the data types and their associated modifiers are described in Table 1.2.

In Table 1.2, other than `char` (which has a size of exactly one byte), none of the fundamental types has a standard size (only a minimum size, at most). This does not mean that these types are of an undetermined size, but that there is no *standard size* across all compilers and machines; each compiler implementation can specify the sizes that best fit the architecture where the program is going to be executing. This rather generic size specification of data types allows the C++ language a lot of flexibility in adapting to work optimally on all kinds of platforms, both present and future.

1.3.1   Characters and Strings

When using the `char` data type, we use single quotes, for example:

```
char Stock = 'MSFT';
```

Certain characters, such as single (' ') and double (" ") quotes have special meaning in C++ and have to be treated with care. In addition, C++ reserves special characters for formatting text and other processing tasks known as *character escape sequences* (or *backslash character constants*) as shown in Table 1.3.

A more versatile data type than `char` is `string` which can be a combination of characters, numbers, spaces and symbols of any length. C++ does not have a built-in data type to hold `strings` instead it is defined in the C++ Standard Library through the inclusion of the header file `<string>`. An example of using `string` variables is shown in Source 1.2.

TABLE 1.2   Common C++ data types

Name	Description	Size (Bytes)	Range
char		1	-128 to 127
unsigned char	Character	1	0 to 255 (ASCII characters)
signed char		1	-128 to 127 (ASCII characters)
int		4	-2,147,483,648 to 2,147,483,647
unsigned int		4	0 to 4,294,967,295
signed int		4	-2,147,483,648 to 2,147,483,647
short int	Integer number	2	-32,768 to 32,767
unsigned short int		2	0 to 65,535
signed short int		2	-32,768 to 32,767
long int		4	Same as `int`
unsigned long int		4	Same as `unsigned int`
signed long int		4	Same as `signed int`
float	Floating point number	4	3.4E-38 to 3.4E+38
double	Double precision	8	1.7E-308 to 1.7E+308
long double	floating point number	10	3.4E-4932 to 1.1E+4932
bool	Boolean value	1	True or False
string	As required		Any length
wchar_t	Wide character	2	0 to 65,535

TABLE 1.3   Character escape sequences

Sequence	Output
\n	New line
\t	Tab
\b	Back space
\?	Question mark
\f	Page feed
\a	Alert (beep)
\\	Backslash
\'	Single quote
\"	Double quote

SOURCE 1.2: STRING VARIABLES

```cpp
// main.cpp
#include <windows.h>
#include <iostream>
#include <string>
using std::cout;
using std::cin;
using std::string;

int main()
{
   SetConsoleTitle(L"Console Output"); // Set title of console
   window

   //declare two string variables
   string strFirstName = "Paul";
   string strLastName = "Darbyshire";

   //concatenate the two strings
   string strFullName = strFirstName + " " + strLastName;

   cout << "\n " << strFullName;

   cin.get(); // Pause console window
   return 0; // Return null integer and exit
}
```

In Source 1.2, two `string` variables are declared and initialised and then joined together to form another string. The (+) symbol is used for joining (or *concatenating*) two variables together, and in this context the (+) symbol is often referred to as the *concatenation operator*.

1.3.2 Variable Declarations

Before a variable can be used in a program it must first be *declared* as shown in Source 1.3. Declaring the variable and its data type allows the compiler to set aside the appropriate amount of memory for storage and subsequent manipulation.

SOURCE 1.3:   DECLARING VARIABLES

```
// ...

// Declare variables
int x, y;
int result;
// Assign values
x = 4;
y = 2;
x = x + 1;
//Do something
result = x - y;

cout << "\n " << result << "\n ";

// ...
```

Console Output

```
3
```

It is possible to declare more than one variable of the *same* type in the same declaration statement. It is also possible to assign initial values to variables whilst they are being declared through the process of *initialisation*, for example:

```
int x, y = 4, z = 3;
```

There is another useful method of initialising a variable known as *constructor initialisation*:

```
int x(0);
```

1.3.3 Type Casting

One way to force an expression to produce a result that is of a different type to the variables declared in the expression is to use a construct called `cast` (i.e. *type casting*). Source 1.4 shows an example of declaring two variables as `int` and dividing them to produce an `int` and `double` division through type casting.

SOURCE 1.4:   TYPE CASTING

```
// ...

int a = 6, b = 4;

cout << "\n " << a/b << "\n"; // Integer division
cout << " " << (double)a/b << "\n "; // Type casting to double
division

// ...
```

Note that type casting will not change the type of the variables from integer only the type of the result to double.

1.3.4 Variable Scope

A variable can have either *global* (i.e. *public*) or *local* (i.e. *private*) scope depending on where it is declared within the program. Any variables declared with global scope should be prefixed with the keyword `const`. An example is shown in Source 1.5.

SOURCE 1.5: VARIABLE SCOPE

```
// ...

// GLOBAL variable
int globalN = 144;

int main()
{
    SetConsoleTitle(L"Console Output"); // Set title of console
    window

    // LOCAL variable
    int localN = 72;

    cout << "\n " << "# of data points (LOCAL) = " << localN;
    cout << "\n " << "# of data points (GLOBAL) = " << globalN;

    cin.get(); // Pause console window
    return 0; // Return null integer and exit
}
```

```
# of data points (LOCAL) = 72
# of data points (GLOBAL) = 144
```

In Source 1.5, you can see that the variable `globalN` has been declared globally and initialised to the value `144`. Global variables can be accessed from anywhere in the program once they have been declared. Local variables, on the other hand, such as `localN` can only be used within the block enclosed by the braces (`{}`) in which it is declared.

1.3.5 Constants

Constants are fixed values assigned to variables that cannot be changed once they have been declared and initialised. We have already used *literal constants* when a variable was declared and initialised in Source 1.2:

```
string FirstName = "Paul";
```

Or, as in Source 1.5:

```
int localN = 72;
```

With *symbolic constants* the `const` keyword is used in front of the declaration and initialisation, for example:

```
const double Volatility = 0.18;
```

Enumerated constants are an alternative way of creating a series of integer constants. Suppose you wanted to assign an integer value of 0 to 6 to the days of the week starting at Sunday. This could be achieved using a list of symbolic constants written as:

```
const int Sun = 0;
const int Mon = 1;
const int Tue = 2; etc.
```

However, with enumeration it is possible to write:

```
enum WeekDays
{
  Sun,
  Mon,
  Tue,
  Wed,
  Thu,
  Fri,
  Sat
};
```

If each week day is not explicitly initialised, they are *automatically* assigned the values 0, 1, 2, 3, etc., starting with the variable Sun. Note that the default value starts at 0 and not 1. Alternatively, it is possible to initialise one or more of the variables to any integer value, for example:

```
enum WeekDays
{
 Sun = 10,
 Mon,
 Tue,
 Wed = 6,
 Thu,
 Fri,
 Sat
};
```

Variables that are not explicitly initialised are given initial values count-ing upwards from the preceding initialised variable i.e. Sun = 10, Mon = 11, Tue = 6, Wed = 7, Thu = 8 and so on.

1.4 OPERATORS

Operators are used to perform a specific operation on a set of operands in an expression. Operators can be of two types:

Unary – take only one argument and

Binary – take two arguments.

1.4.1 The Assignment Operator

The *assignment operator* simply assigns a value to a variable, for example:

```
x = 4;
```

The statement above assigns to the variable x the value 4. Note that the assignment operator always reads from *right -> left*, and never the other way around. The following statement is valid in C++:

```
x = y = z = 3;
```

In this statement, the value 3 is assigned to all three variables x, y and z. Expressions that are evaluated within the assignment operator, such as:

```
x = x + 1;
```

are read as '*add the value* 1 *to* x *and assign this value to* x' i.e. increase the value of x by 1. Indeed, this statement can also be written in a more compact form using *compound assignment operators*, written as:

```
x += 1;
```

In this statement, as before, x is simply *incremented* by 1 and the value assigned to x. Alternatively, if x is *decremented* by 1 we can write:

```
x -= 1;
```

The *increase* (++) and *decrease* (--) operators can also be used to get the same result as above, that is:

```
x++; and x--;
```

An interesting characteristic of the increase and decrease operators is that they can be used either *prefix* or *postfix*. If the increase operator is used as a prefix i.e. ++x; the value of x is increased *before* the expression is evaluated. When used as a postfix i.e. x++; the value of x is increased *after* being evaluated. Sourcc 1.6 shows an example of the prefix and postfix increase operators.

SOURCE 1.6: PREFIX AND POSTFIX OPERATORS

```
// ...

// Declare variable
int y = 3;

// Prefix
cout << "\n " << "Prefix ++y" << "\n ";
cout << "x = " << ++y << "\n ";
cout << "y = " << y << "\n\n";

// Reset y
y = 3;

// Postfix
cout << "\n " << "Postfix y++" << "\n ";
cout << "x = " << y++ << "\n ";
cout << "y = " << y << "\n ";
```

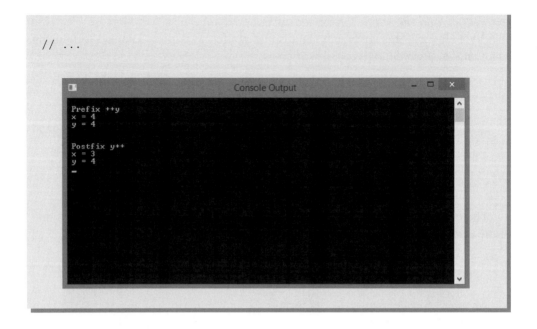

1.4.2 Arithmetic Operators

There are five basic C++ *arithmetic operators* as shown in Table 1.4. The only one that may not be familiar is the *modulo operator* (%) used for determining the remainder of *integer* division as shown in Source 1.7.

TABLE 1.4 Arithmetic operators

Operator	Name
+	Addition
-	Subtraction
*	Multiplication
\	Division
%	Modulo

SOURCE 1.7: MODULO OPERATOR

```
// ...

// Declare variables
int x = 11, y = 3;
```

```
cout << "\n " << "Remainder of 11 divided by 3 = " << x%y << "\n ";

// ...
```

```
Console Output                                        –  □  x
Remainder of 11 divided by 3 = 2
```

1.4.3 Relational Operators

Sometimes it is necessary to test the relationship between two expressions so that some action can be performed based on the outcome of the result. *Relational operators* can be used to perform such tasks. The most common C++ relational operators are shown in Table 1.5.

The only result of a relational operator expression when evaluated is either 1 (*true*) or 0 (*false*) i.e. a *Boolean* value. C++ automatically converts a Boolean value to an integer as shown in Source 1.8.

TABLE 1.5 Common relational operators

Operator	Name
==	Equal to
!=	Not equal to
>	Greater than
>=	Greater than or equal to
<	Less than
<=	Less than or equal to

SOURCE 1.8: RELATIONAL OPERATORS

```
// ...

cout << "\n " << "4 is greater than 3 = " << (4 > 3) << "\n ";
cout << "4 is less than 3 = " << (4 < 3) << "\n ";
cout << "4 is equal to 3 = " << (4 == 3) << "\n ";
cout << "4 is not equal to 3 = " << (4 != 3) << "\n ";

// ...
```

```
Console Output                              _  □  ×

4 is greater than 3 = 1
4 is less than 3 = 0
4 is equal to 3 = 0
4 is not equal to 3 = 1
```

In Source 1.8, the relational expressions are enclosed in parentheses so that C++ evaluates the relationship first and then sends the result to cout. Note that the relation operator to test for *equality* is == and not a single = which refers instead to the assignment of a value to a variable.

1.4.4 Logical Operators

In order to test for more complex expressions, *logical operators* can be combined with relational operators. Logical operators are normally associated with *Boolean algebra*[4] and as such, produce a Boolean result. The three most common C++ logical operators are shown in Table 1.6.

---

[4] *Boolean algebra* is a logical calculus of truth values 0 and 1 developed by George Boole in the 1840s.

TABLE 1.6 Common logical operators

Operator	Boolean Operation
&&	AND
||	OR
!	NOT

For example, suppose you wanted to select only those equities that had a price (Price) above P and market capitalisation (MarketCap) above MC. This could be expressed in C++ as follows:

```
(Price > P) && (MarketCap > MC)
```

1.4.5 Conditional Operator

The *conditional operator* (?) can be used in the following shorthand format:

```
(condition) ? result1 : result2
```

Which is read '*if* condition *is* true *the expression returns* result1, *if it is not it will return* result2'. Source 1.9 shows a typical example of using the conditional operator in this format.

SOURCE 1.9: THE CONDITIONAL OPERATOR (?)

```
// ...

// Declare variables
int a, b, c;
// Assign values to a and b
a = 4;
b = 6;
// Use conditional expression
c = (a > b) ? a : b;

cout << "\n " << "Conditional expression gives " << c << "\n ";

// ...
```

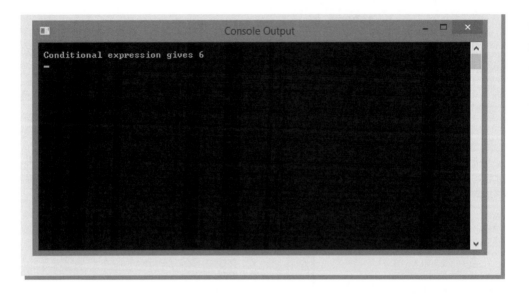

In Source 1.9, a and b are assigned the values of 4 and 6, respectively, which makes the expression (a > b) evaluate to false, thus the first value after the question mark is ignored and the second value (after the colon) accepted; resulting in the value of 6 for the conditional expression.

1.5 INPUT AND OUTPUT

For the majority of cases, programs will require *inputs* from the keyboard and *outputs* to the console window. We have already encountered the <iostream> header file from the C++ Standard Library which allows us to handle I/O in our programs. As we have already seen in all of the above programs, output to the console window is handled with cout along with the *insertion operator* (<<). Inputs from the keyboard are handled by cin along with the *extraction operator* (>>). Source 1.10 shows an example of using both cout and cin.

SOURCE 1.10: INPUT AND OUTPUT

```
// ...

// Declare variable
int n;
// Get value from keyboard
cout << "\n " << "Enter # of data points: ";
```

```
// Assign value to a
cin >> n;
// Output result
cout << " " << "You entered " << n << "\n ";

system("PAUSE"); // Pause console window
return 0; // Return null integer and exit
}
```

```
Console Output                                    –  □  ×

Enter # of data points: 1000
You entered 1000
Press any key to continue . . . _
```

In Source 1.10, an integer a holds the value entered by the user when prompted by the cout statement. Once the user inputs a value and presses Enter the value is stored in a and subsequently output to the screen through the second cout statement. cin can only store the value into a once the Enter key has been pressed. It is possible to allow the user to input several values when prompted by using the concept of *chaining* as shown in Source 1.11.

SOURCE 1.11: CHAINING

```
// ...

// Declare variables
int a, b;
// Get values from keyboard
```

```
cout << "\n " << "Enter two values: ";
// Assign valuse to a and b using chaining
cin >> a >> b;

cout << " " << "The two values were " << a << " and " << b << "\n ";

// ...
```

```
Enter two values: 4 5
The two values were 4 and 5
Press any key to continue . . . _
```

In Source 1.11:

```
cin >> a >> b;
```

is equivalent to the two statements:

```
cin >> a;
cin >> b;
```

In both cases the user must input two values before pressing `Enter` for the program to continue. Note that in Source 1.10 and 1.11 I used `system("PAUSE")` to hold the console window instead of `cin.get()` so as not to confuse the compiler when using console input within the main body of the program.

1.6 CONTROL STRUCTURES

It is possible to *control* the order of execution of statements in a program through two special types of structure, namely *branching* and *looping*.

1.6.1 Branching

The most common type of branching statement is the *decision-making* (or *selection*) structure. Decision-making structures control program execution through the dependence on one or more specified conditions being satisfied. The if structure is by far the most popular type of decision-making structure and there are two basic forms, namely:

```
if (condition) statement;
and
if (condition)
{
statement;
}
```

The if ... else and if ... else if structures are extensions of the if structure that allows further conditions to be tested, that is:

```
if (condition)
{
statement1;
}
else
{
statement2;
}
and
if (condition)
{
statement1;
}
else if
{
statement2;
}
else
{
statement3;
}
```

By mixing relational and logical operators it is possible to create increasingly complex decision-making structures. The `if` structure can also be *nested* (or *embedded*) within a set of `if` structures. Source 1.12 and 1.13 show examples of using the `if` and `if … else if` structures.

SOURCE 1.12:   IF … ELSE STATEMENT

```
// ...

int x;

cout << "\n " << "Enter a number: ";
cin >> x;

//if...else statement
if (x > 100)
{
    cout << "\n " << "Number greater than 100" << "\n ";
}
else
{
    cout << " " << "Number less than 100" << "\n ";
}

// ...
```

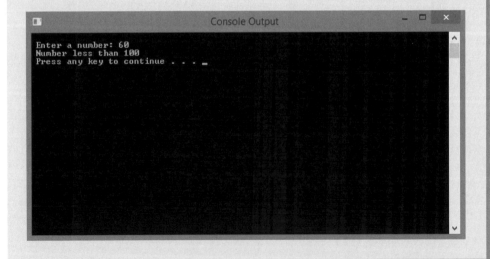

```
Enter a number: 60
Number less than 100
Press any key to continue . . .
```

SOURCE 1.13:   IF … ELSE … IF STATEMENT

```cpp
// ...

int a;

cout << "\n " << "Enter a +ve or -ve number (a): ";
cin >> a;

// if ... else if statement
if (a > 0)
{
   cout << " " << "a is positive" << "\n ";
}
else if (a < 0){
   cout << " " << "a is negative" << "\n ";
}
else
{
   cout << " " << "a is 0" << "\n ";
}

// ...
```

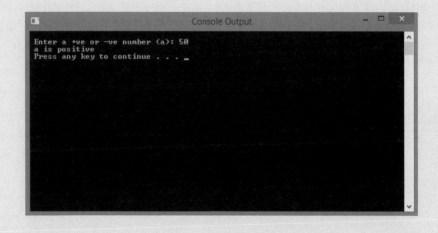

Another type of decision-making structure in C++ is the switch statement that allows the execution of different sets of statements depending on the value of one expression. The syntax for the switch structure is as follows:

```
Switch (expression)
{
Case constant1:
statement1;
break;
Case constant2:
statement2;
break;
.

.

.
default:
statement;
}
```

The `switch` statement works in the following way:

`switch` evaluates `expression` and checks to see if it is equivalent to `constant1`, if it is, execute `statement1` until it reaches `break`. When the `break` statement is reached the program jumps to the end of the `switch` structure. If `expression` is not equal to `constant1` it is checked against `constant2` and if it is equal to this, the program will execute `statement2` until `break` is reached when it then jumps to the end of the `switch` structure. If `expression` does not match any of the `constants`, the program executes the `statement` after `default`, if it exists (optional).

Unlike `if` structures that can test for a variety of conditions, switch structures can only test for equality. Also, only constants can follow the `case` statement and not variables or expressions. Source 1.14 shows an example of using the `switch` structure.

SOURCE 1.14: THE `switch` STATEMENT

```
int n;
...
cout << "\n " << "Choose 1, 2, 3 or 4: ";
cin >> n;

// Switch statement
switch (n)
{
        case 1:
            cout << " " << "You chose 1" << "\n ";
    break;
```

```
       case 2:
          cout << " " << "You chose 2" << "\n ";
       break;
       case 3:
          cout << " " << "You chose 3" << "\n ";
       break;
       case 4:
          cout << " " << "You chose 4" << "\n ";
       break;
       default:
          cout << " " << "1, 2, 3, or 4 not chosen!" << "\n ";
}

// ...
```

```
┌────────────────────────────────────────────────────────────────┐
│ ▫                         Console Output              _  ☐   ✕  │
├────────────────────────────────────────────────────────────────┤
│ Choose 1, 2, 3 or 4: 2                                        ^ │
│ You chose 2                                                     │
│ Press any key to continue . . . _                              │
│                                                                │
│                                                                │
│                                                                │
│                                                                │
│                                                                │
│                                                                │
│                                                              v │
└────────────────────────────────────────────────────────────────┘
```

1.6.2 Looping

In C++, *looping* involves using *iteration* structures in which a particular statement is repeated a certain number of times, or, while a condition is satisfied.

1.6.3 The for Loop

The for loop performs a repetitive task with a counter which is initialised and changes on each iteration. The general syntax of the for loop is as follows:

```
for (initialisation; condition; action) statement;
```

Alternatively, the `for` loop with a statement block is written as follows:

```
for (initialisation; condition; action)
{
statements;
}
```

In general, the `action` involves *incrementing* or *decrementing* the value of the counter. Source 1.15 shows an example of using the `for` loop.

SOURCE 1.15:   THE FOR LOOP

```
// ...

cout << "\n";

// for loop
for (int i = 3; i > 0; i--)
{
    cout << " " << i << ",";
}
    cout << " " << "Go!" << "\n ";

// ...
```

Console Output

```
3, 2, 1, Go!
```

It is possible to specify more than one expression in any of the fields in the parentheses using the *comma operator* (,) which acts as a separator for more than one expression. For example, suppose you wanted to initialise more than one variable in the for loop, that is:

```
for (n = 0, m = 10; n! = m; n++, m--)
{
        statements;
}
```

In this case, n and m are initialised with a value of 0 and 10, respectively. Since n is incremented by one and m decremented by one after each iteration, n! = m (i.e., n not equal to m) condition will become false after the 10th iteration when both n and m equal 10. Also note that any of the fields inside the parentheses of the for loop can be omitted although there must be a semi-colon (;) in their place. For example:

```
for (; i < 100; i++) statement;
```

is perfectly valid if there is no need to initialise the counter i.

1.6.4 The while Loop

The syntax for the while loop is written as:

```
while (condition) statement;
```

Alternatively, the while loop with a statement block is written as:

```
while (condition)
{
statements;
}
```

The while loop repeats the statement while the condition is true, when the condition is false, looping ends. A key difference between the while and for loops is that the former does not require an initialisation (or action) in the loop structure. Source 1.16 shows an example of using the while loop.

SOURCE 1.16:   THE WHILE LOOP

```
// ...

int n;

cout << "\n " << "Enter countdown number: ";
```

```cpp
cin >> n;
cout << " ";

// while loop
while (n > 0)
{
    cout << n << ", ";
    -n;
}
cout << "Go!" << "\n ";

// ...
```

```
Console Output                                        —  □  ✕

Enter countdown number: 8
8, 7, 6, 5, 4, 3, 2, 1, Go!
Press any key to continue . . . _
```

Source 1.16 can be interpreted in the following steps:

Step 1:   User assigns a value to integer n.

Step 2:   The while condition (n > 0) is checked:

    − true: go to Step 3.

    − false: go to Step 5.

Step 3:   Execute statement block.

Step 4:   Return to Step 2.

Step 5:   End program.

Note that the `while` loop must end at some point, therefore a provision must be made inside the statement block to force the condition to become `false`. In Source 1.16, n is decremented by 1 after each loop until it reaches 0 when the condition n > 0 is no longer satisfied and the loop is forced to end.

1.6.5 The do ... while Loop

The do ... while loop is exactly the same as the `while` loop, except that the statement block (or single statement) is evaluated at least once even if the condition is not satisfied. The do ... while loop is written as:

```
do
{
    statements
}
while(condition)
```

A typical use of the do ... while loop is when the condition that determines the end of the loop is determined within the loop as shown in Source 1.17.

SOURCE 1.17: THE DO ... WHILE LOOP

```
// ...

int n;

// do...while loop
do
{
    cout << "\n " << "Enter number (0 to end loop): ";
    cin >> n;
    cout << " " << "The number was " << n << "\n ";
}
while(n != 0);
    cout << "0 ends the loop!" << "\n ";

// ...
```

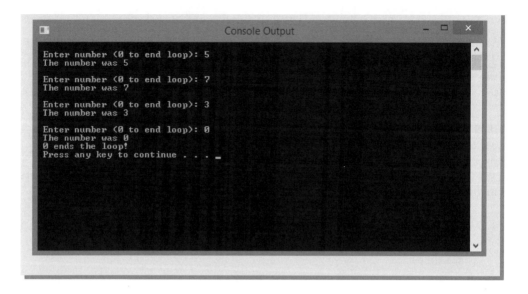

1.7 ARRAYS

C++ provides a data structure, the array, which stores a fixed-size sequential collection of elements (data) of the same type. All arrays consist of contiguous memory locations with the lowest address corresponding to the first element and the highest address to the last element. Source 1.18 shows a typical initialisation and implementation of an array structure. Note that in C++ the first element of an array is [0] i.e. indexing starts at 0 not 1.

SOURCE 1.18: ARRAYS

```cpp
// ...

// Declare an array of 10 integers
int n[10];

// Initialise elements of array
for (int i=0; i<10; i++)
{
    n[i] = i + 100; // Set element at location i to i + 100
}

cout << "\n " << "Element" << setw(13) << "Value" << "\n";
```

```
// Output each array element and value
for (int j=0; j<10; j++)
{
    cout << setw(7) << j << setw(13) << n[j] << "\n";
}
cout << " ";

cin.get();
return 0;
}
```

```
┌──────────────────────────────────────────────────────────────────────┐
│ ▣                          Console Output                  _ ▢  ✕      │
├──────────────────────────────────────────────────────────────────────┤
│ Element         Value                                               ▲  │
│       0          100                                                   │
│       1          101                                                   │
│       2          102                                                   │
│       3          103                                                   │
│       4          104                                                   │
│       5          105                                                   │
│       6          106                                                   │
│       7          107                                                   │
│       8          108                                                   │
│       9          109                                                   │
│ ▬                                                                      │
│                                                                        │
│                                                                        │
│                                                                     ▼  │
└──────────────────────────────────────────────────────────────────────┘
```

In Source 1.18, we have made use of setting field width to make the output look more tidy using `setw()` which is declared in the header `<iomanip>`.

1.8 VECTORS

Just like arrays, vectors use contiguous storage locations for their elements (data) within so-called sequence containers. However, unlike arrays, their size can change dynamically, with their storage being handled automatically by the container. Internally, vectors use a dynamically allocated array to store their elements. Arrays need to be reallocated in order to grow in size when new elements are inserted, which implies allocating a new array and moving all elements to it. This is a relatively expensive task in terms of processing time, and thus, vectors do not reallocate each time an element is added to the container. Instead, vector containers may allocate some extra storage to accommodate for possible growth, and thus the container may have an actual capacity greater than the storage strictly needed to contain its elements (i.e. its size). Source 1.19 shows a typical initialisation and implementation of a vector.

SOURCE 1.19:   VECTORS

```
// ...

vector<double> v; // Vector of doubles

v.push_back(3.796);
v.push_back(7.56989857);
v.push_back(0.054);
v.push_back(12.33);
v.push_back(3987.231);

cout << "\n ";
cout << fixed << setprecision(4); // Set number precision

for (unsigned int i=0; i<v.size(); i++)
{
    cout << v.at(i) << "\n ";
}

// ...
```

```
Console Output                              _ □  ×
3.7960
7.5699
0.0540
12.3300
3987.2310
```

In Source 1.19, we include the header <vector> to use the functions to manipulate vectors e.g. push_back() and size(). Note that when using vectors within
for loops it is often necessary to explicitly set the increment counter to unsigned
int. For example, when using the size() method of vector the returned value is
always going to be positive and so declared unsigned int in the official C++ doc-
umentation. If we just use an int for the increment counter in the for loop the two
variable types will clash since unsigned int is not the same as int. The at()
function returns a reference to the element at position n in the vector and automatically checks whether n is within the bounds of valid elements in the vector, throwing
an out_of_range exception if it is not (e.g. if n is greater than its size). Note that
we have made use of setting number precision using the statement:

```
cout << fixed << setprecision(4)
```

where both fixed and setprecision() are declared in the header <iomanip>.

1.9 FUNCTIONS

Often programs can become long and hard to follow making them difficult to understand and debug. In C++ it is possible to break down a program into smaller more
manageable units of code known as *modules*, or more formally *functions*. A function
is a unit of code that operates on one or more parameters passed into the function
which, in general, returns a value based on a set of mathematical operations. The general structure of a function is written as:

```
type function_name(type param1, type param2, ...)
{
statements;
return expression;
}
```

The first line of the function is known as the *function* header where the type,
function name and parameter list are declared. The function header and body together
are known as the *implementation* of the function. A function can return only *one* value
(e.g. int, double, etc.) or if there is no value to return the function is declared of
type void. A function can have as many parameters, each separated by a comma, as
necessary or no parameters at all. Indeed, functions can also pass other functions as
parameters provided they are declared correctly. Note that the data type returned by a
function must *match* that of the header declaration. Source 1.20 below shows a simple
program for multiplying two type double variables.

SOURCE 1.20:   A SIMPLE FUNCTION

```cpp
// ...

// Function prototype
double Product(double a, double b);

int main()
{
    SetConsoleTitle(L"Console Output"); // Set title of console window

    // Declare variables
    double x, y;

    cout << "\n " << "Enter x and y: ";
    cin >> x >> y;

    cout << " " << "Product = " << Product(x,y) << "\n ";

    system("PAUSE");
    return 0;
}

// Function definition
double Product(double a, double b)
{
    return(a*b);
}
```

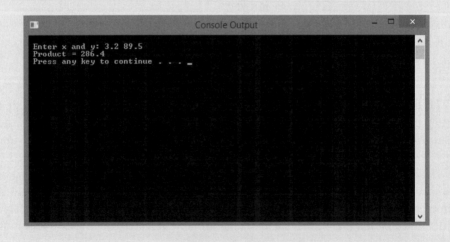

In Source 1.20, the function is first declared using a function *prototype* above the `main()` subroutine. The prototype is a *copy* of the function header terminated with a semi-colon (;). Be aware that when declaring a function (through the *function prototype*) we refer to *parameters*, however, when calling the function, we refer to *arguments*. Arguments are the parameters passed to the function when it is called, and once inside the function, these parameters can be used, and changed, just like any other variable. Within a function prototype, it is possible to omit their names, for example we could have written the prototype for the `Product()` function as:

```
double Product(double, double);
```

In Source 1.20, x and y are the parameters of the `Product()` function and a and b are the arguments of the `Product()` function call. When `Product()` is called the values entered for a and b are *passed* to x and y and subsequently used in the function body. The function can change the values of x and y but cannot change the values of a and b. If it is a requirement that the value of a parameter passed to a function is only allowed to read it and not *change* the value inside the function, the parameter can be set to *constant* in both the prototype and header declaration. For example:

```
double Product(const double x, double y);
```

In this case, the value of x cannot be changed in the body of the function; however, y still can be changed. When using arguments in a function call it is also possible to *initialise* the values for the parameters in the function prototype. For example:

```
int Init(int x, int y = 10, int = 30);
```

Note that once a parameter has an initial value then all other parameters to the right of it must also be declared with initial values. We have already seen that it is not explicitly necessary to state parameter names in function prototypes, so the third parameter in `Init()` is equally acceptable.

In C++, function prototypes are usually put in files with extension *.h*, known as *header files*, while function definitions go into files with the extension *.cpp*, known as *source files* (see Classes later). *Preprocessor directives* (#) can be used to avoid multiple includes during compilation, for example:

```
#ifndef HEADERNAME_H
#define HEADERNAME _H
... contents of the header file.
#endif
```

On most modern compilers it is possible to replace the above statements with a single `pragma` statement as follows:

```
#pragma once
```

1.9.1 Call-by-Value vs. Call-by-Reference

When function arguments are *call-by-value* it implies that *copies* of any variables within the parameter list are made as they are called. So, in Source 1.20, copies of a and b in the body of Product() are made during execution and not a and b themselves. This works fine but can be *inefficient* when dealing with large numbers of parameters and function calls in a program. In order to get around this problem, we can use *call-by-reference* which passes the *memory address* of the argument variables to the function rather than the variables themselves. The function body can then act directly on the variables and dynamically change them in memory as required. Changing the value of the variable stored in the allocated memory address is the same as changing the value of the variable itself. If we are passing an argument a by reference to a parameter variable x, then x is said to be an *alias* for a and both share the same address in memory. That is, when the function acts on x in its body, it essentially also acts on a, so when it changes x, it changes a as well. In order to pass an argument by reference, the *reference operator* (&) is placed in front of the parameter name in both the function prototype and definition.

A major disadvantage of using references in argument lists is that the function is able to modify the input arguments. What we would ideally need is the address of a variable while at the same time not being able to modify it in any way. In this case, we can define the variable to be a *constant reference*. Source 1.21 shows how call-by-value, call-by-reference and constant reference are used to control access to arguments in a function.

SOURCE 1.21: CALL-BY-VALUE, CALL-BY-REFERENCE AND CONSTANT REFERENCE

```
// ...
// Function prototype
void swap(int i, int j);

int main()
{
    SetConsoleTitle(L"Console Output");

    //declare variables
    int i = 1, j = 2;

    cout << "\n " << " i = " << i << " j = " << j << "\n ";
    swap(i,j);
    cout << " i = " << i << " j = " << j << "\n ";
```

```
    cin.get();
    return 0;
}

// Function definition
void swap(int i, int j)
{
    int t;
    t=i;
    i=j;
    j=t;
}
```

```
// ...
// Function prototype
void swap(int &i, int &j);

int main()
{
    SetConsoleTitle(L"Console Output");

    //declare variables
    int i = 1, j = 2;

    cout << "\n " << " i = " << i << " j = " << j << "\n ";
    swap(i,j);
    cout << " i = " << i << " j = " << j << "\n ";
```

```
    cin.get();
    return 0;
}


// Function definition
void swap(int &i, int &j)
{
    int t;
    t=i;
    i=j;
    j=t;
}
```

```
 ▢▮                          Console Output                      _ ▢ ✕
  i = 1 j = 2
  i = 2 j = 1
  ▬
```

```
// ...
// Function prototype
void swap(const int &i, const int &j);

int main()
{
    SetConsoleTitle(L"Console Output");

    //declare variables
    int i = 1, j = 2;

    cout << "\n " << " i = " << i << " j = " << j << "\n ";
    swap(i,j);
    cout << " i = " << i << " j = " << j << "\n ";
```

```
        cin.get();
        return 0;
}


// Function definition
void swap(const int &i, const int &j)
{
        int t;
        t=i;
        i=j;
        j=t;
}



        error C3892: 'i' : you cannot assign to a variable that is const
        error C3892: 'j' : you cannot assign to a variable that is const
```

In Source 1.21, when we make i and j const and pass-by-reference (&), both i and j are shown as errors in the swap() function since we cannot change a variable that is declared const.

Also, note that vectors are very large on memory and as such should *always* be passed into functions by *reference*, for example:

```
void fillVector(vector<int>&);
```

If you do not plan to make any changes to the vector it is still necessary to pass it in by reference but in this case add a const modifier, for example:

```
void fillVector(const vector<int>&);
```

1.9.2 Overloading Functions

In C++, it is possible to create functions that have the same type and name but different number of parameters or data types. This is known as *overloading a function* (or *polymorphism*). The main reason for overloading functions would be where two or more functions perform similar tasks but have different parameters. For example, we could use operator overloading to declare two swap() functions; one that accepts integer values and another that accepts doubles as shown in Source 1.22.

SOURCE 1.22: OVERLOADING THE FUNCTION swap()

```cpp
// ...
// Function prototype
void swap(int &i, int &j);
void swap(double &k, double &m);

int main()
{
    SetConsoleTitle(L"Console Output");

    //declare variables
    int i = 1, j = 2;
    double k = 2.86, m = 3.84;

    cout << "\n " << " i = " << i << " j = " << j << "\n ";
    swap(i,j);
    cout << " i = " << i << " j = " << j << "\n ";

    cout << "\n " << " k = " << k << " m = " << m << "\n ";
    swap(k,m);
    cout << " k = " << k << " m = " << m << "\n ";

    cin.get();
    return 0;
}

// Function definition (integers)
void swap(int &i, int &j)
{
    int t;
    t=i;
    i=j;
    j=t;
}

// Function definition (doubles)
void swap(double &k, double &m)
{
    double t;
    t=k;
    k=m;
    m=t;
}
```

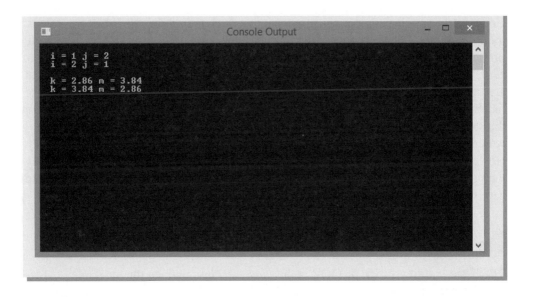

In Source 1.22, the compiler decides the definition to use based on the arguments provided when the function is called. To choose the definition to use, the compiler first searches for a definition with parameters that match an invocation exactly. If an exact match is not found, the compiler tries to match by converting types where possible. If a suitable definition cannot be found, a compilation error occurs.

1.10 OBJECT ORIENTED PROGRAMMING

As already mentioned, only those parts of the C++ language that we need to success-fully implement the tools and techniques in the rest of the book have been covered. However, one very useful development in C++, and something we will make great use of in this book, is the concept of *Object-Oriented Programming* (OOP). OOP allows the building of large and complex programs that can be broken down into smaller self-contained reusable code units known as *classes*. In OOP, data and its manipula-tion are brought together into a single entity called an *object*. Programs then consist of one or more objects interacting with each other to solve a particular problem. The object is responsible for its data and its data can only be manipulated by a predefined list of acceptable operations. In essence, OOP aims to emulate the way humans inter-act with the world around them. In this way, pretty much anything can be modelled as an object. Consider a typical day, get out of bed, have a cup of coffee, catch a bus to work, go to a restaurant for lunch, go to your home, eat your dinner with a knife and fork, watch television etc. It is possible to look on life as a series of interactions with things. These things we call objects. We can view all of these objects as con-sisting of data (*properties*) and operations that can be performed on them (*methods*).

Consider the simple example of a motor car that has hundreds of properties e.g. colour, model type, year, engine capacity, leather interior etc. Let us concentrate on a single property: velocity. Every car has the property of velocity. If it is parked the velocity is zero, if it is on the road it is moving at a certain speed in a particular direction. What are the methods that can modify the car's velocity? We can press the accelerator to increase the speed, we can press the brake to reduce the speed and finally we can turn the steering wheel to alter the direction of the motion. The speedometer is a method we can consult at any time to access the value of the speed component of velocity. However, it is clear that without using any of the other methods we cannot directly manipulate the velocity (unless we have a crash in which case the velocity goes to zero very rapidly).

1.10.1 Classes and Abstract Data Types

The basic building block of OOP is the *class*. A class defines the available characteristics and behaviour of a set of similar objects. A class is an *abstract* definition that is made concrete at run-time when objects based upon the class are *instantiated* and take on the behaviour of the class. Data abstraction is the process of creating an object whose implementation details are *hidden* (or *encapsulated*) and the object is used through a well-defined *interface*. Data abstraction leads to an *abstract data type* (ADT), e.g. when you use a floating point number in a program you are not really bothered about exactly how it is represented inside the computer, provided it behaves in the manner you expect. ADTs should be used independent of their implementation meaning that even if the implementation changes the ADT can be used without modification. Most people would be unhappy if they took their car to the garage for a service and afterwards the mechanic said *'She's running lovely now, but you'll have to use the pedals in reverse from now on'*. If this were the case, we could not think of the car as an ADT. However, the reality is that we can take a car to a garage for a major overhaul (which represents a change of implementation) and still drive it in exactly the same way afterwards.

Consider the concept of a 'Vehicle' class. The class would include *methods* such as Steer(), Accelerate() and Brake(). The class would also include *properties* such as Colour, NumberOfDoors, TopSpeed. The class is an abstract design that becomes real when objects such as Car, RacingCar and Tank are created, each with its own version of the class's methods and properties. Furthermore, *message passing* (or *interfacing*) describes the communication between objects using their *public interfaces*. There are three main ways to pass messages: *properties*, *methods* and *events*:

- *Properties* can be defined in a class to allow objects of that type to advertise and allow changing of state information, such as the 'TopSpeed' property.

- *Methods* can be provided so that other objects can request a process to be undertaken by an object, such as the `Steer()` method.
- *Events* can be defined that an object can raise in response to an internal action.

Other objects can subscribe to these so that they can react to an event occurring. An example for vehicles could be an `'ImpactDetected'` event subscribed to by one or more `'AirBag'` objects.

1.10.2 Encapsulation and Interfaces

Encapsulation refers to the process of *hiding* the implementation details of an object. A washing machine is a good example of an encapsulated object. We know that inside a washing machine are a whole series of complex electronics, however, we do not need to understand them to wash our clothes. In terms of our concept of an object, encapsulation hides the properties, some methods, and all method implementation details of an object from the outside. For example, the velocity of a car cannot be magically changed, we have to press the accelerator or brake – methods that we do not need to know the details of. In this respect the velocity of the car is hidden from outside interference, but can be changed by visible methods.

An *interface* is a simple *control panel* that enables us to use an object. The great benefit of the interface is that we only need to understand the simple interface to use the washing machine or drive the car. This is much easier than understanding the internal implementation details.

Another benefit is that the implementation details can be changed or fixed and we can still use the washing machine or car. For example, suppose your car breaks down and you take it to the garage and they replace the engine with a bigger and better one. The car operates in exactly the same way since the interface has remained unchanged. So, it is extremely important to design a good interface that will not change. The inner workings can be modified and cause no external operational effect. That is, once the user understands the interface, the implementation details can be modified, fixed or enhanced, and once the interface is unchanged the user can seamlessly continue to use the object.

The interface establishes *what* requests you can make for a particular object. However, there must be code somewhere to satisfy that request. This, along with the *hidden data*, comprises the *implementation*. The goal of the *class creator* is to build a class that exposes only what's necessary to the user and keeps everything else hidden. Why? Because if it's hidden, the programmer cannot use it, which means that the class creator can change the hidden portion at will without worrying about the impact on anyone else. The hidden portion usually represents the tender insides of an object that could easily be corrupted by a careless or uninformed programmer, so hiding the implementation reduces program bugs. Once a class has been created and tested, it should (ideally) represent a useful *unit of code*. Code reuse is one of the greatest advantages that OOP languages provide. The simplest way to reuse a class is to just use an object of that class directly.

1.10.3 Inheritance and Overriding Functions

It seems a pity, however, to go to all the trouble of creating a class and then be forced to create a brand new one that might have similar functionality. It would be nicer if we could take the existing class, *clone it* and then make additions and modifications to the clone. This is effectively what you get with *inheritance*, with the exception that if the original class (the *base* class) is changed, the modified '*clone*' (the *derived* class) also reflects those changes. For example, consider the base type Shape in which each shape has a size, a colour, a position and so on. Each shape can be drawn, erased, moved, coloured, etc. From this, specific types of shapes are derived (*inherited*) e.g. circle, square, triangle and so on, each of which may have additional characteristics and behaviours. Certain shapes can be flipped, for example. Some behaviours may be different, such as when you want to calculate the area of a shape. The type *hierarchy* embodies both the similarities and differences between the shapes as shown in Figure 1.1.

When you inherit from an existing type, you create a *new type*. This new type contains not only all the members of the existing type but more importantly it *duplicates the interface* of the base class.

So, all the messages you can send to objects of the base class you can also send to objects of the derived class. Since we know the type of a class by the messages we can send to it, this means that the derived class *is the same type as the base class* e.g. a circle is a shape. This type equivalence through inheritance is one of the fundamental gateways to understanding the meaning of OOP.

In reality, you have two ways to differentiate your new derived class from the original base class. You can simply *add brand new functions* to the derived class. These new functions are not part of the base class interface. This means that the base class simply does not do as much as you wanted it to, so you added more functions.

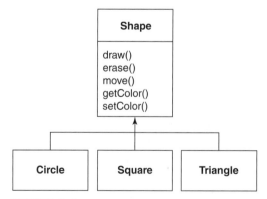

FIGURE 1.1 Schematic of a typical class hierarchy

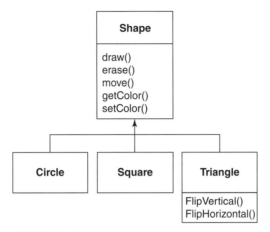

FIGURE 1.2   Adding new functions to the derived class

This simple and primitive use for inheritance is, at times, the perfect solution to your problem (see Figure 1.2).

The second and more important way to differentiate your new class is to *change* the behaviour of an existing base-class function. This is referred to as *overriding* that function.

To override a function, you simply create a new definition for the function in the derived class. You're saying, '*I'm using the same interface function here, but I want it to do something different for my new type*', as shown in Figure 1.3.

1.10.4 Polymorphism

We briefly touched upon *polymorphism* when discussing functions above. It is generally perceived as the most feared part of object orientation. Polymorphism, which

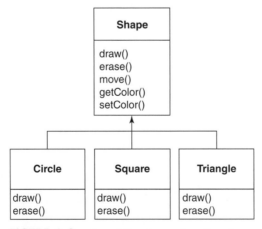

FIGURE 1.3   Overriding base-class functions

literally means *poly* (*many*) and *morph* (*forms*), will again only be mentioned here for completeness. Objects interact by calling each other's methods. How does some object *A* know the supported methods of another object *B*, so that it can call a valid method of *B*? In general, there is no magic way for *A* to determine the supported methods of *B*. *A* must know in advance the supported methods of *B*, which means *A* must know the class of *B*. However, polymorphism means that *A* does not need to know the class of *B* in order to call a method of *B*. In other words, an instance of a class can call a method of another instance, without knowing its exact class. The calling instance need only know that the other instance supports a method, it does not need to know the exact class of the other instance. It is the instance receiving the method call that determines what happens, not the calling instance.

1.10.5 An Example of a Class

Source 1.23 shows an example of a simple class named `AClass` created using the Generic C++ Class Wizard in Visual Studio Express 2012 Windows Desktop as shown in Figure 1.4. Source 1.24 shows an implementation of the simple `AClass`

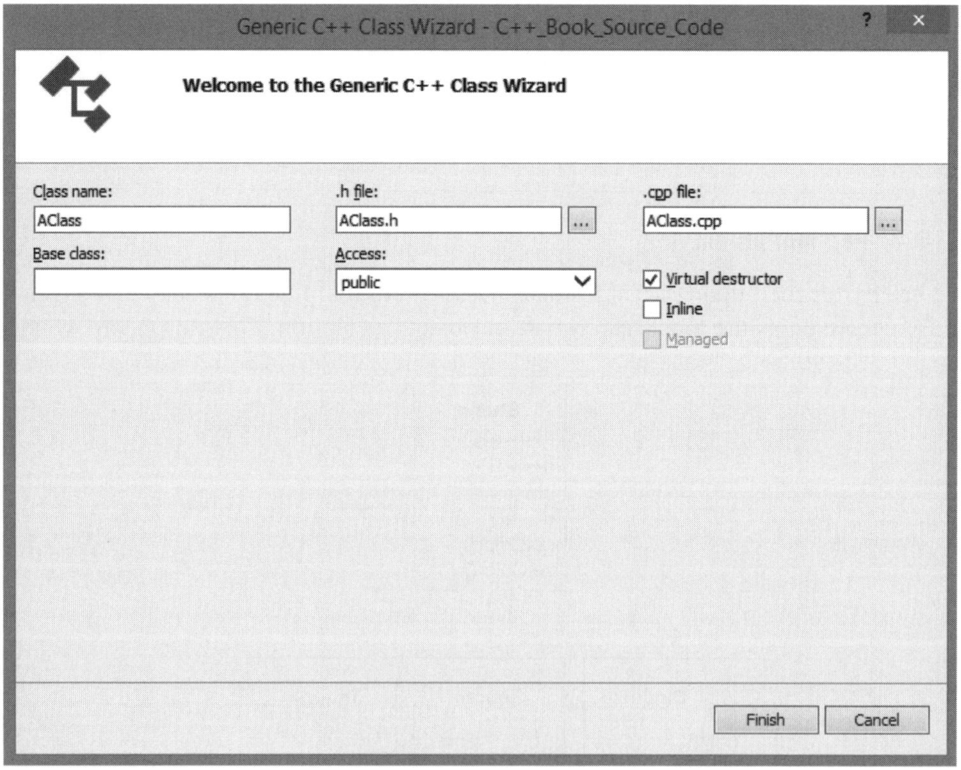

FIGURE 1.4   The Generic C++ Class Wizard dialogue box

class. Note that for all classes, the ending brace (}) is followed by a semi-colon (;) to indicate it is a class.

SOURCE 1.23:   THE .h AND .cpp FILES AUTOMATICALLY GENERATED BY THE VISUAL STUDIO 2013 CLASS WIZARD

```cpp
// AClass.h
#pragma once

class AClass
{
public:
    AClass();
    virtual ~AClass();
private:
};

// AClass.cpp
#include "AClass.h"

AClass::AClass()
{
}
AClass::~AClass()
{
}
```

SOURCE 1.24:   A SIMPLE IMPLEMENTATION OF THE AClass CLASS

```cpp
// AClass.h
#pragma once

class AClass
{
public:
    AClass();
    virtual ~AClass();
```

```cpp
    // Function declaration
    void sayHello();
private:
};

// AClass.cpp
#include <iostream>
using std::cout;

#include "AClass.h"

// Default constructor
AClass::AClass()
{
}

// Default destructor
AClass::~AClass()
{
}

// Function definition
AClass::sayHello()
{
    cout << " Hello\n";
}
// main.cpp
#include "AClass.h"

#include <windows.h>
#include <iostream>
using std::cout;
using std::cin;

int main()
{
    SetConsoleTitle(L"Console Output");

    // Create an instance of the AClass class (instantiation)
    AClass obj;
    // Call the sayHello() function using the dot operator
    obj.sayHello();

    cin.get();
```

```
        return 0;
}
```

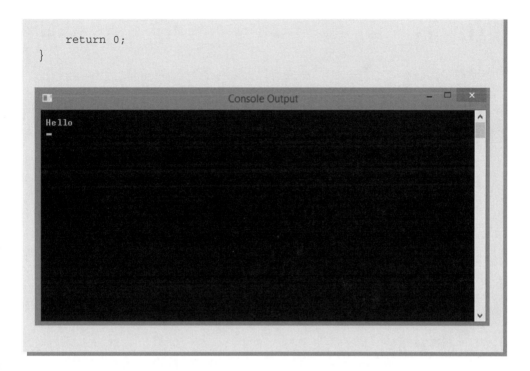

1.10.6 Getter and Setter Methods

Both member data and functions can be declared either `private` or `public` (`protected` will not be discussed in this book). Those declared `public` can be accessed from any part of a program that includes the class with use of the *dot notation* (`.`). Those declared as `private` can only be accessed by member functions of the class. The default declaration for member data and functions is `private` and to access these `private` variables from outside of the class we generally use public *setter* (or *mutator*) and *getter* (or *accessor*) methods as shown in Source 1.25. In general, getters do not modify any of the member variables in the class and so it is good practice to make them constant by adding the `const` modifier.

SOURCE 1.25:   USING SETTER AND GETTER METHODS

```
// AClass.h
#pragma once

#include <string>
using std::string;
```

```cpp
class AClass
{
public:
    AClass();
    void setName(string x); // Setter prototype
    string getName() const; // Getter prototype with const
    modifier

    virtual ~AClass();
private:
    string m_name; // Member variable
};

// AClass.cpp
#include <iostream>
using std::cout;

#include "AClass.h"

AClass::AClass()
{
}

AClass::~AClass()
{
}

// Setter function
void AClass::setName(string name)
{
    m_name = name;
}

// Getter function with const modifier
string AClass::getName() const
{
    return m_name;
}

// main.cpp
#include "AClass.h"

#include <windows.h>
#include <iostream>
```

```
using std::cout;
using std::cin;

int main()
{
    SetConsoleTitle(L"Console Output");

    // Create an instance of the AClass class (instantiation)
    AClass obj;
    // Call the sayHello() funtion using the dot operator
    obj.setName("Paul");
        cout << '\n' << obj.getName() << '\n'; // Call getter
        using dot operator

    cin.get();
    return 0;
}
```

In Source 1.25, each function prototype in the *.h* file is attached to the relevant class definition in the *.cpp* file using the *scope resolution operator* (: :). Subsequently, each member function of the class is accessed in the main body using the *dot operator* notation. When we instantiate an object (obj) of the class in the main program, the compiler creates a *copy* of all member data and functions of the class for that particular object. If more objects of the same class are declared additional copies of the member data and functions are created for each object. The compiler actually handles all of the same data and functions for each of the objects so that nothing gets mixed up. Although the code will work correctly it is not necessarily efficient. A more practical solution is to use the address of the object and the *call-by-reference* technique as described above for functions.

1.10.7 Constructors and Destructors

The *default constructor* is a member function that has the same name as the class and invoked *automatically* once an instance of an object is *created*. Similarly, the *default destructor* has the same name as the class prefixed with a tilde (~) *and* invoked *automatically* once an object is *destroyed*. In practice, there is only ever *one* default destructor although the constructor can have several *overloaded* methods. It is generally considered good practice to include the keyword `virtual` before the destructor so as to alleviate any potential *memory leaks*. An example of the default constructor and destructor is shown in Source 1.26.

SOURCE 1.26: THE DEFAULT CONSTRUCTOR AND DESTRUCTOR

```
// AClass.h
#pragma once

#include <string>
using std::string;

class AClass
{
public:
    AClass(); // Default constructor
    void setName(string x); // Setter prototype
    string getName() const; // Getter prototype with const modifier

    virtual ~AClass();// Default destructor
private:
    string m_name; // Member variable
};

// AClass.cpp
#include <iostream>
using std::cout;

#include "AClass.h"
```

```cpp
// Default constructor
AClass::AClass()
{
    cout << " Default constructor called ...\n";
}

// Default destructor
AClass::~AClass()
{
    cout << " Default destructor called ...\n";
}

// Setter function
void AClass::setName(string name)
{
    m_name = name;
}

// Getter function with const modifier
string AClass::getName() const
{
    return m_name;
}

// main.cpp
#include "AClass.h"

#include <windows.h>
#include <iostream>
using std::cout;
using std::cin;

int main()
{
    SetConsoleTitle(L"Console Output");

    // Create an instance of the AClass class (instantiation)
    AClass obj;
    // Call the sayHello() funtion using the dot operator
    obj.setName("Paul");
        cout << '\n' << obj.getName() << '\n'; // Call getter using
        dot operator
```

```
        cin.get();
        return 0;
}
```

```
┌──────────────────────────────────────────────────────────┐
│ [C:\]            Console Output              _ □  ✕        │
├──────────────────────────────────────────────────────────┤
│ Default constructor called!                           ▲  │
│                                                          │
│ Paul                                                     │
│ Press any key to continue . . .                          │
│                                                          │
│ Default destructor called!                               │
│ Press any key to continue . . . _                        │
│                                                          │
│                                                          │
│                                                          │
│                                                          │
│                                                       ▼  │
└──────────────────────────────────────────────────────────┘
```

Both default constructors and destructors are provided automatically in C++ so do not have to be explicitly implemented in the class. However, experienced programmers usually include them for completeness and especially if any member variables need to be *initialised* with default values. Constructors are generally used to initialise data whereas destructors are used to tidy up any outstanding code issues once an object has been destroyed. There are several methods of initialising data with constructors, for example initialising the data inside the constructor:

```
AClass::AClass()
{
        m_x = 5;
}
```

It is also possible to write *parameterised* constructors, for example:

```
AClass::AClass(int x, int y, int z)
{
        m_x = x;
        m_y = y;
        m_z = z;
}
```

Obviously in all cases the prototype function for the constructor must match the function definition. The above constructor can also be written using the following notation:

```
AClass::AClass(int x, int y, int z)
{
            m_x(x);
            m_y(y);
            m_z(z);
}
```

It is also possible to initialise member variables using the *colon operator* (:), that is:

```
AClass::AClass : x(5)
{
}
```

Any additional member variables are initialised by separating with commas, for example:

```
AClass::AClass : x(5), y(4), z(3)
{
}
```

1.10.8 A More Detailed Class Example

Source 1.27 shows a more detailed example of a class dealing with bank accounts and balances. Many of the issues already discussed are covered in the example as well as some new concepts.

SOURCE 1.27: A DETAILED IMPLEMENTATION OF A BANK ACCOUNT AND BALANCES CLASS

```
// Bank.h
#pragma once

#include <string>
using std::string;


class Bank
```

```cpp
{
public:
    // Default constructor
    Bank();

    // Overloaded constructor
    Bank(string, int, double);

    // Default destructor
    virtual ~Bank();

    // Accessor functions
    string getName() const;
    int getAccNum() const;
    double getBalance() const;

    // Mutator functions
    void setName(string);
    void setAccNum(int);
    void setBalance(double);

    // Member functions
    void withdraw(double);
    void deposit(double);

    // We are printing static variables so must prefix the
    function with the keyword static.
    // NOTE: only add static in the declaration (.h) NOT
    definition (.cpp)
    static void printBankInfo();

private:
    // Member variables
    string m_name;
    int m_accNum;
    double m_balance;

    // Static member variables
    static int m_totalAccounts;
    static double m_bankBalance;
};

// Bank.cpp
```

```
#include "Bank.h"

#include <iostream>
using std::cout;

// Initialise static member variables
int Bank::m_totalAccounts = 0;
double Bank::m_bankBalance = 10000;

// Every time we instantiate a new user in the bank either tho-
rugh the default
// or overloaded constructor we must increment the number of accounts.
Bank::Bank()
{
    m_accNum = 0;
    m_balance = 0.0;
    m_totalAccounts++;
}

// We do not need to modify the default constructor wrt the bank
balance because it is simply
// initialised to zero and there are no parameters.
However, for the overloaded constructor there
// is a newBalance parameter for user deposits. So every time a
user deposits  some money the
// new balance must be added to  m_bankBalance.
Bank::Bank(string name, int accNum, double balance)
{
    m_name = name;
    m_accNum = accNum;
    m_balance = balance;
    m_totalAccounts++;
    m_bankBalance += balance;
}

// Once an object is destroyed, m_totalAccounts and m_bankBalance
change i.e, we must decrement
// totalAccounts and bankBalance of the user being destroyed.
Bank::~Bank()
{
    m_totalAccounts--;
    m_bankBalance -= m_balance;
}
```

```
// Accessor functions
string Bank::getName() const
{
    return m_name;
}


int Bank::getAccNum() const
{
    return m_accNum;
}


double Bank::getBalance() const
{
    return m_balance;
}


// Mutator functions
void Bank::setName(string name)
{
    m_name = name;
}


void Bank::setAccNum(int accNum)
{
    m_accNum = accNum;
}


// The setBalance mutator must also be updated. So before doing
anything we
// must take m_bankBalance and substract the balance they may
already have
// (it could be zero but we don not know). Then add on the new
balance to the
// m_bankBalance.
void Bank::setBalance(double balance)
{
    m_bankBalance -= balance;
    m_balance = balance;
    m_bankBalance += balance;
}


// Member functions
void Bank::withdraw(double withdraw)
```

```
{
    m_balance -= withdraw;
    m_bankBalance -= withdraw;
}

void Bank::deposit(double deposit)
{
    m_balance += deposit;
    m_bankBalance += deposit;
}

void Bank::printBankInfo()
{
    cout << "\n " << "Number of Accounts: " << m_totalAccounts << "\n ";
    cout << "Total Balance: " << m_bankBalance << "\n ";
}
// main.cpp
#include <windows.h>
#include <iostream>
using std::cout;
using std::cin;

#include "Bank.h"

int main()
{
    SetConsoleTitle(L"Console Output");

    cout << '\n' << "Adam created an account and deposited 500";
    Bank Adam("Adam", 0001, 500); // Calling overloaded constructor

    Bank::printBankInfo(); // Calling printBankInfo() inside a class
    without instantiating an object

    Bank Sarah; // Calling default constructor

    cout << '\n' << "Sarah created an account and deposited 1000";

    Sarah.setName("Sarah"); // Calling mutator function setName()
    Sarah.setAccNum(0002);   // Calling mutator function setAccNum()
    Sarah.setBalance(1000);  // Calling mutator function setBalance()

    Bank::printBankInfo();
```

```cpp
cout << '\n' << "Eric created an account and deposited 1500";
Bank Eric("Eric", 0003, 1500); // Calling overloaded constructor

Bank::printBankInfo(); // Calling printBankInfo() inside a class
without instantiating an object

cout << "\n" << "\n" << "Eric set his balance to 1200";
Eric.setBalance(1200);

Bank::printBankInfo(); // Calling printBankInfo() inside a class
without instantiating an object

cout << "\n" << "\n" << "Sarah deposited 700";
Sarah.deposit(700);

Bank::printBankInfo(); // Calling printBankInfo() inside a class
without instantiating an object

cout << "\n" << "Adam's account was terminated due to lack of
use";
Adam.~Bank(); // Calling destructor

Bank::printBankInfo(); // Calling printBankInfo() inside a class
without instantiating an object

cin.get();
return 0;
}
```

```
Console Output                                          _ □ ×

Adam created an account and deposited 500
Number of Accounts: 1
Total Balance: 10500

Sarah created an account and deposited 1000
Number of Accounts: 2
Total Balance: 10500

Eric created an account and deposited 1500
Number of Accounts: 3
Total Balance: 12000

Eric set his balance to 1200
Number of Accounts: 3
Total Balance: 12000

Sarah deposited 700
Number of Accounts: 3
Total Balance: 12700

Adam's account was terminated due to lack of use.
Number of Accounts: 2
Total Balance: 12200
```

In Source 1.27, we have *overloaded* the Bank() constructor, that is:

```
Bank();
Bank(string, int, double);
```

This gives us several methods of instantiating an object of the class within the main body of the program e.g. both Adam and Sarah objects are created using different constructors. We have also added some tidying up code to the default destructor for dealing with closing or terminating accounts.

```
Bank::~Bank()
{
    m_totalAccounts--;
    m_bankBalance -= m_balance;
}
```

Another important concept we have included is that of *static member variables* and *functions*. Static member variables e.g. m_totalAccounts and m_bankBalance have the same value in any instance of a class and do not even require an instance of the class to exist. However, we must initialise static member variables using a specific scope operator (::) syntax, that is:

```
int Bank::m_totalAccounts = 0;
double Bank::m_bankBalance = 10000;
```

It is also possible to have *static member functions* of a class, for example:

```
static void printBankInfo();
```

Static member functions are functions that do not require an instance of the class, and are called the same way as you access static member variables i.e. with the class name rather than a variable name, for example:

```
Bank::printBankInfo();
```

Be clear that static member functions can only operate on static members, as they do not belong to specific instances of a class.

1.10.9 Implementing Inheritance

Recall our initial discussion of inheritance above. Suppose you have a Class A that has several functions and variables you want to access in another Class B. In this case, it is possible to *inherit* the functions and variables from Class A and use them as you would in Class B. Whenever you inherit from a class, the main class you inherit from is called the *base* class and the class that does the inheriting is called the *derived* class. Source 1.28 shows an example of implementing inheritance.

SOURCE 1.28: INHERITANCE

```cpp
// Mother.h
#pragma once

class Mother
{
public:
    Mother();
    void sayName();

    virtual ~Mother();
};

// Mother.cpp
#include "Mother.h"
#include <iostream>
using std::cout;

Mother::Mother()
{
}

void Mother::sayName()
{
    cout << "I am part of the Partridge family" << "\n ";
}

Mother::~Mother()
{
}

// Daughter.h
#pragma once

class Daughter: public Mother
{
public:
```

```
    Daughter();

    virtual ~Daughter();
};

// Daughter.cpp
#include "Mother.h"
#include "Daughter.h"

Daughter::Daughter()
{
}

Daughter::~Daughter()
{
}

// main.cpp
#include <windows.h>
#include <iostream>
using std::cout;
using std::cin;

#include "Mother.h"
#include "Daughter.h"

int main()
{
SetConsoleTitle(L"Console Output");

Mother mum;
cout << "\n " << "Mother" << "\n ";
mum.sayName();

// Daughter object inherits sayName() from the Mother class
Daughter helen;
cout << "\n " << "Daughter" << "\n ";
helen.sayName();

cin.get();
return 0;
}
```

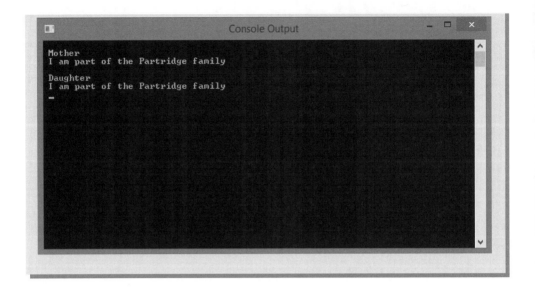

1.10.10 Operator Overloading

Operator overloading allows the manipulation of standard C++ operators to change the way they are implemented. For example, suppose you had two class objects that you wanted to add together, operator overloading allows you to treat the operator + differently for these objects. Table 1.7 shows a list of operators that can be overloaded in C++.

TABLE 1.7   Operators that can be overloaded in C++

```
+   -   *   /   =   <   >   +=  -=    *=   /=   <<   >>
<<=   >>=   ==   !=   <=   >=
++ --  %  &  ^  !  |  ~  &=  ^=  |=  &&  ||  %=  []  ()  ,  ->*  ->
new delete   new[]   delete[]
```

Source 1.29 shows an example of overloading the (+) operator.

SOURCE 1.29: OVERLOADING THE (+) OPERATOR

```cpp
// Vec2D.h
#pragma once

#include <iostream>
using std::ostream;
```

```cpp
class Vec2D
{
public:
    int m_x, m_y;

    Vec2D();
    Vec2D(int, int);

    // Oveloaded (+) operator declared constant and by reference
    Vec2D operator+(const Vec2D&) const;

    virtual ~Vec2D();
};

// Vec2D.cpp
#include "Vec2D.h"

#include <iostream>
using std::cout;

Vec2D::Vec2D() : m_x(0), m_y(0)
{
}

Vec2D::Vec2D(int x, int y) : m_x(x), m_y(y)
{
}

Vec2D Vec2D::operator+(const Vec2D& v) const
{
    // Uses an anonymous Vec2D object
    return Vec2D(m_x + v.m_x, m_y + v.m_y);
}

Vec2D::~Vec2D()
{
}

// main.cpp
#include <windows.h>
#include <iostream>
using std::cout;
using std::cin;
```

```
#include "Vec2D.h"

int main()
{
    SetConsoleTitle(L"Console Output");

    Vec2D a(3,3); // Create Vec2D object a
    Vec2D b(4,2); // Create Vec2D object b

    // Use (+) overloaded operator
    Vec2D c = a + b;

    cout << '\n' << c.m_x;
        cout << '\n' << c.m_y; << '\n';

    cin.get();
    return 0;
}
```

Note that there are *three* objects involved in the `operator+` member function: the *current* object that plays the role of the *left operand*, the argument v that plays the role of the *right operand* and a *new* object with a return type the same as that of the member function. Furthermore, neither the current object nor the v object are modified by the operation so we can add the `const` keyword. What if we wanted to print out c directly? For example:

```
cout << "\n " << c << "\n ";
```

This would lead to an error of the type '*no operator "<<" matches these operands*'. Source 1.30 shows how we can overload the *insertion* (<<) operator in Source 1.29 so that we can overcome this error and print out object c directly without needing to call its individual member variables i.e. c.m_x and c.m_y.

SOURCE 1.30:   OVERLOADING THE (<<) OPERATOR

```cpp
// Vec2D.h
#pragma once

#include <iostream>
using std::ostream;

class Vec2D
{
public:
    int m_x, m_y;

    Vec2D();
    Vec2D(int, int);

    // Oveloaded (+) operator declared constant and by reference
    Vec2D operator+(const Vec2D&) const;

    // Overload (<<) operator
    // ostream is not a member of the Vec2D class but wants to
    consume its
    // member variables so we make it a friend of the Vec2D class.
    friend ostream& operator<<(ostream& stream, const Vec2D&);

    virtual ~Vec2D();
};
// Vec2D.cpp
#include "Vec2D.h"

#include <iostream>
using std::cout;

Vec2D::Vec2D() : m_x(0), m_y(0)
{
}

Vec2D::Vec2D(int x, int y) : m_x(x), m_y(y)
```

```cpp
{
}

Vec2D Vec2D::operator+(const Vec2D& v) const
{
    // Uses an anonymous Vec2D object
    return Vec2D(m_x + v.m_x, m_y + v.m_y);
}

ostream& operator<<(ostream& stream, const Vec2D& v)
{
    cout << "(" << v.m_x << ", " << v.m_y << ")";
    return stream;
}

Vec2D::~Vec2D()
{
}

// main.cpp
#include <windows.h>
#include <iostream>
using std::cout;
using std::cin;

#include "Vec2D.h"

int main()
{
    SetConsoleTitle(L"Console Output");

    Vec2D a(3,3); // Create Vec2D object a
    Vec2D b(4,2); // Create Vec2D object b

    // Use (+) overloaded operator
    Vec2D c = a + b;

    cout << "\n " << c;
    cout << "\n " << c << "\n ";

cin.get();
return 0;
}
```

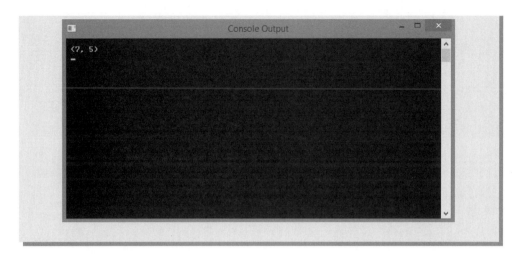

With the statement:

```
cout << "\n " << c << "\n ";
```

the first ≪ invokes the *left shift* operator and shifts c into `cout`, then it reads the next ≪ and invokes the left shift operator again and shifts "\n " into `cout` i.e. it reads *left -> right*. In Source 1.30, since we are constantly modifying the `ostream` object (i.e. using multiple insertion operations) we must pass it by *reference* so that it takes into account this *operator chaining* process. Note also that `ostream` is not a member (i.e. it is a *non-member*) of the `Vec2D` class but wants to be able to access the *private* members of the class. In this case, we make `ostream` a *friend* of the `Vec2D` class. By default, a non-member function cannot access the private member data of a class unless the class *explicitly* states that that function is allowed to do so, i.e. a class must *give away* its friendship, a friend cannot be simply *assumed* by a non-member function.

Chapter 1 has provided an overview of the key C++ programming ideas and concepts required to develop and build fairly robust quantitative analysis models. All of the programs introduced throughout the book will reply on methods and principles discussed in this chapter. By no means is this a complete resource for developing commercial level software systems but does give an adequate level of experience to begin prototyping such systems. We have also introduced the very powerful concept of OOP hopefully without burdening the reader with too much information and syntax. The idea, as with the other content, is to cover the necessary requirements needed to understand, develop and implement object-oriented programs in order to efficiently solve many of the problems encountered throughout the book. However, there may be several instances when we will be introducing some new C++ not covered explicitly here to solve a particular challenging problem. These will likely rely on more advanced methods in C++ and it makes more sense to discuss these implementations on an individual basis as they are encountered.

CHAPTER 2

The Hedge Fund Industry

The global credit crisis originated from a growing bubble in the US real estate market which eventually burst in 2008. This led to an overwhelming default of mortgages linked to subprime debt to which financial institutions reacted by tightening credit facilities, selling off bad debts at huge losses and pursuing fast foreclosures on delinquent mortgages. A liquidity crisis followed in the credit markets and banks became increasingly reluctant to lend to one another causing risk premiums on debt to soar and credit to become ever scarcer and costlier. The global financial markets went into meltdown as a continuing spiral of worsening liquidity ensued. When the credit markets froze, hedge fund managers were unable to get their hands on enough capital to meet investor redemption requirements. Not until the early part of 2009 did the industry start to experience a marked resurgence in activity realising strong capital inflows and growing investor confidence.

The aftermath of the financial crisis has clearly highlighted many of the shortcomings of the hedge fund industry and heightened the debate over the need for increased regulation and monitoring. Nevertheless, it has since been widely accepted that hedge funds played only a small part in the global financial collapse and suffered at the hands of a highly regulated banking system.

Chapter 2 introduces the concept of hedge funds and how they are structured and managed as well as a discussion of the current state of the global hedge fund industry in the aftermath of the last financial crisis. Several key investment techniques that are used in managing hedge fund strategies are also discussed. This chapter aims to build a basic working knowledge of hedge funds, and along with Chapter 3, develop the fundamentals necessary in order to approach and understand the more quantitative and theoretical aspects of modelling and analysis developed in later chapters.

2.1 WHAT ARE HEDGE FUNDS?

Whilst working for *Fortune* magazine in 1949, Alfred Winslow Jones began researching an article on various fashions in stock market forecasting and soon realised that it was possible to neutralise *market risk*[1] by buying undervalued securities and *short selling*[2] overvalued ones. Such an investment scheme was the first to employ a *hedge* to eliminate the potential for losses by cancelling out adverse market moves, and the technique of *leverage*[3] to greatly improve profits. Jones generated an exceptional amount of wealth through his *hedge fund* over the 1950s and 1960s and continually outperformed traditional money managers. Jones refused to register the hedge fund with the Securities Act of 1933, the Investment Advisers Act of 1940 or the Investment Company Act of 1940, with the main argument being that the fund was a *private* entity and none of the laws associated with the three Acts applied to this type of investment. It was essential that such funds were treated separately from other regulated markets since the use of specialised investment techniques, such as short selling and leverage were not permitted under these Acts; neither was the ability to charge performance fees to investors.

So that the funds maintained their *private* status, Jones would never publicly advertise or market the funds but only sought investors through word of mouth keeping everything as secretive as possible. It was not until 1966, through the publication of a news article about Jones's exceptional profit-making ability, that Wall Street and *High Net Worth*[4] (HNW) individuals finally caught on and within a couple of years there were over 200 active hedge funds in the market. However, many of these hedge funds began straying from the original *market neutral* strategy used by Jones and employed other more seemingly volatile strategies. The losses investors associated with highly volatile investments discouraged them from investing in hedge funds. Moreover, the onset of the turbulence in financial markets experienced in the 1970s practically wiped out the hedge fund industry altogether. Despite improving market conditions in the 1980s, only a handful of hedge funds remained active over this period. Indeed, the lack of hedge funds around in the market during this time changed the regulator's views on enforcing stricter regulation on the industry altogether. Not until the 1990s did the hedge fund industry begin to rise to prominence again and attract renewed investor confidence.

Nowadays, hedge funds are still considered *private investment schemes* (or *vehicles*) with a collective pool of capital only open to a small range of institutional investors and wealthy individuals and having minimal regulation. They can be as diverse as the manager in control of the capital wants to be in terms of the investment strategies and the range of financial instruments which they employ, including

---

[1] *Market risk* (or *systematic risk*) is the risk that the value of an investment will decrease due to the impact of various market factors, for example changes in interest and foreign currency rates.

[2] See Section 2.4.1.

[3] *Leverage* is the use of a range of financial instruments or borrowed capital to increase the potential return of an investment (see Section 2.4.2).

[4] A *High Net Worth* (HNW) individual (or family) is generally assumed to have investable assets in excess of $1 million, excluding any primary residence.

stocks, bonds, currencies, futures, options and physical commodities. It is difficult to define what constitutes a hedge fund, to the extent that it is now often thought in professional circles that a hedge fund is simply one that incorporates any *absolute return*[5] strategy that invests in the financial markets and applies non-traditional investment techniques. Many consider hedge funds to be within the class of *alternative* investments along with private equity and real estate finance that seek a range of investment strategies employing a variety of sophisticated investment techniques beyond the longer established traditional ones, such as *mutual funds*.[6]

The majority of hedge funds are structured as limited partnerships with the manager acting in the capacity of general partner and investors as limited partners. The general partners are responsible for the operation of the fund, relevant debts and any other financial obligations. Limited partners have nothing to do with the day-to-day running of the business and are only liable with respect to the amount of their investment. There is generally a minimum investment required by *accredited investors*[7] of the order of $250 000–$500 000, although many of the more established funds can require minimums up to $10 million. Managers will also usually have their own personal wealth invested in the fund, a circumstance intended to further increase their incentive to consistently generate above average returns for both the clients and themselves. In addition to the minimum investment required, hedge funds will also charge a fee structure related to both the management and performance of the fund. Such fees are not only used for administrative and ongoing operating costs but also to reward employees and managers for providing positive returns to investors. A typical fee basis is the so-called *2 and 20* structure which consists of a 2% annual fee (levied monthly or quarterly) based on the amount of *Assets under Management* (AuM) and a 20% performance-based fee i.e. an incentive-oriented fee. The performance-based fee, also known as carried interest, is a percentage of the annual profits and only awarded to the manager when they have provided positive returns to their clients. Some hedge funds also apply so-called *high water marks* to a particular amount of capital invested such that the manager can only receive performance fees, on that amount of money, when the value of the capital is more than the previous largest value. If the investment falls in value, the manager must bring the amount back to the previous largest amount before they can receive performance fees again. A *hurdle rate* can also be included in the fee structure representing the minimum return on an investment a manager must

---

[5] *Absolute return* refers to the ability of an actively managed fund to generate positive returns regardless of market conditions.

[6] *Mutual funds* are similar in structure to hedge funds but are subject to much stricter regulation and limited to very specific investments and strategies.

[7] An *accredited investor* is one with a net worth of at least $1 million or who has made $200,000 each year for the past two years ($300,000 if married with a spouse) and have the capacity to make the same amount the following year.

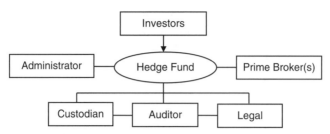

FIGURE 2.1   A schematic of the typical structure of a
hedge fund

achieve before performance fees are taken. The hurdle rate is usually tied to a market
benchmark, such as LIBOR[8] or the one-year T-Bill[9] rate plus a spread.

2.2 THE STRUCTURE OF A HEDGE FUND

In order for managers to be effective in the running of their business a number of
internal and external parties covering a variety of operational roles are employed in the
structure of a hedge fund as shown in Figure 2.1. As the industry matures and investors
are requiring greater transparency and confidence in the hedge funds in which they
invest, the focus on the effectiveness of these parties is growing as is their relevant
expertise and professionalism. Hedge funds are also realising that their infrastructure
must keep pace with the rapidly changing industry. Whereas in the past, some funds
paid little attention to their support and administrative activities, they are now aware
that the effective operation of their fund ensures the fund does not encounter unnecessary and unexpected risks.

2.2.1 Fund Administrators

Hedge fund *administrators* provide many of the operational aspects of the successful running of a fund, such as compliance with legal and regulatory rulings, financial reporting, liaising with clients, provision of performance reports, risk controls
and accounting procedures. Some of the larger established hedge funds use specialist in-house administrators whilst smaller funds may avoid this additional expense by
outsourcing their administrative duties. Due to the increased requirement for tighter
regulation and improved transparency in the industry, many investors will only invest
with managers that can prove a strong relationship with a reputable third-party admin-
istrator and that the proper processes and procedures are in place (see Table 2.1).

---

[8] LIBOR is the *London Interbank Offered Rate*, a rate that banks lend to other banks in the London
interbank market.
[9] A treasury bill (or T-bill) is a short-term debt obligation backed by the US government with a maturity
of less than one year.

TABLE 2.1 Top five global administrators as of 2015 (Based on SEC filings)

Administrator
CITCO
State Street
SS&C GlobeOp
BNY Mellon
Northern Trust

Hedge funds with offshore operations often use external administrators in offshore locations, to provide expert tax, legal and regulatory advice for those jurisdictions. Indeed, it is a requirement in some offshore locations (e.g. the Cayman Islands) that hedge fund accounts must be regularly audited. In these cases, administrators with knowledge of the appropriate requirements in those jurisdictions would fulfil this requirement.

2.2.2 Prime Brokers

The *prime broker* is an external party who provides extensive services and resources to a hedge fund, including brokerage services, securities lending, debt financing, clearing and settlement and risk management. Some prime brokers will even offer incubator services, office space and *seed* investment for start-up hedge funds. The fees earned by prime brokers can be quite considerable and include trade commissions, loan interest and various administration charges. Due to the nature of the relationship between the prime broker and a hedge fund, in particular being the counterparty to trades and positions, only the largest financial institutions are able to act in this capacity (see Table 2.2).

For this reason, the prime brokerage market is relatively small and each prime broker tends to service a large number of hedge funds and therefore takes on an extremely

TABLE 2.2 Top five global prime brokers as of 2015 (Based on SEC filings)

Prime Broker
Goldman Sachs
Morgan Stanley
JP Morgan
Credit Suisse
Deutsche Bank

TABLE 2.3 Top five global custodians as of 2015 (Based on SEC filings)

Custodian
JP Morgan
BNY Mellon
Goldman Sachs
Morgan Stanley
Credit Suisse

high degree of risk. Some major restructuring occurred amongst prime brokers in 2008 and 2009, for example the acquisitions of Bear Stearns by JP Morgan and Merrill Lynch by Bank of America, and the takeover of Lehman Brothers by Barclays Capital. This resulted in a shift in market share from some former investment banks to commercial banks and saw the prime brokerage industry begin to consolidate. In order to alleviate investor concerns since the collapse of some major financial institutions, many fund managers are cautious in employing a single prime broker and prefer to subscribe to multiple prime brokers.

2.2.3 Custodian, Auditors and Legal

Hedge fund assets are usually held with a *custodian*, including the cash in the fund as well as the actual securities.[10] The custodian is normally a bank which will offer services, such as safekeeping the hedge fund assets, arranging settlement of any sales or purchases of securities and managing cash transactions (see Table 2.3). The general structure of a hedge fund exempts them from the requirement to have their financial statements audited by a third party. However, in order to satisfy investors, many hedge funds have their accounts and financial reviews audited annually by an external audit firm. It is important that the auditing firm is seen to be independent of the hedge fund to give credence to their reports and services.

The legal structure of a hedge fund is designed to provide investors with limited liability i.e. if a fund suffers a severe loss the maximum amount an investor can lose is the level of capital invested in the fund. They cannot be made liable for losses over this amount or any other outstanding debt or financial obligation. In addition, the legal structure is also chosen to optimise the tax status and legal liability of the hedge fund itself. To facilitate this, there are a small number of standard hedge fund structures e.g. the master-feeder structure, which is adopted by a large number of funds. These

---

[10] This is true except when the assets are used as *collateral* for gaining leverage. In these cases, the assets used as collateral are held by the prime broker. As most hedge funds use some degree of leverage, it is common for assets to be held by both custodians and prime brokers.

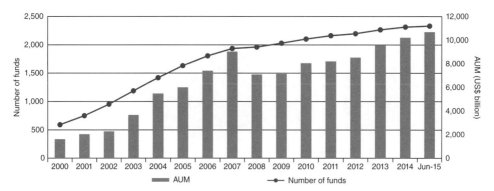

FIGURE 2.2 Growth in the global hedge funds industry since 2000
Source: Eurekahedge

comply with the legal requirements of the various jurisdictions where the hedge funds operate and obtain the optimal tax treatment. The master-feeder structure is a two-tier structure where investors invest through a feeder vehicle which itself invests in the hedge fund. There can be a number of feeder vehicles, located and domiciled in a number of different jurisdictions. Each can have a different legal form and framework. Depending on their tax status, investors can decide which feeder vehicle they wish to invest in. As a general rule the tax regime of an investor will depend on the location of the investor i.e. *on-* or *offshore*.[11]

2.3 THE GLOBAL HEDGE FUND INDUSTRY

After exceptional growth since 1998, total assets managed by the hedge fund industry peaked at $1.97 trillion in 2007. After the credit crunch and financial crisis of 2008, with well-publicised frauds and scandals as well as the collapse of several major financial institutions, the hedge fund industry suffered severe losses and investor loyalty. Not until the early part of 2009 did the industry start to experience a marked resurgence in activity realising strong capital inflows and growing investor confidence as shown in Figure 2.2.

It is estimated that the total amount of AuM in the industry by the first half of 2015 stood at $2.23 trillion with a strong stream of asset flows into hedge funds over the past several years, managed by a total of 11 211 hedge funds globally (see Figure 2.2). Of the global hedge fund market, North American funds still remain the prominent market making up around two-thirds of the global industry followed, quite a way behind, by Europe and then Asian sectors as shown in Figure 2.3.

---

[11] *Onshore* (or *domestic*) locations include the US and UK, and to a lesser degree Switzerland and some other European countries. *Offshore* locations include the Cayman Islands, Bermuda, Bahamas, Luxembourg and Ireland.

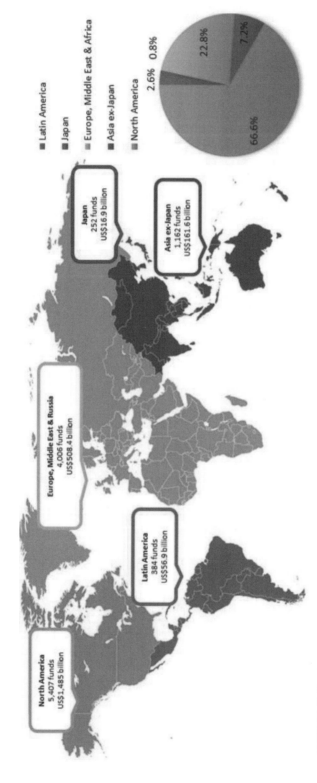

FIGURE 2.3 Global hedge fund industry map as of first half 2015
Source: Eurekahedge

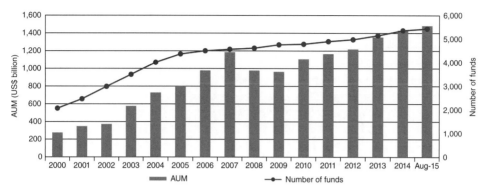

FIGURE 2.4 Growth of the North American hedge fund industry since 2000
Source: Eurekahedge

2.3.1 North America

The North American hedge fund industry has steadily grown on the back of renewed strong investor inflows accounting for roughly two-thirds of total asset growth in the region. Despite mixed economic performance in the US during 2014 and into 2015, total AuM of the North American hedge fund industry stood at US$1.485 trillion managed by 5407 hedge funds midway through 2015 (see Figure 2.4).

Despite periods of high volatility and market swings, North American hedge funds have consistently posted record returns since reaching their lowest point in early 2009. This is a clear indication of the confidence investors began to show in North American funds after the fallout from the global financial crisis of 2008 when billions of dollars were redeemed and funds suffered massive performance-based losses. Since then, hedge fund managers have provided significant protection against market downturns as well as addressing investors' concerns over counterparty risk by engaging multiple prime brokers instead of the usual singular relationship. Moreover, managers have increased redemption frequencies allowing investors better access to their capital, allowed for more transparency across investment strategies and implemented more stringent risk management controls. Such changes, together with a much improved outlook on the US economy and the introduction of *quantitative easing*,[12] have led to increased investor confidence and substantial asset flows into North American hedge funds which look set to continue well into 2017.

---

[12]*Quantitative easing* is a monetary policy that has been employed by the US, the UK and the Eurozone, especially since the financial crisis of 2008. When a county's interest rate is either at, or close to zero, normal expansionary monetary policy fails so the central bank creates new money which it uses to buy government bonds and increase the money supply and excess reserves of the banking system. A further lowering of interest rates follows and it is anticipated that this will lead to a stimulus in the economy.

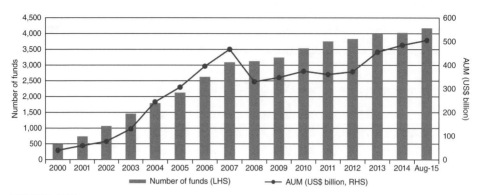

FIGURE 2.5 Growth of the European hedge fund industry since 2000
Source: Eurekahedge

2.3.2 Europe

The rapid growth of the European hedge fund industry over the first seven years of the last decade was eventually slowed by the onset of the financial downturn in 2008. The onset of the global financial crisis, which was followed by the *sovereign debt crisis* in the *Eurozone* sector, dealt a serious blow to the industry with managers seeing large redemptions and heavy performance-based losses. As with North American hedge funds, the European sector experienced huge losses and increased pressure for redemptions from investors which continued until early 2009 when the global economy began to see a potential recovery (see Figure 2.5).

However, by the end of 2011, confidence in the European hedge fund industry declined, following a resurgence of debt woes in member EU sovereigns as the crisis intensified amid fears over Greece exiting the Euro. Throughout 2012, industry assets stayed at their lows as the crisis continued to put a damper on investor sentiment. The *European Central Bank's* (ECB) stance to keep interest rates low and support the Eurozone's recovery has restored market confidence to some extent. Following signs of economic recovery in the region, European hedge funds have enjoyed a period of sustained growth starting in 2013 and into 2015. In addition, the European region has shown some interesting trends with regards to fund launches since the market began to rebound in 2009. Although attrition rates have been relatively high, launches have gained strength on the back of the new *UCITS III regulation*.[13] The popularity of UCITS III has seen the launch of many new start-ups seeking investment capital in the increasingly competitive hedge fund arena. However, many new hedge fund launches have suffered from the investment bias towards allocating to much more well-known and larger based hedge fund names. Nevertheless, it is anticipated that this trend is

---

[13]UCITS III is the *Undertakings for Collective Investment in Transferable Securities*, an EU investment regulation for the creation and distribution of pooled investment funds, such as mutual funds and hedge funds (see Section 2.5.1).

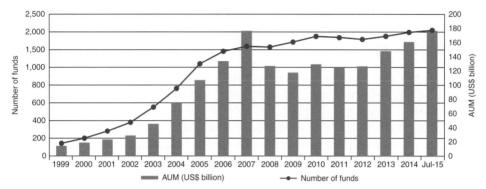

FIGURE 2.6 Growth of the Asian hedge fund industry since 1999
Source: Eurekahedge

likely to change as a result of the increased diversification offered by European hedge funds and growing confidence in a new regulatory environment over the coming years.

2.3.3 Asia

The Asian hedge fund industry grew steadily in 2015 with the asset base growing at twice the rate seen over the same period last year. With strong investor inflows during the year, total AuM increased by midway through 2015, bringing the total size of the Asian hedge fund industry to US$178 billion managed by 1414 hedge funds (see Figure 2.6).

The Asian hedge fund industry witnessed tremendous growth from 1999 over the next eight years until end-2007. Gains realised into 2008 were partially reversed by the advent of the global financial crisis which resulted in a spate of fund liquidations as managers struggled to deal with negative returns and redemption requests from investors. The industry bottomed out early in 2009 mainly due to speculation that the Asia markets may suffer from a possible double-dip recession as a result of the debt contagion passing from Europe. By the second half of 2009, the Asian hedge fund industry witnessed a rebound amid rallying equity markets and some positive asset flows. After another short downturn in 2011, the industry has since realised strong performance-based growth.

Despite this, the Asian sector has never seen the growth experienced pre-2008. In general, hedge fund managers have struggled to generate asset flows and this together with the highly volatile markets has led investors to be extremely cautious about investing in the current climate. However, the desire for Asian governments to attract global hedge fund managers to the region, reductions in hedge fund set-up costs compared to other western locations, the availability of a growing range of financial products and the easing of access and market restrictions in regions such as China and India, should see a steady sustained growth in the sector through 2017 and beyond.

2.4 SPECIALIST INVESTMENT TECHNIQUES

2.4.1 Short Selling

A *short sale* is the sale of a security that a seller does not own or that is completed by delivery of a borrowed security. The short seller borrows the securities from a prime broker in return for paying a daily fee, and promises to replace the borrowed securities at some point in the future. The transaction requires the prime broker to borrow the shares from a securities lender and make delivery on behalf of the short seller. Prime brokers can borrow securities from custodians who hold large institutional investments e.g. mutual and pension funds or from their own proprietary trading accounts. The cash from the transaction is held in an *escrow account*[14] until the short seller is in a position to replace the borrowed shares (or they are called back by the lender). Since the short seller borrows the securities from the prime broker and has a future commitment to replace them, collateral must be posted in the form of cash, securities or other financial assets. The collateral, in addition to the fee for borrowing the securities, provides the prime broker with additional income in the form of interest until the shares are returned.[15] In addition, the short seller must cover any dividends paid on the shares during the period of the loan and in the case of any stock splits e.g. two-for-one, the short seller must pay back twice as many shares.

The eventual buyer of the shares from the short seller is usually unaware that it is a short sale so the seller must make arrangements to cover the delivery obligations. The shares are transferred to the buyer with full legal ownership, including voting rights which can pose a severe problem for the short seller if the prime broker requires the securities back (or *called-away*), for example if the original securities lender requires them for a company shareholder meeting. Although this rarely happens in practice short selling does carry a great deal of risk, especially if the shares are held over a long period of time and the stock fails to decline as expected causing them to have to post further margin and eventually forcing the short seller to close out their position at a significant loss. However, when stock prices fall, short sellers make a profit from the short sale, and also between 60 and 90% of the interest income charged by the prime broker on the cash deposit (i.e. the *short rebate*).

It is often the case that hedge funds do not disclose the names of companies they are selling short to investors for fear of a *short-squeeze*. Unexpected news on short selling activity can cause share prices to suddenly rise due to potential price manipulation through long investors buying additional shares or forcing securities lenders to recall

---

[14] An *escrow account* is an account set up by a broker for the purpose of holding funds on behalf of the client until completion of a transaction.

[15] Borrowing money to purchase securities is generally known as *buying on margin*. It is usually necessary for a hedge fund to open a margin account with a prime broker and maintain the margin with available cash reserves when market prices move adversely in order to meet a *margin call*.

loaned shares. In this case, short sellers' demand for stocks to cover their short positions can cause a mismatch between the availability of shares and thus drive prices up further. To avoid short-squeezes, hedge funds employing short selling only normally invest in large cap companies which have a greater amount of liquidity and volume of shares available from prime brokers. In the US, hedge funds are only allowed to engage in short sales with those securities whose recent price change was an upward movement.[16] Such restrictions are used to prevent hedge funds investing in stocks that are already declining so as avoid the possibility of sending the market into free fall. However, short sellers are often thought of as providing efficient price discovery as well as market depth and liquidity. It is important to investors that they are confident that prices represent fair value and that they can get easy access to liquid markets in which they can readily convert shares into cash. Hedge funds through short selling provide this level of confidence by forcing down overvalued stocks and generating liquidity within the markets.

2.4.2 Leverage

Leverage is using borrowed cash, or a margin account, to increase the purchasing power and exposure to a security (or investment) with the aim of generating higher returns. Financial instruments, such as options, swaps and futures (i.e. derivatives) are also used to create leverage. A premium is paid to purchase a derivative in the underlying asset which gives them various rights and obligations in the future. This premium is far less than the outright price of the underlying asset and thus allows investors to buy an economic exposure to considerably more of the asset than they could otherwise.

Although generally misunderstood, leverage is an extremely widespread investment technique, especially in the hedge fund industry. A great deal of confusion often arises from the various definitions and measurements of leverage. In terms of hedge fund leverage, the debt-to-equity ratio or percentage is often the preferred indicator, for example, if a hedge fund has $50 million equity capital and borrows an additional $100 million, the fund has a total of $150 million in assets and a leverage of *2x equity* or 67% (=100m/150m). Leverage ratios are typically higher than traditional investments and generally more difficult to measure due to the sophisticated use of certain financial instruments and strategies. Since adding leverage to an investment inherently increases risk, investors often equate a highly leveraged hedge fund with a high risk investment. However, this is not normally the case since hedge funds often use

---

[16]The *up-tick* rule was introduced in the US by the Securities and Exchange Commission (SEC) in 1938 to restrict the short selling of stocks unless there was an upward movement in the price. The restriction was lifted in 2007, but there has since been a growing debate on reinstating the ruling to prevent the potential for market manipulation through short selling (see Section 2.5.3).

leverage to offset various positions in order to reduce the risk on their portfolios.[17] For this reason, it is not advisable for investors to solely rely on leverage ratios as proxies for hedge fund risk. It makes more sense to correctly analyse the nature of the strategy in more detail before making a decision on the riskiness of the hedge fund.

2.4.3 Liquidity

Although hedge funds can generate abnormal returns by exploiting the value from investing in *illiquid*[18] assets, there is always a need to access market liquidity. Liquidity is the degree to which an asset can be bought or sold without adversely affecting the market price or value of the asset.[19] Liquidity plays a critical role in the financial markets providing investors with an efficient mechanism to rapidly convert assets into cash. During the recent financial turmoil, hedge funds experienced an unprecedented amount of requests from investors to withdraw their capital creating a serious liquidity problem.

The global credit crisis originated from a growing bubble in the US real estate market which eventually burst in 2008. This led to an overwhelming default of mortgages linked to subprime debt to which financial institutions reacted by tightening credit facilities, selling off bad debts at huge losses and pursuing fast foreclosures on delinquent mortgages. A liquidity crisis followed in the credit markets and banks became increasingly reluctant to lend to one another causing risk premiums on debt to soar and credit to become ever scarcer and costlier. The global financial markets went into meltdown as a continuing spiral of worsening liquidity ensued.

Hedge funds that had assets linked to the subprime debt disaster and other related securities suffered huge losses. Problems were amplified further when investors tried to withdraw capital from their funds and it became apparent that there was a liquidity mismatch between assets and liabilities. When the credit markets froze, hedge fund managers were unable to source sufficient capital to meet investor redemption requirements. This forced managers to restructure their liquidity terms and impose further *gate provisions*,[20] increase the use of *side-pocketing*[21] and enforce

---

[17]The amount of leverage that hedge funds can take on is usually limited by margin supplied by the prime broker and on certain restrictions set by regulators or other organisations. In circumstances where the amount of leverage rises above a certain limit, the lender can take possession of the hedge fund investments, sell them and use the proceeds to offset any losses on the debt financing.

[18]*Illiquid* assets include low volume traded stocks, real estate and other capital holdings.

[19]A highly liquid market can also be considered a *deep* market.

[20]*Gated provisions* are a restriction on the amount of capital that can be withdrawn from a fund during a redemption period. Such provisions are subject to management discretion and normally referred to in the hedge fund prospectus.

[21]A *side-pocket* (or *designated investment*) is an account used by hedge funds to separate illiquid assets from more liquid ones. Holding illiquid assets in a hedge fund can cause a great deal of complexity when investors try to withdraw their capital.

lock-ups.[22] Not only did this negatively affect investor relations but this was further damaged by the selective and insufficient disclosure of performance being made by hedge fund managers. For example, many managers were seen to be reporting side-pocket performance only to investors while relaying much better liquid performance in publications with only a passing note of disclosure about the exclusion of side-pockets. In the case of lock-ups, there exists a clear conflict of interest between locking up investors' capital and continuing to charge management fees. Investors have since argued that it would be more acceptable for gate provisions and the issue of involuntary side-pockets to be tied to deferrals or a reduction in management fees until the fund returns to an appropriate liquid position. The aftermath of the financial crisis has clearly highlighted many of the shortcomings of the hedge fund industry and heightened the debate over the need for increased regulation and monitoring. Nevertheless, it has since been widely accepted that hedge funds played only a small part in the global financial collapse and suffered at the hands of a highly regulated banking system. Indeed, many prominent institutional and economic bodies argue that their very presence provides greater market liquidity and improved price efficiency whilst aiding in the global integration of the financial markets.

2.5 RECENT DEVELOPMENTS FOR HEDGE FUNDS

2.5.1 UCITS Hedge Funds

One of the major developments in the hedge fund industry over the past several years has been the exceptional growth in the *Undertakings for Collective Investment in Transferable Securities* (UCITS) hedge funds. UCITS was designed to meet investor demand for well-regulated instruments monitored by improved compliance standards in the areas of investor protection, regulation and disclosure. The regulatory bodies of the EU are continually updating and improving upon the product to maintain its relevance to investors, with UCITS V being the most recent set of regulations implemented. The implementation of UCITS IV in mid-2011 repealed the previous UCITS III Directive, and provided many enhancements to address pressing concerns from investors, such as transparency, liquidity and risk management aspects of their investments. UCITS IV addressed investor concerns with frequent liquidity, strict requirements to curb fraudulent activities, portfolio concentration limit to counteract excessive risk taking and standardised reporting guidelines, among many others. UCITS V supplements the UCITS IV Directive by addressing some of the weaker points regarding investor protection such as in the areas of remuneration, risk-taking behaviour, duties and liabilities of depositories and administrative sanctions, gradually aligning

---

[22] A *lock-up* is a period of time designated by the hedge fund manager in which an investor may not withdraw any investment in a fund.

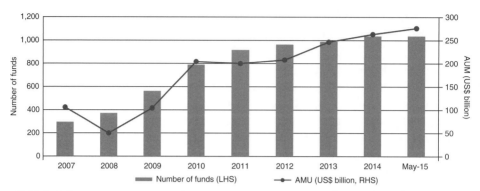

FIGURE 2.7 Growth in number of UCITS hedge funds since December 2007
Source: Eurekahedge

the UCITS Directive and *Alternative Investment Fund Managers Directive* (AIFMD) together (see Section 2.5.2).

As of September 2010, the UCITS hedge fund industry stood at an estimated $131 billion managed by over 600 individual funds (see Figure 2.7). UCITS is a set of directives developed by the EU member states to allow cross-border investments. The aim of the Directives is to improve the financial opportunities offered to UCITS-compliant hedge fund managers whilst addressing the needs of investors in terms of effective risk management procedures, increased transparency and liquidity, especially in light of the recent financial crisis.

UCITS hedge funds have maintained a strong pattern of growth since 2008. By the end of 2014, with the industry delivering modest returns and also attracting plenty of new capital from investors, the industry size was at US$263.2 billion managed by a total of 1038 funds. The UCITS growth trend continued in 2015, with its current size at US$275.7 billion, overseen by a population of 1041 funds.

The original version of the Directive was introduced in 1985 with the goal of establishing a common legal framework for open-ended funds investing in transferable securities set up in any EU member state. That is, to develop a pan-European market in collective investment schemes. Unfortunately, the framework suffered from many obstacles, such as the extent of different marketing rules and taxation allowed across member states. Not until December 2001 was a directive formally adopted under the UCITS III banner which has since undergone several further amendments with a view to including the use of additional asset classes (e.g. hedge fund indices) and a more diverse range of derivative products. Such inclusions have allowed UCITS funds to pursue a number of different investment possibilities, such as absolute return strategies, in ways that were simply not possible under previous UCITS frameworks.

The increased number of eligible asset classes and available use of derivatives has led to a greater number of multi-strategy funds being launched in the UCITS sector in comparison to that of the European multi-strategy industry. Despite this, however, almost half of UCITS funds over the last several years have adopted the long/short equity strategy for several reasons:

1. Long/short equity is by far the largest global hedge fund strategy and therefore those existing managers launching new UCITS vehicles would naturally prefer this strategy
2. Operating the long/short equity strategy under the UCITS framework is relatively straightforward
3. The simplicity of the long/short equity strategy lends itself well to marketing and liaising with retail investors who may not have the knowledge and understanding of the markets like a typical hedge fund client.

Despite the common use of long/short equity strategies in Europe, the regulatory constraints within the UCITS framework mean there are very few similarities elsewhere across industry sectors. For example, there are very few event-driven UCITS hedge funds and practically no distressed-debt-based funds, primarily due to the liquidity restrictions placed on UCITS compliancy. Nevertheless, a major advantage of UCITS funds is the ability of managers to utilise their experience in a proven investment strategy whilst offering potential investors the added incentive of investing in a regulated market. Some of the key features of UCITS hedge fund regulation and fund structure include:

1. Only investment in liquid securities is permitted i.e. those that can be sold within 14 days without substantial loss of value
2. Funds cannot have exposure to more than 10% in one stock
3. Managers can utilise leverage up to 100% of the *Net Asset Value*[23] (NAV) of the fund
4. Managers can employ shorting techniques through the use of derivatives
5. Funds can be easily marketed across the EU and registered in member states and
6. Funds must be domiciled in an EU member state as opposed to offshore locations.

The development of UCITS funds has also opened up the sector to new sources of capital, for example, from retail investors wishing to make use of the alternative investment market but with the assurance of stricter regulatory controls. In addition, improved redemption rules and transparency have helped in building investor confidence, especially after the much debated issue surrounding the use of gated provisions that stopped investors withdrawing large amounts of capital from their funds during the period of huge losses following the financial crisis in 2008. Indeed, the much anticipated release of UCITS V and the development of other European directives, such

---

[23] *Net Asset Value* (NAV) is used to put a value on a hedge fund and is the total of all the hedge fund assets minus all the hedge fund liabilities.

as the directive providing for the new EU "passport", which will give hedge funds marketing rights throughout the EU, will broaden the investment appeal of UCITS-compliant funds even further.

2.5.2 The European Passport

In November 2010 the EU passed a new set of laws governing the use and regulation of the alternative investment industry, named the *Alternative Investment Fund Managers Directive* (AIFMD). The AIFMD aims to provide hedge funds (and private equity funds) with a so-called *passport* to allow funds that meet EU standards access to all EU markets. The passport gives hedge funds the opportunity to market to investors throughout the EU with only a single authorisation. In addition, the Directive will subject hedge funds to increased supervision, regulation and transparency providing pan-European investors with the confidence to invest and operate in a stable European financial market.

The newly formed Paris-based *European Securities and Markets Authority* (ESMA) will act as the EU financial supervisory authority and issue passports, especially to non-EU funds that wish to operate in the EU markets under a single authorisation. The ESMA will also demand non-EU funds to grant the same rights that their funds will enjoy in the European markets. However, the controversial passport scheme did not come into effect for some EU funds until 2013, and later for many non-EU funds, despite formal warnings from the European Commission.

2.5.3 Restrictions on Short Selling

Short selling can result in unlimited losses if the hedge fund incorrectly anticipates the direction of movement of share prices. Moreover, short selling can also be used to manipulate market prices. It has been argued for some time that hedge funds can engage in collective short selling to create an imbalance in supply and force down the price of a security. During the recent financial turmoil and substantial falls in stock prices, hedge funds were often accused of short selling to exacerbate and profit from the declining markets. During 2008 and 2009, regulators announced several actions to protect against abusive short selling and to make short sale information more readily available to the public.

One of the main methods of market abuse was the use of *naked* short sales i.e. the activity of selling short without having borrowed or arranged to borrow the securities to make delivery to the buyer. Such a *failure-to-deliver* is a gross violation of ethical market practice and something the regulators were determined to address. New temporary rulings forced prime brokers to first ascertain, before undertaking a short sale transaction, whether the securities were available for short selling or could be borrowed against delivery. Market participants were also required to provide detailed information on short sale activity and their overall short positions. Although the rulings curbed short sale abuses during the financial crisis of 2008 many hedge fund managers have since argued that such regulation hinders the efficient workings of the financial markets and causes a negative effect on liquidity. Restrictions and other regulation on short sales is a contentious area of debate amongst market professionals and regulators and under continual review. Nevertheless, regulators are keen to address issues associated with short selling and the provision of detailed information on short sale activity for public disclosure and may certainly impose further restrictions on the practice in the near future.

In this chapter we have provided an introduction to the concept of hedge funds, how they are structured and the key players within such an investment vehicle. Each of the major markets within the global hedge fund industry has been reviewed with focus on the current financial crisis and how hedge funds have performed over this period. In fact, it has been publicly stated that hedge funds have played only a minimal part in the global financial collapse and have instead suffered at the hands of a highly regulated financial system. Nevertheless, some of the specialist investment techniques employed by hedge fund managers have since come under increased scrutiny and regulatory pressures.

Hedge Fund Data Sources

O btaining accurate, reliable and timely data on hedge funds is of extreme importance to a manager or analyst wishing to measure, monitor and assess the returns and performance of such investment opportunities. The need for consistent and robust hedge fund indices, as well as trustworthy benchmarks for the industry, is also of enormous value and a necessity when trying to obtain a clear representation of a hedge funds track record.

Chapter 3 reviews a variety of prominent commercial hedge fund databases and the subsequent indices and benchmarks they produce. In addition, the many pitfalls and problems that need to be fully understood when interpreting and using such summary statistics are discussed. In particular, the inherent heterogeneity and lack of representativeness within the hedge fund universe is highlighted as a major concern in the industry. Moreover, some of the most innovative products developed in order to overcome some of these shortfalls are reviewed.

3.1 HEDGE FUND DATABASES

Many hedge fund managers provide, on a voluntary basis, monthly hedge fund performance data to a variety of commercial databases. These hedge fund databases collect, assimilate and produce informative reports, indices and benchmarks based on this data for potential investors, consultants, analysts and academics involved in investment and research on hedge funds. Such data allows the construction and publication of numerous *non-investable* and *investable* indices that purport to give an indication of the state of the hedge fund industry and act as important benchmarking indicators. However, due to the voluntary nature of a fund manager's requirement to supply informative monthly data, the indices produced by these vendors can be misleading and contain several *biases* and *anomalies*. Moreover, a complete record of every single hedge fund in the industry is simply not available; relevant information comes only from samples of the hedge fund universe. The quality and quantity of such data varies between vendors and an investor is left to their own judgement in accepting one set of hedge fund performance statistics over another. For this reason, it is important to note that any given database provides only a sample of the entire hedge fund universe, requiring investors to access multiple data sources to get a clearer understanding of the investment opportunities and the state of the hedge fund industry.

3.2 MAJOR HEDGE FUND INDICES

In traditional finance, the use of indices is a useful investment tool for managing the exposure of a portfolio of investments to market risk i.e. a so-called *passively* managed investment style. In the hedge fund world, where performance is generally driven by a manager's skill and expertise, reflecting an *active* management style, the use of hedge fund indices is more surprising, since the concept of an index is commonly associated with the notion of passive management. However, many of the commercial databases, and a selection of traditional index providers e.g. FTSE and Dow Jones, have developed and published a range of hedge fund indices and relevant benchmarks.[1] The way such indices are designed and constructed varies considerably amongst providers and should be fully understood before accepting the index has a valued industry benchmark or performance measurement. Many of the index providers purport to have the best index methodology and construction process with strict inclusion criteria and thorough due-diligence procedures. Nevertheless, many investors, as well as the industry itself, are wary of considering one index better than another and approach the hedge fund index and benchmark arena with caution.

3.2.1 Non-Investable and Investable Indices

The hedge fund industry is highly heterogeneous making the construction of a satisfactory performance index that comprises the available hedge fund universe extremely difficult. Non-investable hedge fund indices try, at best, to represent the performance of a sample of the hedge fund universe taken from a relevant database. However, such databases have diverse selection criteria and methods of index construction leading to many differing published indices. Although aiming to be representative of the hedge fund universe, non-investable indices suffer from many unavoidable *biases*.[2] A further difficulty associated with the heterogeneity of hedge funds is the classification of investment styles. With over 12 000 active hedge funds in the industry, determining each manager's investment style is virtually impossible. Some index providers have developed their own classification system that attempts to capture a high level of homogeneity within each investment group and a subsequent level of heterogeneity

---

[1] Over the past decade, many hedge fund databases and index providers have merged, been acquired by larger firms or developed into *boutiques* offering specialist hedge fund services and consultancy.
[2] See Section 3.3.

between individual groups. Unfortunately, many hedge fund managers do not report their investment style correctly or often change styles without giving prior notice to the database vendor. Clearly then, hedge fund indices are subject to a greater lack of representativeness than traditional indices. Such a problem goes beyond an insufficient classification of investment styles. Instead, it concerns the actual managers themselves who have a great deal of freedom and choice at their disposal.

By early 2000, many index providers had launched a series of investable indices offering a low-cost investment opportunity to gain exposure to the hedge fund industry. An index is investable when the investors are able to replicate the index by obtaining and maintaining a certain level of *tracking error*.[3] Generally based on platforms of separate *managed accounts*,[4] this new generation of indices has been able to provide investors with improved *liquidity* and a low-cost method of gaining access to the hedge fund world. In addition, the composition, construction methodology and management principles are overseen by an independent committee and disclosed to the public, allowing increased transparency. To create an investable index, the index provider selects a range of hedge funds and develops structured products or derivative instruments that deliver the performance of the investable index. To make them investable, each hedge fund agrees to accept investments on the terms given by the index provider. When investors buy an investable index the provider makes the investments in the underlying hedge funds, making such an index similar in many ways to a *fund of hedge fund* (FoHF)[5] investment. In fact, some refer to investable indices as merely FoHFs in disguise or with additional constraints. However, by their very construction, investable hedge fund indices are unable to represent the hedge fund universe. Such indices cannot, for example, represent an *open* funds universe, since they are not composed of funds belonging to this subset of the complete universe. They contain many *partially* closed hedge funds i.e. funds that accept new investments only from investors that have reserved capacity. Hedge funds generally do have capacity issues as certain strategies only work well within certain limits of investment capital. Indeed, many hedge fund managers refuse further investment of capital into the fund after they have reached a maximum level of AuM and assign them as *closed* funds. As a result, it is very difficult for hedge fund indices to remain investable when the composite hedge funds have closed their doors to new investors. Most index providers argue that to be a truly representative index that acts as a gauge for hedge fund performance, both open and closed funds should be included in the hedge fund index.

---

[3] See Section 3.4.1.

[4] *Managed accounts* are a rapidly-growing, fee-based investment management product for High Net Worth (HNW) individuals. Such accounts allow access to professional money managers, high degrees of customisation and greater tax efficiencies. They are also said to provide the added benefits of greater TLC i.e. Transparency, Liquidity and Control.

[5] A *fund of hedge fund* (FoHF) is a common investment vehicle for inexperienced investors or those that have limited exposure to the alternative investment market.

The trade-off, therefore, is between having as broad a representation as possible of hedge fund performance against having a smaller sample of hedge fund managers representing the performance accessible through investment.

By the end of 2006, hedge fund *replication* aimed to eliminate many of the problems associated with hedge fund indices. Instead of accessing the performance of hedge funds directly they take a statistical approach to the analysis of historic hedge fund returns, and use this to construct a model of how hedge fund returns react to movements in a range of investable financial instruments. This model is then used to construct an investable portfolio of those assets. This makes the index investable, and in principle they can be as representative as the hedge fund database from which they were constructed. As the hedge fund industry becomes increasingly diversified, offering greater opportunity for investors to gain exposure to hedge fund returns without direct involvement, the growth in such indices is set to increase.

3.2.2 Dow Jones Credit Suisse Hedge Fund Indices (www.hedgeindex.com)

The *Credit Suisse/Tremont Hedge Fund Indices* were rebranded in 2010 after Credit Suisse joined forces with Dow Jones Indices to provide the flagship *Dow Jones Credit Suisse* (DJCS) *Hedge Fund Index*. Dow Jones is responsible for the calculation, distribution and marketing of the indices whilst Credit Suisse affiliates continue to manage the financial instruments associated with them.

The *DJCS Hedge Fund* (or *Broad*) *Index* is one of the industry's most respected indices which tracks approximately 9000 funds from the proprietary Credit Suisse database and includes around 400 hedge funds as of July 2014. The index comprises only hedge funds with a minimum of $50m AuM[6] and audited accounts,[7] although hedge funds with an AuM of more than $500m and a track record of less than a year may be considered under special circumstances. In terms of index participation, AuM does not include managed accounts and reflects only the assets of the fund, not the AuM of the investment company. For index inclusion, fund managers must report performance returns, in the form of *net asset values* (NAVs), on a monthly basis. The index is asset-weighted (see Box 3.1) and broadly diversified across 10 style-based investment strategies (see Table 3.1) which seek to be representative of the entire hedge fund universe. The DJCS Hedge Fund Index construction is based on a transparent, unbiased rule-based selection process. The methodology analyses the percentage of assets invested in each subcategory and selects funds for the index based on those percentages, matching the shape of the index to the shape of the universe. Fund *weight caps* can be applied to enhance diversification and limit concentration

---

[6] AuM can be difficult to determine, since hedge fund managers combine managed accounts and onshore/offshore vehicles, and also use different amounts of leverage, either through margins or by short selling.

[7] A hedge fund must have a minimum one-year track record to have audited financial accounts.

TABLE 3.1 Asset weights by investment
strategy for the DJCS Hedge Fund Index

Investment Style	Asset Weight (%)
Convertible arbitrage	1.70
Dedicated short bias	0.30
Emerging markets	7.20
Equity market neutral	2.10
Event driven	26.10
Fixed income arbitrage	4.50
Global macro	19.30
Long/short equity	20.80
Managed futures	4.50
Multi-strategy	13.50

Source: Hedge Index

risk. The index is calculated and rebalanced monthly and funds are reselected on a
quarterly basis as required.

BOX 3.1: ASSET WEIGHTING SCHEMES

When measuring the performance of a portfolio of hedge funds or an average
of a group of funds, it is necessary to assign a particular weight to each of the
individual funds. There are three major weighting schemes used in the hedge
fund industry, namely *equal*, *asset* and *arbitrary* weightings.

Equal

If there are N hedge funds in the group of funds, then, each fund return has an
equal weight, w_i in the average that is given by:

$$w_i = \frac{1}{N}$$

The average is a measure of the average behaviour of the fund returns irre-
spective of the amount of AuM (or *market capitalisation*) of each hedge fund.

Asset

Each hedge fund return is weighted with respect to the amount of AuM in proportion to the total assets managed within the group of funds i.e. dollar-weighted

averages. If a particular fund i has AuM denoted by A_i, then the weight of fund i in the average is given by:

$$w_i = \frac{A_i}{\sum_{i=1}^{N} A_i}$$

Arbitrary

Each hedge fund return is given an arbitrary weight w_i within the average which can be changed over time. However, the total of all the arbitrary weights must always sum to 100%.

Suppose we have a number of hedge funds, N in a group where the return on fund i is denoted by r_i and respective weight w_i, then a performance measurement (or index) for the group can be determined as the weighted average of the individual hedge fund returns, such that:

$$r_{index} = \sum_{i=1}^{N} w_i r_i$$

The index family currently consists of 17 indices, including a range of geographical and strategy-specific hedge fund indices. The current family includes:

- The *DJCS AllHedge Index*, formerly the CSFB/Tremont Sector Invest Index, is a diversified investable index comprised of an aggregate of all 10 DJCS AllHedge Strategy Indices and asset-weighted based on the sector weights of the Broad Index. The AllHedge Index was launched in October 2007, and any performance of the index predating October 2007 is simulated from returns on the underlying AllHedge Strategy Indices as of October 2004. AllHedge seeks to represent the investable hedge fund universe and encompasses around 80 funds as of November 2013;
- The *DJCS Blue Chip Hedge Fund Index*, formerly the CSFB/Tremont Investable Hedge Fund Index, is an investable index made up of the 60 largest hedge funds from the 10 style-based sectors comprising the Broad Index; and
- The *DJCS LEA Hedge Fund Index* is an emerging market asset-weighted composite[8] index covering the regions of Latin America, Europe, Middle East, Africa, and Asia emerging economies. The index was launched in April 2008.

---

[8] A composite index consists of individual hedge funds that cover a range of different investment strategies.

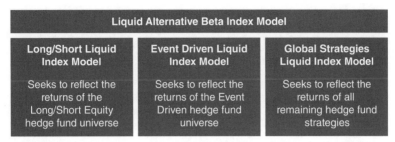

FIGURE 3.1 The Liquid Alternative Beta Index model
Source: Hedge Index

3.2.2.1 Liquid Alternative Betas In addition to the above index family, Credit Suisse publishes a series of *Liquid Alternative Beta* (LAB) indices.[9] LAB indices aim to replicate (or *clone*) the aggregate return characteristics of alternative investments strategies using commonly traded instruments with high liquidity. LABs reflect the returns of a dynamic basket of investable market factors selected and weighted so as to approximate the aggregate returns of the universe of hedge funds represented by the family of DJCS hedge fund indices. Such liquid replication strategies seek to provide hedge fund returns without direct hedge fund investment and thus enhance liquidity and eliminate hedge fund *headline*[10] risk (see Box 3.2). The range of LAB indices currently includes the CS Event Driven Liquid Index, CS Global Macro Liquid Index, CS Long/Short Equity Liquid Index and CS Merger Arbitrage Liquid Index as shown in Figure 3.1.

BOX 3.2:   A LIQUID REPLICATION STRATEGY

Problem: A pension plan with a traditional 60/40 (equity/fixed income) portfolio is planning a 5% hedge fund allocation. To implement the program, the plan starts due diligence on several hedge fund managers, a lengthy process that may delay capital deployment. If the funds remain in cash or short maturity fixed income, expected returns could be negatively impacted.

Solution: To better manage the transition and speed up the exposure of the plan to potential hedge-fund like returns, the plan makes an allocation to a liquid alternative beta strategy with daily liquidity. The risk/return profile of this interim allocation is expected to provide a reasonably close match to that of the direct hedge funds in which it plans to invest. The plan can then draw down

---

[9] Alternative beta refers to alternative systematic risks i.e. those risks that cannot be diversified away and are compensated through risk premia or the expected rate of return above the risk-free interest rate.
[10] *Headline* risk is the impact that a negative news story could have on the value of an investment.

its replication exposure gradually to reallocate to the selected hedge funds as it completes the due diligence process (see Figure 3.2).

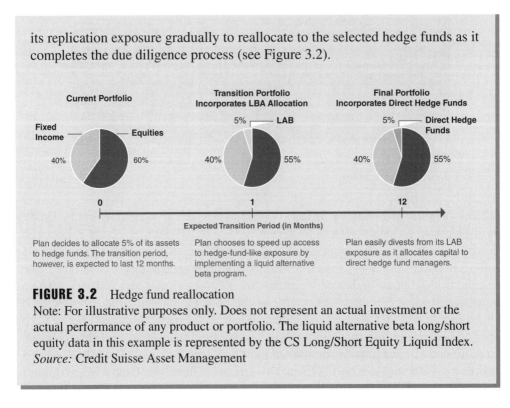

FIGURE 3.2   Hedge fund reallocation
Note: For illustrative purposes only. Does not represent an actual investment or the actual performance of any product or portfolio. The liquid alternative beta long/short equity data in this example is represented by the CS Long/Short Equity Liquid Index. *Source:* Credit Suisse Asset Management

The three main components that drive hedge fund performance can be identified as:

1. Traditional beta
2. Alternative beta and
3. Alpha.

Traditional beta returns are based on long-only investment strategies and have exposure to traditional market factors, such as equity and credit risk that act as a *proxy*[11] for well-known benchmark indices e.g. the S&P 500 and Russell 2000 indices. Alternative beta involves other factors, such as *currency carry* and *equity momentum*, that can be captured using various investment strategies and proxies through *systematic* trading.[12] Alpha is attributable to the skill and expertise of the hedge fund manager and is often difficult to capture. Fung and Hsieh (2004), pioneers in the field of

---

[11] A *proxy* is an efficient approximation for another investment.
[12] *Systematic* (or *rule-based*) trading involves using an automated system to trade on behalf of the trader. The system makes all trading decisions with respect to the rules set by the trader and the information available at the time. The other type of trading is discretionary; where the trader uses his intelligence and knowledge to make trading decisions with respect to the information available at the time.

TABLE 3.2 Traditional and alternative beta factors driving aggregate hedge fund returns and their respective proxies

	Strategy	Factors	Proxies
Traditional Beta Examples	Long/short equity	US large cap	S&P 500 index
	Long/short equity	US small cap	Russell 2000 index
	Event driven	High yield fixed income	IBOX high yield liquid index
Alternative Beta Examples	Global macro	Currency carry	Custom currency carry proxy: long high-yielding currencies; short low-yielding currencies
	Long/short equity	Equity momentum	Custom trend-following proxy: long well-performing companies; short poorly performing companies
	Event driven	Merger arbitrage	Custom M&A proxy: long companies being acquired; short companies that are acquirers

Source: Credit Suisse

hedge fund replication, have shown traditional and alternative beta to be the largest contributors to aggregate hedge fund returns. For this reason, one of the first steps in hedge fund replication is to identify traditional and alternative beta factors that represent the exposure of individual hedge fund strategies. These factors then have to be represented by proxies. These turn out to be fairly straightforward in terms of traditional betas (e.g. S&P 500); however, custom proxies have to be developed for many of the alternative beta factors (see Table 3.2).

Once the factors and proxies have been determined it is necessary to ascertain the combination of exposure and weights that best replicate the hedge fund strategies. Investors can gain market exposure to the factors identified by the analysis using a variety of liquid commonly traded financial instruments, such as index funds, *Exchange Traded Funds* (ETFs),[13] swaps, listed futures and option contracts. Any factor exposures and their respective weights can be updated periodically based on ongoing quantitative analysis e.g. factor modelling. Figure 3.3 shows the hypothetical

---

[13]ETFs are a security that tracks an index, a commodity or a basket of assets like an index fund, but can be traded like a stock on an exchange.

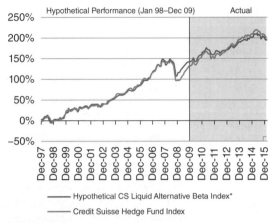

FIGURE 3.3   Hypothetical performance of the
CS LAB Index from Jan 1998 to Dec 2009 and
actual historical performance from Jan 2010
through Feb 2016
*Simulations for the CS LAB Index were used to
measure how a portfolio of securities and market
indices designed to track hedge fund indices
would have performed in the period beginning
December 1997. The LAB Index was launched in
January 2010 and shown by the vertical black line.
Source: Credit Suisse

and actual performance of the CS LAB index from January 1998 through to February
2016. Figure 3.4 shows a schematic of the LAB index construction process.

3.2.3 Hedge Fund Research (www.hedgefundresearch.com)

Hedge Fund Research (HFR) produces numerous indices of hedge fund performance
ranging from industry-aggregate levels down to specific, focused areas of sub-strategy
and regional investment. The *HFRI Fund Weighted Composite Index*, created in 1994,
is one of the most widely used standards of global hedge fund performance. The HFRI
index is constructed using equally weighted composites of over 2200 single-manager
hedge funds reporting to the HFR database. The *HFRI FoHF Index* is another equally
weighted index composite from the HFR database of over 800 FoHFs. Figure 3.5
shows the growth of $1000 since the inception of the HFRI Fund Weighted Composite
Index against several global industry indices.

Since 2003, HFR has also produced a range of investable HRFX indices constructed from a variety of quantitative methods, multi-level screening, cluster analysis,
Monte-Carlo simulation and optimisation techniques (see Figure 3.6) to ensure each
index is a unique representation of its investment criteria. HFRX Indices are designed

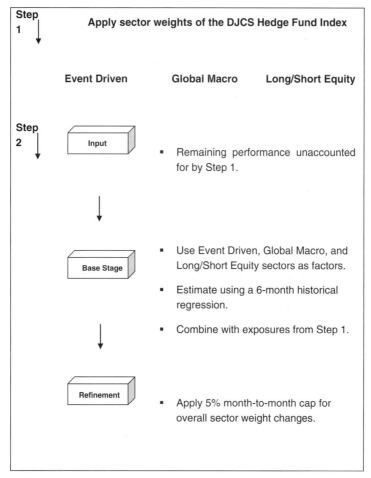

FIGURE 3.4 A schematic of the CS LAB Index construction process
Source: Credit Suisse

to offer full transparency, daily pricing and consistent fund selection, as well as stringent risk management and strict reporting standards.

HFRX Indices use four constituent weighting methodologies and each strategy, sub-strategy and regional investment focus has a corresponding index. The four constituent weighting methodologies are defined as:

1. *HFRX Global Hedge Fund Index* – represents the overall composition of the hedge fund universe comprised of a range of hedge fund strategies; including but not limited to convertible arbitrage, distressed securities, equity hedge, equity market neutral, event driven, macro, merger and relative value arbitrage. The underlying constituents and indices are asset weighted based on the distribution of assets in the hedge fund universe.

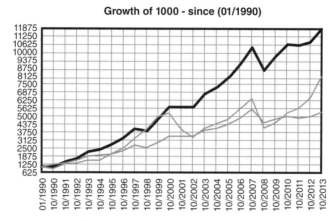

FIGURE 3.5   The growth of $1000 since inception of the
HFRI Fund Weighted Composite Index and FoHFs
Composite Index against the S&P 500
Source: HFR

2. *HFRX Equally Weighted Strategies Index* – applies an equal weight to all selected
constituents.

3. *HFRX Equally Weighted Sub-Strategies Index* – is constructed by equally weighting the sub-strategies included in the HFRX Global Hedge Fund Index.

4. *HFRX Absolute Return Index* – incorporates hedge funds that exhibit low volatilities and correlations to standard directional benchmarks of equity market and
hedge fund industry performance.

5. *HFRX Market Directional Index* – incorporates hedge funds that exhibit high
volatilities and correlations to standard directional benchmarks of equity market
and hedge fund industry performance.

Table 3.3 shows a summary comparison of the HFRI and HFRX indices.

3.2.4 FTSE Hedge (www.ftse.com)

Since December 1997, FTSE Hedge has provided a series of global indices based on
a detailed quantitative and qualitative screening process of 9000 hedge funds from
the FTSE database. The indices give a daily measure of the aggregate risk and return
characteristics of a broadly based global universe of investable hedge funds that allow
a sound basis for the creation of liquid and structured investment products within a
high degree of transparency. For index inclusion, hedge funds must have a minimum of
$50m AuM and have audited accounts for the past 24 months. *FTSE Hedge* currently
includes the *FTSE Hedge Index*, eight trading strategy indices (equity hedge, CTA,

Cluster Analysis	HFR screens over 7500 hedge funds to identify those firms with minimum 24-month track record, at least $50 million AUM, willing to trade on a transparent basis and are open to new investments.
	↓
Correlation Analysis	Cluster and correlation analyses are performed to group managers by true strategy categories and to eliminate outliers.
	↓
Monte-Carlo Simulation	Monte-Carlo Simulation helps determine the adequate number of managers to replicate each strategy.
	↓
Due Diligence	Selected managers must provide daily transparency and pass extensive qualitative screening.
	↓
Strategy Weighting	Manager investments are then weighted to maximise representation with their group.

FIGURE 3.6 A dynamic, bottom-up approach to HFRX index construction
Source: HFR

global macro, merger arbitrage, distressed securities, convertible arbitrage, equity arbitrage and fixed income relative value), and three management style indices (directional, event-driven and non-directional).

The construction methodology follows four main stages, namely a classification process, quantitative screening, statistical sampling and a due diligence stage as shown in Figure 3.7. In essence, the funds are classified into strategic categories within the FTSE Hedge Index, which results in around 450–500 funds remaining. These funds are then further screened, by mathematical sampling to ensure transparency, down to 80 funds. Finally, 40 hedge funds are selected, by an independent committee of leading market professionals, for the actual index.

3.2.4.1 FTSE Hedge Momentum Index Since January 2000, FTSE Hedge also produces the *FTSE Hedge Momentum Index*, an investment strategy index designed

TABLE 3.3   A summary comparison of the HFRI and HFRX indices

Category	HFRI Monthly Indices	HFRX Indices
Created	1994	2003
Weighting	Equally	Index specific
Reporting style	Net of all fees	Net of all fees
Index calculated	Three times a month: Flash Update (5th business day of the month), a Mid Update (15th of the month), and an End Update (1st business day of following month)	Monthly or daily
Index rebalanced	Monthly	Quarterly
Criteria for inclusion	Listing in HFR Database; Reports monthly net of all fees monthly performance and assets in USD	In addition to meeting HFRI criteria, funds must be open to new investment
Minimum asset size and/or track record for fund inclusion	$50 million or greater than a 12-month track record	$50 million and 24-month track record
Investable index	No	HFR Asset Management, LLC constructs investable products that track HFRX
Number of funds	Over 2000 in HFRI Fund Weighted Composite Over 800 in HFRI FoFs Composite	Over 250 in total constituent universe

Source: HFR

to outperform the underlying FTSE Hedge Index. All constituents of the FTSE Hedge Momentum Index are selected from the FTSE Hedge Index based on strictly defined quality, liquidity and capacity criteria. By under- or over-weighting the constituent funds in terms of whether they show persistent positive return (i.e. momentum), the index can be shown to outperform the FTSE Hedge Index. Indeed, over an eight-year period the FTSE Hedge Momentum Index has returned a 10.1% annualised performance, representing a 3.9% outperformance over and above the FTSE Hedge Index.

3.2.5 Greenwich Alternative Investments (www.greenwichai.com)

First published in 1995, the *Greenwich Alternative Investments* (GAI) *Global Hedge Fund Indices* provide more than 22 years of risk and return history that represents both

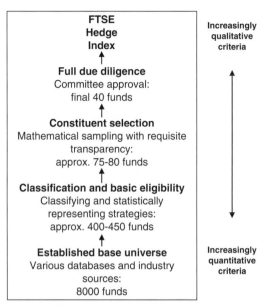

FIGURE 3.7 FTSE Hedge Index quantitative and qualitative index construction
Source: FTSE Hedge

the overall hedge fund universe as well as various constituent groups of hedge funds as defined by their investment strategies. The flagship index, the GAI Global Hedge Fund Index, is designed to reflect the dynamic nature of the hedge fund universe and does not have a fixed set of constituent funds. Instead, GAI attempts to include as many funds as possible, excluding all FoHFs, based on monthly return data. Funds are not excluded on the basis of size, location or other factors but must have a minimum three-month track record. Currently in excess of 2000 hedge funds are used to calculate the GAI Global Hedge Fund Index at month-end. Each hedge fund is categorised by investment strategy based on the information supplied by the fund manager and according to the GAI hedge fund strategy definitions. In 2004, four broad Strategy Groups were introduced in the GAI Global Hedge Fund Index, namely Market Neutral Group, Long/Short Equity Group, Directional Trading Group and Specialty Strategies Group. In January 2010, 10 regional indices were introduced as a result of an increasing number of funds focused exclusively on specific geographic regions. The indices were created in two sets i.e. Developed Markets and Emerging Markets with each set containing five indices, namely Composite, Global, Asia, Europe and Americas.

3.2.5.1 GAI Investable Indices The *GAI Investable Hedge Fund Indices* are an additional series of hedge fund benchmarks designed to represent expected performance of investable hedge funds that are open and considered suitable for institutional

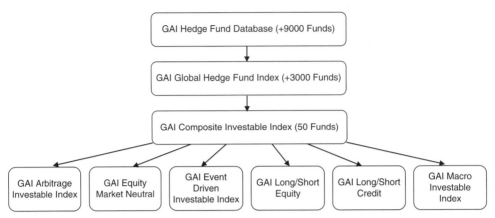

FIGURE 3.8 The family of GAI Investable Indices
Source: GAI

investment. The GAI Investable Indices are designed to replicate the performance of the unique strategies of the hedge fund universe (see Figure 3.8).

The GAI Global Hedge Fund Indices form the basis for the construction of the *GAI Investable Indices*. Asset weights of the Greenwich Investable Indices follow those of the GAI Global Hedge Fund Indices in order to most accurately represent the current asset allocation within the hedge fund index. The GAI Investable Indices provide sophisticated investors with an investable benchmark for the hedge fund industry designed to track the various strategies of the GAI Global Hedge Fund Indices. Table 3.4 shows the family of GAI investable indices along with their respective replicating performance index.

TABLE 3.4 GAI Investable Indices and associated replicating index

GAI Investable Index Name	# Funds	GAI Replicating Index
Composite Investable Index (Monthly)	50	Global Hedge Fund Index
Composite Investable Index (Quarterly)	50	Global Hedge Fund Index
Arbitrage Investable Index	10	Global Arbitrage Index
Equity Market Neutral Investable Index	10	Global Equity Market Neutral Index
Event-Driven Investable Index	10	Global Event-Driven Index
Futures Investable Index	10	Global Futures Index
Long-Short Credit Investable Index	10	Global Long-Short Credit Index
Long-Short Equity Investable Index	20	Global Long-Short Equity Index
Macro Investable Index	10	Global Macro Index

Source: GAI

The fund selection process begins with a quantitative review of the performance of all the funds in the GAI Global Hedge Fund Index. Each one is then ranked within their assigned strategy according to the Greenwich Value Score™ (GVS). The GVS is a multi-factor model designed to identify persistent top-quartile funds and provide a relative performance rating and risk assessment based on:

- Risk adjusted performance
- Volatility
- Downside risk and
- Correlations.

Potential candidates are then examined on a qualitative basis and subjected to a rigorous due diligence procedure, including a detailed review of the hedge fund model to determine strategy, style and expected returns whilst also highlighting a manager's ability to effectively create alpha and consistently deliver positive returns. During this process, an in-depth analysis of the fund strategy and risk control procedures are also undertaken as well as stress testing at various points within the fund's performance (see Figure 3.9). In addition to meeting the above quantitative and qualitative

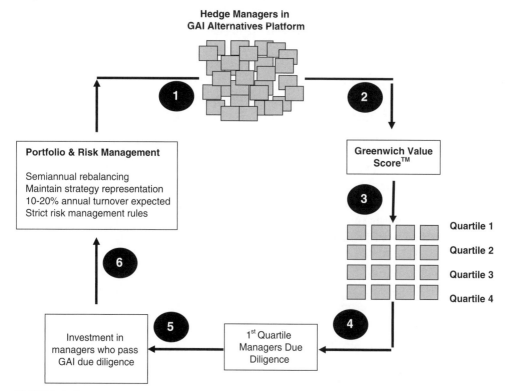

FIGURE 3.9 Schematic of the fund selection process
Source: GAI

processes, the constituent fund must also have a minimum one-year track record and AuM exceeding $50m (overall company assets greater than $100m).

3.2.6 Morningstar Alternative Investment Center (www.morningstar.com/advisor/alternative-investments.htm)

In September 2008, Morningstar acquired the *Morgan Stanley Capital International* (MSCI) *Hedge Fund Index* family and agreed to use their industry-leading categorisation and index construction methodology. The Morningstar MSCI Hedge Fund Indices currently consist of over 190 indices.

3.2.6.1 MSCI Hedge Fund Classification Standard   In July 2002, MSCI launched the *MSCI Hedge Fund Classification Standard* (HFCS), one of the most comprehensive hedge fund classification models to date. The HFCS uses three Primary Characteristics, namely the hedge fund investment style, asset class and geography in order to classify funds and define hedge fund strategies. In addition, Secondary Characteristics are defined through the *Global Industry Classification Standard* (GICS), and cover capitalisation size for equity-oriented strategies, and fixed income focus for credit-oriented strategies (see Table 3.5). The investment process determines the approach managers use to select investments in order to generate returns and manage risk. They are grouped into five broad categories, or investment process groups i.e. Directional Trading, Relative Value, Security Selection, Specialist Credit and Multi-Process. The indices are equal weighted at all four levels of aggregation and asset weighted at the two highest levels as can be seen in Table 3.6.

Classification schemes attempt to group hedge funds based on their strategy and characteristics; however, such meaningful groupings are challenging due to the inherent heterogeneity of hedge fund investing. Such diversification does not allow the development of a simple group-based system and any classification is likely to be subject to a large degree of subjectivity. The MSCI HFCS attempts to overcome this problem by attempting to capture the multi-dimensional nature of hedge fund investing through the use of Primary and Secondary Characteristics, as described above, to more accurately and effectively identify and define hedge fund strategies. The MSCI HFCS strives to offer a balance between a suitable level of detail which permits an accurate classification of a large number of strategies whilst also allowing an intuitive understanding of its interpretation and implementation.

3.2.6.2 MSCI Investable Indices   In addition to the family of MSCI Hedge Fund Indices, MSCI developed an index construction methodology to build a range of *MSCI Investable Hedge Fund Indices*. Their aim was to develop a set of replicable and tradable hedge fund indices reflecting the aggregate performance of a diversified range of hedge fund strategies. Such objectives require that the investable hedge fund indices

TABLE 3.5 MSCI Primary and Secondary Characteristics breakdown

Primary Characteristics					Secondary Characteristics		
Investment Process		Asset Class	Geography		GICS Sector	Fixed Income Sector	Market Cap
Process Group	Process		Area	Region			
Directional Trading		Commodities	Developed Markets		Consumer Discr.	Asset-Backed	Small
	Discretionary	Convertibles		Europe	Consumer Staples	Gov. Sponsored	Small & Mid Cap
	Tactical	Currencies		Japan	Energy	High Yield	Mid & Large Cap
	Systematic	Equity		North America	Financial	Investment Grade	No Size Focus
	Multi-Process	Fixed Income		Pacific ex Japan	Health Care	Mortgage-Backed	
		Diversified		Diversified	Industrials	Sovereign	
Relative Value			Emerging Markets		IT	No Sector Focus	
	Arbitrage			EMEA	Materials		
	Merger Arb.			Asia Pacific	Telecom Services		
	Statistical Arb.			Latin America	Utilities		
	Multi-Process			Diversified	No Industry Focus		

(continued)

TABLE 3.5 (*Continued*)

	Primary Characteristics				Secondary Characteristics		
Investment Process			Geography				
Process Group	Process	Asset Class	Area	Region	GICS Sector	Fixed Income Sector	Market Cap
Security Selection			Global Markets				
	Long Bias			Europe			
	No Bias			Asia ex Japan			
	Short Bias			Asia			
	Variable Bias			Diversified			
Specialist Credit							
	Credit Trading						
	Distressed						
	Private						
	Multi-Process						
Multi-Process Group							
	Event Driven						
	Multi-Process						

Source: MSCI

TABLE 3.6 The MSCI Hedge Fund Index classification structure

Hedge Fund Composite Indices					Weighting Asset & Equal
Process Group	**Process Group**	**Process Group**	**Process Group**	**Process Group**	← ——— Asset & Equal
Directional Trading	Relative Value	Security Selection	Specialist Credit	Multi-Process	← ———
Investment Process	**Investment Process**	**Investment Process**	**Investment Process**	**Investment Process**	Equal ← ———
Discretionary Trading	Arbitrage	Long Bias	Distressed Securities	Event Driven	
Tactical Allocation	Merger Arbitrage	No Bias	Long-Short Credit	Multi-Process	
Systematic Trading	Statistical Arbitrage	Short Bias	Private Placements		
Multi-Process	Multi-Process	Variable Bias	Multi-Process		
Strategy Indices	**Strategy Indices**	**Strategy Indices**	**Strategy Indices**	**Strategy Indices**	Equal ← ———

Source: MSCI

be based on well-diversified managed account platforms (or *Platforms*) of hedge fund investments offering more frequent pricing and liquidity than is otherwise possible.

An investable *Hedge Fund Reference Framework* (HFRF) is designed to establish which hedge fund investment processes and strategies will be represented in the investable index. The HFRF is further supplemented by a series of index calculation, maintenance rules and guidelines relating to segment diversification, fund eligibility, concentration, investment capacity, and fund and segment weight allocation. The MSCI *Hedge Fund Composite Index* (HFCI) is used as a proxy for the hedge fund universe. The HFCI is an equally weighted index that measures the performance of a diverse portfolio of hedge funds (AuM greater than $15m) across the range of available investment strategies. Figure 3.10 shows a schematic of the MSCI investable index construction methodology.

A review of the investable hedge fund index is conducted on a quarterly basis where funds are added or deleted and adjustments made to the constituent weights for available investment capacity. Segment weights are also realigned to the HFRF and checked to ensure that they still adhere to the general index construction and maintenance principles.

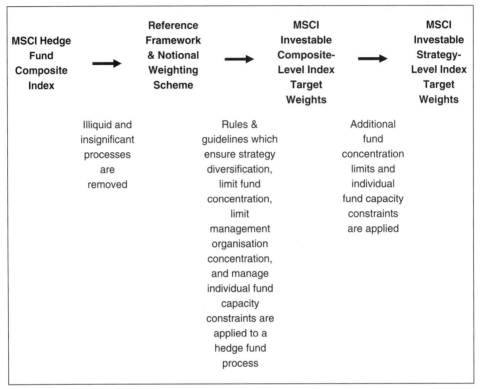

FIGURE 3.10   A schematic of the MSCI investable index construction methodology
Source: MSCI

3.2.7   EDHEC Risk and Asset Management Research Centre (www.edhec-risk.com)

As detailed above, the different hedge fund indices available in the market conform to a range of selection criteria and are developed through a variety of construction methodologies attached to a variety of commercial databases. With such inherent heterogeneity in the hedge fund industry, investors cannot rely on competing hedge fund indices to obtain a *true and fair* representation of hedge fund performance. As a response to this lack of representativeness and *purity* in the hedge fund industry, EDHEC Risk and Asset Management Research Centre (EDHEC) introduced a novel *index of indices* idea to alleviate the problem. Such *Alternative Indices* were first discussed in an EDHEC working paper by Amenc and Martellini (2003) who argued that due to the impossible nature of ascertaining the *best* index available on the market, a better construction method is to use a combination of competing indices to determine a more robust and representative industry benchmark. Since competing indices are based on different sets of hedge funds in their composition, the resulting portfolio of indices must be more exhaustive than any of the competing indices it is derived from.

EDHEC use a method of factor analysis to develop a set of hedge fund indices that are the best possible one-dimensional summaries of information within the competing indices for a given investment style. Mathematically, this involves finding the first component of competing indices using their historical performance data. The first principal component has a built-in element of *optimality*,[14] because there is no other linear combination of competing indices that implies a lower information loss. Indeed, information is lost where the heterogeneity in the competing hedge funds' construction is the most severe. Since competing indices are affected in different ways by measurement biases, determining the linear combination of competing indices that implies a maximisation of the variance explained, leads implicitly to a minimisation of the bias.

3.3 DATABASE AND INDEX BIASES

Hedge funds report monthly returns to commercial databases on a voluntary basis; such participation means that only a portion of the hedge fund universe is observable and represented. For example, hedge fund managers will tend to report to databases only when their performance is good and may stop reporting once they become less attractive. This effect leads to a variety of bias in the databases which can lead to vendors publishing misleading and incomplete return statistics, especially when considering index construction and their subsequent publication. Such a problem does not occur in the mutual fund industry, where public disclosure of net asset values is enforceable by law causing a natural convergence of the universe and database of mutual funds. However, it is well known that hedge fund performance data and their benchmarks inherit measurement biases from the databases on which they are based. As a consequence, it is particularly important to be completely aware of the origin and the consequence of potential measurement biases.

3.3.1 Survivorship Bias

If a database contains only information on funds that are active and report regularly to a database (i.e. *live* funds), then a *survivorship bias* can be introduced into calculated performance measures and indices constructed using such data. It is, however, important to distinguish between funds that have simply exited a database (i.e. *defunct* funds) and those that have ceased operation altogether due to bankruptcy or liquidation (i.e. *dead* funds). A defunct fund is a fund that was in a database but ceases to report information to the vendor for whatever reason (e.g. merger); a dead fund is one that is known to have terminated operations and closed down completely. Clearly, a dead fund must also be a defunct fund, but a defunct fund need not necessarily be a

---

[14]*Optimality* refers to stable, more representative, easy to replicate, non-commercial and with fewer biases.

dead fund. Other funds that are defunct but not dead are those that have reached their capacity and no longer require additional capital or the need to attract new investors. Alternatively, the fund manager may believe their performance is so good that their investment style must remain private and no longer wish to provide sensitive information to a database that may be publicly available.

The effect of survivorship bias has been well known in the mutual fund industry for some time and is fairly straightforward to determine. The standard method of determining the survivorship bias, first proposed by Malkiel (1995), is to obtain the universe of all mutual funds that are active during a given time period. The average return of all funds is compared with that of the surviving funds at the end of the period. The return difference is survivorship bias. However, survivorship bias in hedge funds cannot be measured directly because the universe of hedge funds is not readily observable. Survivorship bias can only be estimated using a sample of hedge funds in a database. Technically, over any sample period, if a complete record of defunct funds is available, survivorship bias can be estimated through tedious data manipulation. The problem is in verifying the completeness of historical records on defunct hedge funds. The magnitude of the survivorship bias generally depends on two parameters, namely:

1. The *attrition rate*[15] and
2. The average returns difference between surviving and dead funds.

The hedge fund industry is all too aware that the exclusion of a fund from a database can lead to an upward bias in hedge fund returns and an understated historical risk. Xu, Liu and Loviscek (2009) studied a major commercial database of hedge funds from January 1994 to March 2009 and found that hedge fund returns were generally much worse than the industry would have us believe since many failing funds stop reporting their performance. The gap in returns between these failing funds and others averaged 0.54% a month, or about 6% per annum. This is an extremely high figure and suggests that average reported hedge fund returns set an unrealistic expectation for hedge fund investors.

With regard to defunct funds, there exists another type of bias, namely liquidation bias. This is a result of the fund stopping reporting hedge fund performance to the database several months prior to the final liquidation value of the fund whilst they concentrate on winding down their operations. This generally causes an upward bias in the returns of defunct funds. The opposite of liquidation bias is participation bias. This bias can occur with a successful hedge fund manager who closes his fund and stops reporting his results because he no longer needs to attract new capital.

Another related concept to survivorship bias, and again a result of voluntary reporting, is self-selection bias. Funds not performing well can hide bad results in

---

[15]The *attrition rate* is the percentage of hedge funds that fail over a given time period e.g. a year.

order to avoid investors withdrawing their money whereas funds performing well may wish to protect their investment strategies, and stop the inflow of capital by ceasing to report and closing the fund. In fact, some hedge fund managers choose to be included in a database, period by period, depending on the fund's performance.[16] The fact that hedge fund managers can choose when to participate in the database leads to a self-selection bias. Such a bias is almost impossible to determine let alone measure.

3.3.2 Instant History Bias

For many databases, there is often a sizeable lag between a fund's inception date and the date at which the fund returns are submitted to a particular database. This time lag typically corresponds to the hedge fund incubation period (12–18 months) where the performance of the fund is evaluated using *seed* investment before being publicly offered to investors in order to attract further capital. Once a manager is in a position to submit attractive performance data to a database, they naturally chose the start date that shows the hedge fund in the most positive light. The database vendor introduces an 'instant history' bias into the data when they decide to *backfill* the data to show the historic performance of the hedge fund even though such data was not available when the database was established. Clearly, such funds are likely to be those that offer higher returns and therefore backfilled data will invariably inflate the performance of the fund in the earlier days. Different databases handle the issue of backfilling data differently, and as a result, the impact of this bias varies between vendors. To reduce or avoid this bias some vendors do not backfill returns at all. Others, however, backfill only a few months; in any event, performance returns obtained from databases should be handled with care.

3.4 BENCHMARKING

The development of traditional indices rests on the assumptions that the underlying instruments are homogeneous, and that an investor follows a simple *buy and hold* strategy. Traditional indices are constructed to represent the return of the *market portfolio*; an asset-weighted combination of all investable instruments in that asset class or a suitably equivalent proxy. These indices are designed to directly define the risk premium available to investors willing to expose themselves to the systematic risk of the asset class. For example, an investor trading in the Dow Jones will be exposed to a broad range of market risks based on 30 US large cap equities i.e. there exists a general equilibrium model. However, such a model is still absent from the hedge fund world. In the early years of hedge funds, investment committees established a type of hedge fund performance indicator based on the idea of an *absolute return*, loosely defined

---

[16]Many hedge fund index compilers prohibit this practice and insist that managers regularly and timely submit performance data in order to be considered for inclusion in the index.

as a flat rate of return obtainable under any market condition (i.e. 14.0% p.a.) with no reference to a market average or *peer* group measure. As the market became more challenging and competitive for hedge fund managers, benchmarking to an absolute return in its purest sense has become practically impossible. Hedge fund managers naturally focus their efforts on liquid markets, where trading opportunities and leverage are readily available. Thus, as the dynamics in the global markets change, the nature of hedge funds in the market also changes. Benchmarking such a dynamic industry in itself is an arduous task, and the difficulty is further exemplified by the fact that the hedge funds that constitute the benchmarks are drawn from a sample of funds managed by managers with diverse investment styles. For this reason, investors are increasingly relying on a range of hedge fund indices, as discussed above along with their inadequacies, as their primary method of benchmarking. Benchmarking with an index only makes sense if the index has the following characteristics and attributes:

- Representative
- Rule-based
- Fully investable
- Transparent
- Diversified
- Timely reported and
- Liquid.

Having a reliable benchmarking system is one of the biggest challenges that institutional investors face when selecting and evaluating hedge fund managers and their returns. Most institutional investors are interested in analysing how hedge fund strategies correlate with and compare to broad market indices for portfolio construction, optimisation and asset allocation purposes. As the hedge fund industry matures and becomes ever more driven by large institutional investment, benchmarking is sure to increase.

3.4.1 Tracking Error

The tracking error is a measure of how closely a portfolio follows the index to which it is benchmarked. The lower the tracking error, the more the fund resembles its benchmark's risk and return characteristics. In all cases, the benchmark is the measured position of neutrality for the hedge fund manager. If a manager were to simply follow the benchmark, the expectation would be that their performance should equal the performance of the benchmark, and their tracking error should be zero. The most common measure is the difference in the return earned by a portfolio and the return earned by the benchmark against which the portfolio is constructed. For example, if a particular hedge fund earns a return of 9.15% during a period when the particular benchmark produces a return of 9.07%, the tracking error is 0.08%, or 8 basis points.

Tracking error may be calculated from historical performance data or estimated for future returns. The former is called *ex-post*, and the latter *ex-ante* tracking error. Mathematically, tracking error (*TE*) can be defined in terms of the standard deviation (*SD*), such that:

$$TE = \sqrt{\frac{1}{N-1} \sum_{i=1}^{N} \left(r_{N-1,N} - r_{N-1,N}^{bm} \right)^2} \tag{3.1}$$

where N is the total number of sample data points, $r_{N-1,N}$ is the hedge fund return and $r_{N-1,N}^{bm}$ is the benchmark return. Many practitioners have argued that the quadratic form of the *TE* is difficult to interpret, and that fund managers generally think in terms of linear and not quadratic deviations from a benchmark. In this case, *TE* in terms of the mean absolute deviations (*MAD*) can be written as:

$$MAD = \frac{1}{N-1} \sum_{i=1}^{N} \left| r_{N-1,N} - r_{N-1,N}^{bm} \right| \tag{3.2}$$

In this chapter we have discussed the major hedge fund databases available in the market and the range of services and products they offer. We have highlighted the fact that the hedge fund industry is highly heterogeneous, which makes the construction of a useful market index that comprises the available hedge fund universe very difficult. Moreover, the issues relating to the different ways in which hedge funds report to commercial databases create a variety of data biases which can lead to vendors publishing misleading and incomplete performance measures. Non-investable hedge fund indices try to represent the performance of a sample of the hedge fund universe taken from a particular database; however, such vendors have diverse selection criteria and methods of index construction leading to many different published indices. More recently, many index providers have developed investable indices that offer a low-cost investment and exposure to the hedge fund industry. Nevertheless, one should be fully aware of the limitations and constraints before accepting a particular index as a valued industry benchmark.

In the following chapters we will build and develop a quantitative and theoretical approach to modelling and analysing hedge funds. Chapter 4 begins this process by introducing the main statistical methods and techniques applied to hedge funds.

Statistical Analysis

In order for hedge fund managers to make informed decisions with regard to their investments it is essential that several key statistical analyses are performed. This will usually involve analysing a time series of periodic hedge fund returns to ascertain relevant statistical properties of the data in order to make critical inference about the characteristics and performance of the hedge fund. Many visual and mathematical methods are available that allow hedge fund managers to understand the underlying data structure and identify potential anomalies that may need further investigation whilst also allowing managers to make better informed decisions. It is also important that a serious investor or hedge fund manager have a working knowledge of many of the probability and statistical concepts encountered in the industry so as to be confident and knowledgeable when explaining and discussing their hedge fund investment strategies to potential investors.

Chapter 4 covers the main concepts, principles and techniques employed in the statistical analysis of hedge fund returns. Both visual and theoretical methods are presented which show how to extract and interpret the informational content and underlying characteristics within a periodic time series of hedge fund returns. However, before delving into those issues we will briefly discuss the basis of the class structure we are going to build upon as we go through each chapter.

4.1 THE STATS CLASS

In order to implement the statistical methods described in this chapter we will be developing a `Stats` class. Source 4.1 shows the basic skeleton of the `Stats` class which will we add to as and when necessary.

SOURCE 4.1:   THE SKELETON OF THE STATS CLASS

```cpp
// Stats.h
#pragma once;

class Stats
{
public:
    Stats() {}
    virtual ~Stats() {}
private:
};

// Stats.cpp
#include "Stats.h"
```

Notice that the default constructor and destructor have been declared and defined in the header file by removing the semi-colon (;) and adding the opening and closing braces ({ }). We can do this since we are not explicitly using either the constructor or destructor to initialise any variables or perform any tasks in the class.

4.2 THE UTILS CLASS

The Utils class contains several helper functions to assist with the other classes and provide methods that we will make use of on many occasions to simplify general tasks, for example printing to the console output and error checking. The Utils class and associated methods are shown in Source 4.2.

SOURCE 4.2:   THE UTILS CLASS

```cpp
// Utils.h
#pragma once

#include <iostream>
#include <string>
#include <vector>
using std::string;
using std::vector;
```

```
// typedef definitions
typedef unsigned int UINT;
typedef double DBL;
typedef vector<int> V1DI;
typedef vector<float> V1DF;
typedef vector<double> V1DD;
typedef vector<vector<int>> V2DI;
typedef vector<vector<float>> V2DF;
typedef vector<vector<double>> V2DD;

class Utils
{
public:
    Utils() {}
    virtual ~Utils() {}

    // Member function declarations
    static void PrintResult(const V1DD& v, const int& WIDTH); //
    PrintResult()
    static void PrintFile(const V2DD& v, const V1DS&, const int& n); //
    PrintFile()   void
    ErrorChk(const string& s); // ErrorChk()
private:
    // Member variable definitions
};


 // Utils.cpp
#include "Utils.h"

#include <iostream>
#include <iomanip>
using std::cout;
using std::setw;
using std::cerr;

// Member function definitions
// PrintResult()
void Utils::PrintResult(const V1DD& v, const int& p, const V1DS& s,
const int& WIDTH)
{
    UINT n = ceil(v.size() / (DBL)WIDTH);

    cout << "\n  ";
```

```cpp
    for (UINT i=0; i<s.size(); i++)
     cout << std::left << setw(p + 4) << s[i];
    cout << "\n";

    cout << fixed << setprecision(p);
    for(UINT i=0; i<WIDTH; i++)
    {
      for(UINT j=0; j<n; j++)
      {
            // Access elements using array flattening i.e., we can
            // index between 1D and 2D arrays using offsets
            // e.g, a 2D array: a[i][j] = 1D array: a[j*WIDTH+i]
            cout << right << setw(p + 4) << v[j*WIDTH+i];
      }
      std::cout << "\n";
    }
}


// PrintFile()
void Utils::PrintFile(const V2DD& v, const V1DS& s, const int& n)
{
    cout << "\n        ";
    for (UINT i=0; i<s.size(); i++)
     cout << std::left << setw(6) << s[i];
    cout << "\n";

    for(UINT i=0; i<n; i++)
    {
     for(UINT j=0; j<v[0].size(); j++)
     {
            cout << right << setw(6) << v[i][j];
     }
     cout << "\n";
    }
}


// ErrorChk()
void Utils::ErrorChk(const string& s)
{
    cerr << "\n Run-time error...\n";
    cerr << " Message: " << s << "\n\n";
    std::cin.get();
    exit(1);
}
```

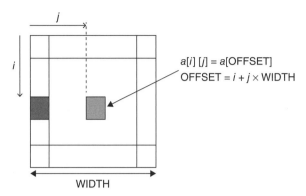

FIGURE 4.1   Using an array OFFSET to index between 1D and 2D arrays

In the `Utils` class we have added several abbreviations for various common type declarations, for example `UINT` has been defined using a `typedef` to represent `unsigned int` and `DBL` for type `double`. We have also included several `typedef` definitions for vectors, for example `V1DF` has been defined to represent `vector<float>`. Similarly, `V2DD` is used to represent `vector o<vector><double>>`. These definitions are not essential but can make code much more readable especially when using lots of repetitive type declarations. `PrintResult()` enables us to display formatted results to the console output whether we are dealing with 1D or 2D data. Here, we have made use of *array flattening* so we can output, for example, a formatted 2D table from a 1D input vector. Array flattening allows us to index between 1D and 2D arrays (i.e. vectors) using relevant offsets e.g. a 2D array, `a[i][j]` can be constructed from a 1D array using an array `OFFSET`, such as `a[j*WIDTH+i]`, where `i` and `j` increment over the array and map to similar locations in the 2D array. Figure 4.1 shows a graphical interpretation of the process of array flattening between 1D and 2D arrays. Conversely, `Print-File()` allows us to display the contents of our data files to the console output in a 2D manner.

The simple `ErrorChk()` routine allows us to add quick error checking for correct parameter input and other useful tests. In a more commercially driven system such error checking would be handled using separate classes and probably a file system for error processing and logging information.

4.3   THE IMPORT CLASS

We have created a file importing method to use with our data samples in an `Import` class as shown in Source 4.3. The example shows a typical output using the `Get-Data()` method using the data file *cta_index.dat*.

SOURCE 4.3:   THE IMPORT CLASS AND EXAMPLE IMPLEMENTATION

```cpp
// Import.h
#pragma once

#include "Utils.h"

#include <string>
using std::string;

class Import
{
public:
    Import() {}
    virtual ~Import() {}

    // Member function declarations
    V2DD GetData(const string& fileName); // GetData()
private:
    // Member variable declarations
    Utils m_utils; // An instance of the Utils class
};

// Import.cpp
#include "Import.h"

#include <fstream>
#include <sstream>
#include <iostream>
using std::cout;
using std::string;
using std::ifstream;
using std::stringstream;

// Member functions definitions
// GetData()
V2DD Import::GetData(const string& fileName)
{
    int ROW = 0, COLS = 0; // Initialise rows and columns
    string line, tmp;
    stringstream ss; // Create a stringstream object

    ifstream file(fileName); // Add file to fstream
```

```cpp
        getline(file, line); // Remove file header
        ss.clear(); // Clear stringstream

        ss << line;
        while (ss >> tmp)
                COLS++; // Determine # columns (COLS) in file

        V2DD data; // Declare a 2D vector of doubles
        V1DD v(COLS); // Declare a 1D vector of doubles

        if(file.is_open())
        {
         while(file.good())
         {
                data.push_back(v); // Add a new row to data
                for (int COL=0; COL<COLS; COL++)
                {
                        file >> data[ROW][COL]; // Fill the row with COL
                        elements
                }
                ROW++; // Keep track of the current ROW and increment
         }
         data.pop_back(); // Remove null values at end of data
         std::cout << "\n File:" << fileName << "\n";
         std::cout << " Imported " << data.size() * (COLS - 1) <<
         " values successfully!\n";
         file.close(); // Close file
       }
       else
       {
         m_utils.ErrorChk("Unable to load file");
       }

        return data;
}

// main.cpp
#include "Import.h"
#include <windows.h>
#include <iostream>
using std::cout;
using std::cin;

int main()
```

```
{
    SetConsoleTitle(L"Console Output");


    V2DD data; // Declare a 2D vector for the data values
    Import ctai; // Create an instance of the Import class

    // Call GetData() member function from the Import class
    data = ctai.GetData("./data/cta_index.dat");

        V1DS v; // Declare a 1D vector for the hedge fund name
    v.push_back("CTA");

    cout << "\n Printing first 18:\n";
    Utils::PrintFile(data, v, 18); // Print first 18 only

    cin.get();
    return 0;
}
```

```
▫                           Console Output                        —  ☐  ✕
File:./data/cta_index.dat
Imported 72 values successfully!

Printing first 18:
        CTA
     1  -0.74
     2   1.45
     3   0.74
     4   1.29
     5   0.24
     6  -0.51
     7   1.57
     8   2.01
     9   0.33
    10  -0.42
    11  -0.29
    12   3.01
    13  -0.87
    14   0.81
    15   1.83
    16   2.17
    17   1.18
    18  -1.94
```

Note that there are numerous other ways of manipulating files in C++ but this gives us a standard working method that we can easily use and is more than adequate for our purposes. In import.h we have instanced the Utils class in the header file with the member variable m_utils. This allows us access to the ErrorChk() method from the Utils class using dot notation i.e. m_utils.ErrorChk(). However, we must include the Utils class header file (Utils.h) within the Import class header to allow this access.

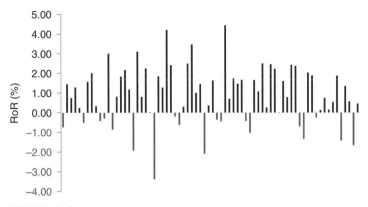

FIGURE 4.2 Bar chart of the monthly returns for the CTA Index

4.4 BASIC PERFORMANCE PLOTS

4.4.1 Value Added Index

Extracting any valuable information from a time series of hedge fund returns is practically impossible with a large set of data in tabular format. Consider the hypothetical monthly[1] returns for a CTA Index; a total of 72 individual positive and negative returns.[2] A simple bar chart of the data, as shown in Figure 4.2, gives an instant visualisation of the historical performance of the CTA Index over the time period as well as identifying areas of highs and lows.

The *Value Added Index* (VAI) is a statistic that shows the performance of a hypothetical $1000 investment based on a set of returns for a hedge fund with a specific reporting frequency e.g. daily, weekly, monthly. The VAI can be calculated for daily, weekly or monthly returns depending on the reporting frequency. The VAI is given by:

$$\text{VAI}_{t+1} = \text{VAI}_{t}(1 + \text{r}_{t}) \tag{4.1}$$

The monthly VAI (VAMI) for the CTA Index of monthly returns is shown in Figure 4.3.

Reading off the final value of the $1000 investment in the CTA Index over the total period gives a VAMI value of $1830; however, it does not really tell us much about

---

[1] Hedge funds can also report daily and weekly returns, but monthly is the most common.

[2] A hedge fund may just provide a series of periodic Net Asset Values (NAV) in which case they can be converted into an equivalent series of periodic returns using $r_{t_1,t_2} = \frac{NAV_{t_2} - NAV_{t_1}}{NAV_{t_1}}$ where r_{t_1,t_2} is the return for the hedge fund between time t_1 and t_2 $(t_2 > t_1)$.

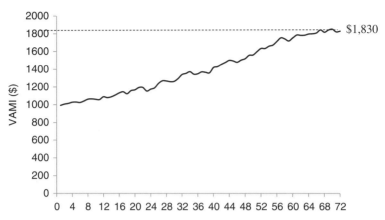

FIGURE 4.3   The VAMI plot for the CTA Index of monthly returns

the performance of the Index since inception. Source 4.4 shows the VAI() member function and method implementation for the Stats class.

SOURCE 4.4:   THE VAI() MEMBER FUNCTION AND METHOD IMPLEMENTATION

```cpp
// Stats.h
#pragma once;

#include "Utils.h"

class Stats
{
public:
    Stats() {}
    virtual ~Stats() {}

    // Member function declarations
    DBL VAI(const V2DD& v); // VAI()
private:
    // Member variable declarations
    Utils m_utils; // An instance of the Utils class
};

// Member functions definitions
// VAI()
DBL Stats::VAI(const V2DD& v)
{
```

```
        UINT n = v.size(); // Declare an unsigned integer
        DBL vai; // Define a double for VAI

        vai = 1000.0; // Initialise to $1,000

            // Calculate VAI using Eqn. (3.1)
        for(UINT i=0; i<n; i++)
        {
         vai *= (1 + v[i][v[0].size()-1] / 100.0);
        }

        return vai;
}

// main.cpp
#include "Import.h"
#include "Stats.h"
#include <windows.h>
#include <iostream>
using std::cout;
using std::cin;

int main()
{
    SetConsoleTitle(L"Console Output");

    V2DD data; // Declare a 2D vector for the data values
    Import ctai; // Create an instance of the Import class

    // Call GetData() member function from the Import class
    data = ctai.GetData("./data/cta_index.dat");

    Stats stats; // Create an instance of the Stats class
    DBL vai; // Declare a double for the VAI value

    // Call VAI() method function from the Stats class
    vai = stats.VAI(data);

    // Output result
    cout << "\n VAI($): " << vai <<"\n";

    cin.get();
    return 0;
}
```

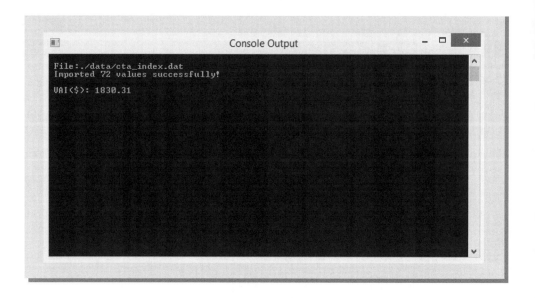

Using `[v[0].size()-1]` in the `for` loop allows us access to the columns in the V2DD container and we have subtracted one since the first column is just period data i.e. 1, 2, 3, etc.

4.4.2 Histograms

A histogram is a graphical summary of the frequency distribution of a set of *empirical data*,[3] for example as a time series of monthly hedge fund returns (or NAVs). The frequency is an absolute value in which each value represents the actual count of the number of occurrences of a particular value in a group of data. Relative frequencies involve *normalising* the frequencies through division of the absolute frequency by the total number of observations in the group of data. Knowing the *max* and *min* values of the monthly returns it is possible to set a range that encompasses all the monthly returns in the data set. This range is then divided into equal intervals (or *bins*) and an absolute frequency determined for each number of values that fall within each bin. Once the absolute values have been determined, a relative frequency can be calculated by dividing each absolute frequency by the sum of absolute frequencies i.e. 72. An example of a histogram for the CTA Index is shown in Figure 4.4.

The histogram is a very useful representation of a set of hedge fund returns over a specific time period, gives a good visual representation of the shape of the distribution and highlights areas of high negative and positive returns.

---

[3] *Empirical data* are those gained by means of a series of observations or by experiment. Empirical measures are those determined from observed values, as opposed to those calculated using theoretical models.

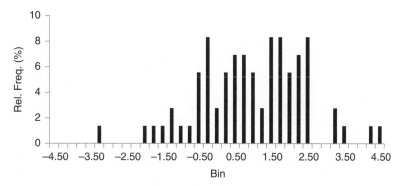

FIGURE 4.4 A histogram plot for the CTA Index of monthly returns

4.5 PROBABILITY DISTRIBUTIONS

In order to understand probability distributions, it is important to know what is meant by a *random variable*. When a numerical value of a variable is determined by an unknown (or chance) event, that variable is said to be random. Random variables can either be *discrete* or *continuous*. For example, suppose an experiment consists of flipping a coin six times and recording the number of heads that appear after each toss. The number of heads results from a *random process* (i.e. flipping the coin) and the actual number recorded is a value between 0 and 6 i.e. a finite integer value. Therefore, the number of heads is said to be a *discrete* random variable. Now suppose the same experiment is performed, but the *average* number of heads after flipping the coin six times is recorded. The average number of heads again results from a random process, however, the actual number recorded can now be any value between 0 and 1 i.e. an infinite number of values. In this case, the average number of heads after six coin flips is said to be a *continuous* random variable.

A *probability distribution* describes all the possible values that a random variable can take within a given range. Probability distributions can also be discrete or continuous. For example, consider an experiment in which a coin is flipped two times and let a random variable[4] X represent the number of heads that occur. The four possible outcomes to this experiment are HH, HT, TH and TT so the discrete random variable X can only have values 0, 1 or 2. That is, the experiment can be described by a discrete probability distribution as shown in Table 4.1.

A continuous probability distribution differs from a discrete probability distribution since the probability that a continuous random variable will equal a certain value is always zero. That is, the continuous random variable can take on an infinite number of values. As a result, continuous probability distributions cannot be expressed in tabular format (as in Table 4.1) but have to be described in terms of a mathematical

---

[4] Generally, a random variable is denoted by an uppercase letter e.g. X and the possible values of the random variable denoted by lowercase letters e.g. $\{x_1, x_2, x_3\}$.

TABLE 4.1 The discrete probability distribution for the random variable X

Number of Heads	Probability
0	$1/4$
1	$1/2$
2	$1/4$
Total Probability	**1**

function known as a *Probability Density Function* (PDF). However, before looking at such density functions, it is worthwhile taking the time to understand the difference between population and samples when discussing probability distributions and associated statistical measures.

4.5.1 Populations and Samples

A population includes every element from a set of possible observations (i.e. the entire data set), whereas a sample consists only of those elements drawn from the population. Depending on the sampling method, it is possible to derive any number of samples from a population (see Figure 4.5). Furthermore, a statistical measure associated with a population, such as mean or standard deviation, is known as a *parameter*; but a statistical measure associated with a particular sample of the population is called a *statistic*. However, most statistical measures in the finance world, although determined from samples of data, are often referred to as parameters.

A sampling method is the process of selecting a sample from the population. When considering random sampling, several properties must hold, for example:

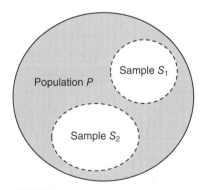

FIGURE 4.5 Several samples taken from the population of the data set

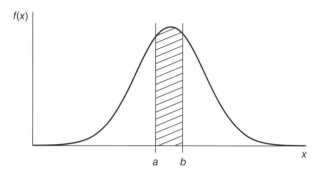

FIGURE 4.6   The PDF and interval [a, b]

- The population consists of N elements
- The random sample consists of n elements and
- All random samples of n elements are equally likely to occur.

Adhering to the above properties ensures that the chosen random sample is representative of the total population and that any statistical assumptions made about the random sample will be valid.[5]

4.6 PROBABILITY DENSITY FUNCTION

Given a continuous random variable, X, the PDF[6] of X is a function $f(x)$ such that for two numbers, a and b with $a \leq b$ we have:

$$P(a \leq X \leq b) = \int_a^b f(x)dx \tag{4.2}$$

where $f(x) \geq 0$ for all x. So, the PDF of a continuous random variable is a function which when integrated over the limits a to b gives the probability that the random variable will have a value within that given interval (or domain). More formally, the probability that X is a value within the interval [a, b] equals the area under the PDF from a to b (see Figure 4.6).

As with discrete probability distributions, the total probability for a continuous probability distribution must also be one. Moreover, the total area under the PDF is always equal to one, that is:

$$\int_{-\infty}^{\infty} f(x)dx = 1 \tag{4.3}$$

---

[5] Although the sample may be subject to a *bias* compared with the population.
[6] The Probability Density Function (PDF) is also known as the probability distribution function, the probability mass function or probability density function.

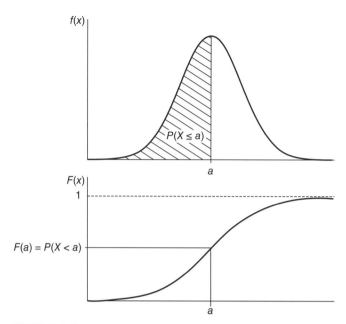

FIGURE 4.7 The relationship between the PDF and CDF

4.7 CUMULATIVE DISTRIBUTION FUNCTION

The *Cumulative Distribution Function* (CDF) describes the probability that a random variable X with a given probability distribution will be found at a value less than or equal to x. The CDF is a function $F(x)$ of a random variable, X, for a number x, such that:

$$F(x) = P(X \leq x) = \int_{-\infty}^{x} f(s)ds \qquad (4.4)$$

That is, for a given value x, $F(x)$ is the probability that the observed value of X will be at most x. Figure 4.7 shows the relationship between a typical PDF and CDF.

4.8 THE NORMAL DISTRIBUTION

A very popular probability distribution is the *normal* (or *Gaussian*[7]) *distribution* which has the following PDF:

$$f(x) = \frac{1}{\sigma\sqrt{2\pi}} \exp\left(-\frac{(x-\mu)^2}{2\sigma^2}\right) \qquad (4.5)$$

---

[7] The *Gaussian distribution* is named after Carl Friedrich Gauss (1777–1855), a German mathematician and scientist who made major contributions in the fields of number theory, statistics, differential geometry, astronomy and optics.

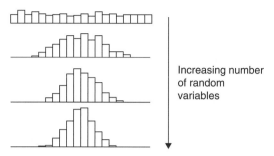

FIGURE 4.8 The central limit theorem

where μ and σ are the mean and standard deviation of the probability distribution. The normal distribution is considered the most prominent in probability and statistical theory (and in finance), and, in many real-life studies, probability distributions tend towards the normal distribution provided there are a sufficient number of random variables. Indeed, the central limit theorem (also known as the law of large numbers) states that the sum of a large number of *independent and identically distributed* (iid) random variables have an approximate normal distribution. The approximation improves as the number of random variables increases as illustrated in Figure 4.8.

In fact, the normal distribution is often used as a first approximation to a random variable that tends to *cluster* around a single mean value i.e. μ. The graph of the normal distribution is symmetric about the mean and usually referred to as the *bell*-shaped curve as shown in Figures 4.8 and 4.9.

A normal distribution can be fully described by only two statistical parameters, the mean and standard deviation. When a random variable X is distributed with a mean μ and standard deviation σ, the normal distribution can be denoted in the following compact form:

$$X \sim N(\mu, \sigma^2) \tag{4.6}$$

The normal distribution is assumed to approximate the model for many financial time series, including the distribution of monthly hedge fund returns, although these

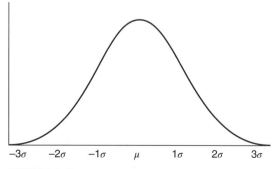

FIGURE 4.9 The normal distribution

can often deviate from normality and this must be taken into account when making inferences from such data.

4.8.1 Standard Normal Distribution

If $\mu = 0$ and $\sigma = 1$ the distribution is said to be a standard normal distribution (or z-distribution), such that:

$$X \sim N(0, 1) \tag{4.7}$$

With the following PDF:

$$f(x) = \frac{1}{\sqrt{2\pi}} \exp\left(-\frac{x^2}{2}\right) \tag{4.8}$$

The normal random variable of a standard normal distribution is known as a z-score (or standard score). Every normal random variable X can be converted into a z-score using the following transformation:

$$z = \frac{X - \mu}{\sigma} \tag{4.9}$$

where X, μ and σ are the random variable, mean and standard deviation from the original normal distribution, respectively. The z-score indicates the number of standard deviations above or below the mean e.g. if the z-score is 2, then the original random variable X is 2 standard deviations above the mean. A negative z-score means that X is below the standard deviation by a certain amount.

4.9 VISUAL TESTS FOR NORMALITY

4.9.1 Inspection

A quick and simple visual test to determine how much a series of hedge fund returns deviate from normality is to plot the histogram of the empirical distribution against a fitted normal distribution. In this case, the bins are additionally used to calculate each normal value across the bin range. So that the empirical values can be plotted against the normal values, it is necessary to *normalise* each value with respect to the total so that each complete set forms a *unit* area. Figure 4.10 shows the empirical distribution plotted against a normal distribution.

Figure 4.10 shows that the distribution of monthly returns for the CTA Index has a reasonable bell-shaped curve which approximates the normal distribution. However, there seem to be several spikes that fall outside the normal which would need to be investigated further by considering *higher moments* of the monthly returns distribution i.e. the *skew* and *kurtosis* measures.

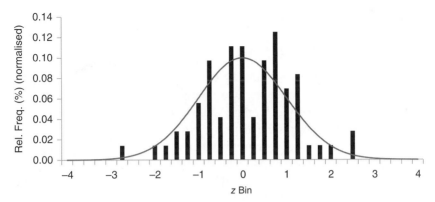

FIGURE 4.10 Empirical vs. normal distribution for the CTA Index

4.9.2 Normal Probability Plot

Another very useful data visualisation technique and test for normality is the *normal probability plot* (or normal *Q-Q* plot). Figure 4.11 shows a typical normal probability plot for a series of hedge fund returns. If the data is normal, the plot should fall more or less on a straight line between the data points. The hypothetical CTA Index data shows a very good fit to normality except around the tails of the distribution which can be seen from the departure of the data around the top and bottom of the straight line. Normal probability plots are often *S*-shaped indicating that the sample data is skewed or has heavier tails in relation to the normal distribution. A statistical measure of the *goodness-of-fit* is the correlation between the ordered data and z-scores. If the data are approximately normally distributed, then the correlation should be a high positive value. Normal probability plots are easy to construct and interpret with the added advantage that outliers within the data are easily identified.

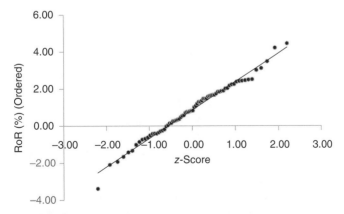

FIGURE 4.11 A normal probability plot for the CTA Index

4.10 MOMENTS OF A DISTRIBUTION

4.10.1 Mean and Standard Deviation

The *mean* and *standard deviation* are the first and second moments of a probability distribution and without doubt the two most quoted statistical measures used in finance.[8] The mean measures the average value of the distribution of a random variable and the standard deviation is the dispersion (or spread) of these values around the mean. The dispersion of returns around the mean is generally considered the amount of risk associated with a hedge fund. That is, the larger the standard deviation, the greater the potential hedge fund risk. For this reason, market practitioners often refer to the standard deviation as the volatility of the hedge fund.

For both the mean and standard deviation it is important to distinguish between individual population and sample measures. The mean for the population is denoted by μ and for the sample by $\bar{x}$. Similarly, the number of independent observations in a population is defined by N and for a sample taken from the population by n (where $n < N$). Mathematically, the means for a population and sample are given by:

$$\mu = \frac{\sum_{i=1}^{N} x_i}{N} \tag{4.10}$$

$$\bar{x} = \frac{\sum_{i=1}^{n} x_i}{n} \tag{4.11}$$

To get the annualised figure, the original mean is multiplied by the frequency representing the original time period e.g. 12 for monthly and 4 for quarterly[9] (see Box 4.1). Source 4.5 shows the `Mean()` and `StdDev()` member functions and method implementations.

The standard deviation for the population is denoted by σ and for the sample by s. Mathematically, the standard deviations[10] for a population and sample are given by:

$$\sigma = \sqrt{\frac{\sum_{i=1}^{N} (x_i - \mu)^2}{N}} \tag{4.12}$$

$$s = \sqrt{\frac{\sum_{i=1}^{n} (x_i - \bar{x})^2}{n-1}} \tag{4.13}$$

---

[8] Such statistical measures are generally known as *point estimates* since they use a sample data set to determine a single value (or statistic) which is a *best guess* for an unknown population parameter. Point estimates can be contrasted with *interval estimates* e.g. confidence intervals.

[9] When considering daily returns, practitioners generally assume there are 252 trading days in a year.

[10] The standard deviation squared is known as the *variance*, however, the resulting formula gives a value in terms of squared units e.g. returns squared ($\%^2$). So, taking the square root of the variance gives the standard deviation and the correct units for returns (i.e. %).

BOX 4.1:   SQUARE ROOT RULE – STANDARD DEVIATION

If a series of hedge fund returns are quoted in monthly or quarterly figures, then they can be transformed into an equivalent annualised series using the so-called *square root rule*. To get the annualised figure, the original standard deviation is multiplied by the square root of the frequency representing the original time period e.g. 12 for monthly and 4 for quarterly. More formally:

$$\sigma_{\text{annual}} = \sigma_{\text{monthly}} \times \sqrt{12}$$

$$\sigma_{\text{annual}} = \sigma_{\text{quarterly}} \times \sqrt{4}$$

SOURCE 4.5:   THE Mean() AND StdDev() MEMBER FUNCTIONS AND METHOD IMPLEMENTATIONS

```cpp
// Stats.h
// ...

    DBL Mean(const V2DD& v, const int& f); // Mean()
    DBL StdDev(const V2DD& v, const char& c, const int& f); // Std-
Dev()


// ...

// Stats.cpp
// ...

// Mean()
DBL Stats::Mean(const V2DD& v, const int& f = 1)
{
    UINT n = v.size(); // Declare an unsigned integer
    DBL mean = 0.0; // Define a double for Mean

    // Calculate Mean using Eqn. (3.10)
    for(UINT i=0; i<n; i++)
    {
     mean += v[i][v[0].size()-1];
    }
    mean /= n;
```

```
      mean *= (double)f; // Cast frequency (f) to double
      return mean;
}

// StdDev() - Sample (s), Population (p)
DBL Stats::StdDev(const V2DD& v, const char& c, const int& f = 1)
  {
      if((c != 's') && (c != 'p')) m_utils.ErrorChk("Type must be 's'
      (sample) or 'p' (population)!");

      UINT n = v.size(); // Declare an unsigned integer
      DBL std = 0.0; // Define a double for St. Dev.
      DBL mean = Mean(v); // Calculate the Mean

      // Calculate St. Dev. using Eqn. (3.12) or (3.13)
      for (UINT i=0; i<n; i++)
      {
       std += pow((v[i][v[0].size()-1] - mean), 2);
      }

      if (c == 's') // Determine Sample or Population
       std /= (n-1);
      else
       std /= n;

      return sqrt(sqrt(tmp) * sqrt((double)f));
  }

// main.cpp
// ...


DBL mean, std;

// Call Mean() and StdDev() member functions of the Stats class
mean = stats.Mean(data, 12);
std = stats.StdDev(data, 's', 12); // Sample (s)

// Output results
cout << fixed << setprecision(3);
cout << "\n Mean:\n";
Utils::PrintResult(mean, 1);
cout << "\n St. Dev.:\n";
Utils::PrintResult(std, 1);

// ...
```

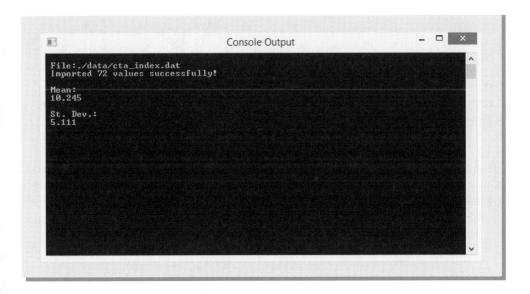

We have added a check to test for the correct input parameter in the `StdDev()` method for whether we are using a sample or population of the data, i.e.:

```
if((c != 's') && (c != 'p')) m_utils.ErrorChk("Type must be 's'
(sample) or 'p' (population)!");
```

We will make use of several such error checks throughout our code. Note that f is set to 1 by default indicating that the reporting frequency will be the period representing the data i.e. monthly in this case. To get annualised figures we simply set the parameter to 12 in the function call e.g. `stats.Mean(data, 12);`

One of the major advantages of using standard deviation, apart from the ease of calculation, is that it gives a direct measure of the *riskiness* of the distribution of returns for a hedge fund. However, most hedge fund returns do not exhibit a normal distribution i.e. the familiar bell-shaped curve, but can be skewed or stretched in some way. In order to fully define a probability distribution, it is necessary to investigate higher moments of the distribution, such as *skew* and *kurtosis*.

4.10.2 Skew

Skew is the third moment of a probability distribution and measures the degree of asymmetry or skew of a distribution. Skew can be either zero, positive or negative. Positive (or *right*) skew indicates a distribution with an asymmetric tail extending toward more positive values, whereas with negative (or *left*) skew the tail extends toward more negative values (see Figure 4.12). The skew of a normal distribution is zero. Hedge fund returns are generally assumed to have either positive or negative skew; knowing the direction of the skew can help fund managers estimate whether a

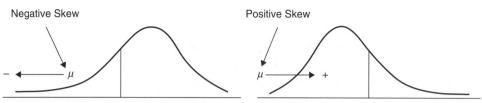

FIGURE 4.12   Positive and negative skew

given (or future) return or price will be larger or smaller than the mean value. That is, if a particular return distribution is skewed, which is generally the case, there is a greater probability that the returns will be either higher or lower than that of a normal distribution. Unlike mean and standard deviation, skew has no units but is a pure number, like a z-score.

Mathematically, the sample skew, s is given by:

$$s = \frac{n}{(n-1)(n-2)} \sum_{i=1}^{n} \left(\frac{x_i - \bar{x}}{s} \right)^3 \tag{4.14}$$

Box 4.2 shows how to calculate the annualised skew based on a similar square root rule as applied to the standard deviation.

BOX 4.2: SQUARE ROOT RULE – SKEW

To get the annualised figure, the original skew is divided by the square root of the frequency representing the original time period e.g. 12 for monthly and 4 for quarterly. More formally:

$$s_{\text{annual}} = s_{\text{monthly}} / \sqrt{12}$$

$$s_{\text{annual}} = s_{\text{quarterly}} / \sqrt{4}$$

4.10.3 Kurtosis

Kurtosis ($m4$), the fourth moment of a probability distribution, measures the degree of peakedness or flatness of a distribution compared to the normal distribution. When calculating kurtosis, it is generally assumed that excess kurtosis is being considered. Positive kurtosis (or leptokurtic) indicates a relatively peaked distribution and heavy tails with more extreme values whilst negative kurtosis (platykurtic) refers to a flatter distribution with thinner tails and relatively fewer extreme values. A distribution with

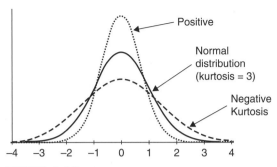

FIGURE 4.13 Positive, negative and zero kurtosis

a kurtosis of three is known as a mesokurtic distribution[11] e.g. the normal distribution (see Figure 4.13). A higher kurtosis usually indicates that the variability in the data is due to a few extreme variations from the mean, rather than many relatively small differences. As with skew, kurtosis also has no units.

Mathematically, the sample excess kurtosis, k is given by:

$$k = \left[\frac{n(n+1)}{(n-1)(n-2)(n-3)} \sum_{i=1}^{n} \left(\frac{x_i - \bar{x}}{s} \right)^4 \right] - \frac{3(n-1)^2}{(n-2)(n-3)} \qquad (4.15)$$

To get the annualised figure, the original kurtosis is divided by the frequency representing the original time period e.g. 12 for monthly and 4 for quarterly. Source 4.6 shows the sample `Skew()` and `XSKurt()` member functions and method implementations.

SOURCE 4.6:   THE Skew() AND XSKurt() MEMBER FUNCTIONS AND METHOD IMPLEMENTATIONS

```
// Stats.h
// ...

DBL Skew(const V2DD& v, const int& f); // Skew()
DBL XSKurt(const V2DD& v, const int& f); // XSKurt()

// ...

// Skew()
DBL Stats::Skew(const V2DD& v, const int& f = 1)
```

---

[11]Rather than saying the kurtosis = 3 for a normal distribution, some talk instead of the *excess kurtosis* being zero i.e. excess kurtosis = kurtosis − 3

```cpp
{
    UINT n = v.size(); // Declare an unsigned integer
    DBL skew = 0.0; // Define a double for Skew

    DBL mean = Mean(v); // Calculate the Mean
    DBL std = StdDev(v, 's'); // Calculate the St. Dev.

    // Calculate Skew using Eqn. (3.14)
    for (UINT i=0; i<n; i++)
    {
     skew += pow((((v[i][v[0].size()-1] - mean) / std), 3);
    }
    skew *= (DBL)n/((n-1)*(n-2));

    return skew;
}

// XSKurt()
DBL Stats::XSKurt(const V2DD& v, const int& f = 1)
 {
    UINT n = v.size(); // Declare an unsigned integer
    DBL xskurt = 0.0; // Define a double for XS Kurt.

    DBL mean = Mean(v); // Calculate the Mean
    DBL std = StdDev(v, 's'); // Calculate the St. Dev.

    // Calculate XS Kurt. using Eqn. (3.15)
    for (UINT i=0; i<v.size(); i++)
    {
      xskurt += pow((((v[i][v[0].size()-1] - mean) / std), 4);
    }
    xskurt *= (DBL)n * (n+1) / ((n-1) * (n-2) * (n-3));
    xskurt -= 3 * pow((DBL)(n-1), 2) / ((n-2) * (n-3));

    return xskurt;
}

// main.cpp
// ...

DBL mean, std, skew, kurt;
...
// Call Mean() and StdDev() member functions of the Stats class
mean = stats.Mean(data, 12);
std = stats.StdDev(data, 's', 12); // Sample (s)
```

```
skew = stats.Skew(data, 12);
kurt = stats.XSKurt(data, 12);

// Output results
cout << fixed << setprecision(3);
cout << "\n Mean:\n";
Utils::PrintResult(mean, 1);
cout << "\n St. Dev.:\n";
Utils::PrintResult(std, 1);
cout << "\n Mean:\n";
Utils::PrintResult(skew, 1);
cout << "\n St. Dev.:\n";
Utils::PrintResult(xskurt, 1);

// ...
```

```
Console Output                                        _  □  ×

File:./data/cta_index.dat
Imported 72 values successfully!

Mean:
10.245

St. Dev.:
5.111

Mean:
-0.050

St. Dev.:
0.024
```

Notice how we have type cast n in the final calculations for both the Skew() and XSKurt() methods since n is originally declared of type UINT so we must force it to be of type double for the calculations to be type consistent. In the following sections we will be using several sets of time series data for several different hedge funds and will need to develop these methods further to make them more robust. Figure 4.14 shows a list of summary statistics (available in the methods of the Stats class) for the CTA Index.

It is evident that the CTA Index has a degree of negative monthly skew (-0.172) and positive kurtosis (0.282) which is a common characteristic of hedge fund return distributions.

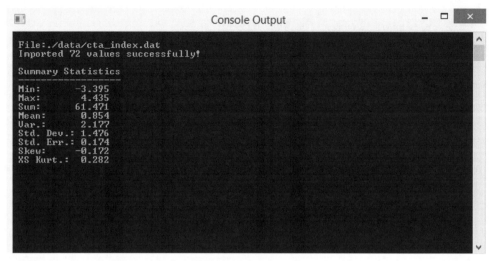

FIGURE 4.14   Summary statistics for the CTA Index

4.11   COVARIANCE AND CORRELATION

Both *covariance* and *correlation* are related measures that indicate the degree of variation between two sets of random variables, for example a set of hedge fund returns and the market benchmark e.g. S&P 500 Index. Given any pair of random variables, X_i and X_j, their covariance is denoted by $\text{cov}(X_i, X_j)$ or, in matrix form, by Σ_{ij}. By definition, the covariance is a *symmetric* matrix[12] i.e. $\Sigma_{ij} = \Sigma_{ji}$. Also, the covariance of any element X_i with itself is the variance, that is:

$$\text{cov}(X_i, X_i) = \text{var}(X_i) \tag{4.16}$$

The covariance matrix Σ can be written as:

$$\Sigma = \begin{pmatrix} \Sigma_{11} & \Sigma_{12} & \Sigma_{13} & . & . & \Sigma_{1n} \\ \Sigma_{21} & \Sigma_{22} & \Sigma_{23} & . & . & . \\ \Sigma_{31} & \Sigma_{32} & \Sigma_{33} & . & . & . \\ . & . & . & . & . & . \\ . & . & . & . & . & . \\ \Sigma_{n1} & . & . & . & . & \Sigma_{nn} \end{pmatrix} \tag{4.17}$$

---

[12]The covariance matrix must also be *positive definite* i.e. a matrix that is analogous to a positive real number.

```
                                              Console Output                                    -  □  ×
File:./data/10_hedge_funds.dat
Imported 720 values successfully!

Printing first 18:

        CTA    CTA2    CTA3    GM1     GM2     LS1     LS2     LS3     MN1     MN2
   1    4.68    0.1   -2.69   0.89   -6.66    0.37    5.8    2.36   -3.09    2.81
   2   -0.18    1.79    3.61   -0.9    2.93   -1.06    4.27    0.32   -0.87   -3.51
   3    0.66    2.04   -0.28  -5.38    6.68    0.62   -3.11   -0.44    0.19   -1.56
   4   -1.45    1.34    2.95    1.33    2.26   -0.62   -4.67    4.89    0.56   -0.07
   5    3.11   -0.16   -4.83    0.88    2.21   -1.4     4.12   -1.54   -0.82    0.38
   6    1.1    -1.4     5.01   -1.02   -6.26    1.36   -0.31    1.02    0.97   -0.07
   7   -5.11    1.15    8.03   -2.88    6.66    2.02    6.87    1.12    1.5    -2.85
   8    4.91   -1.2     3.25    3.81   -0.72    0.74    0.31    4.32    2.41    0.62
   9   -0.7    -1.99   -1.96    5.93    0.38    0.54   -6.94   -0.1     2.23   -0.46
  10    1.33    2.2    -0.75   -6.2     1.3     1.77    1.97   -6.56    0.51   -0.33
  11   -0.52    2.45   -3.79    3.23   -2.85    1.64   -1.8    -0.55    0.93   -0.91
  12    6.15    0.17    2.19    2.46    4.05   -1.42   -3.75    2.79    2.18   -0.97
  13   -1.36   -1.54    2.4    -2.82   -1.01    2.16   -0.45   -0.81    1.63   -1.24
  14    2.07   -1       6.18    1.65   -4.85    0.23    0.77    1.67   -1.52    0.52
  15   -2.32   -0.65   -0.72   -2.1    14.91   -0.8     7.5    -0.25    2.86   -0.58
  16    4.88   -0.97    3.82    7.12   -4.03    2.24   -4.34   -0.57    2.27    0.89
  17    2.96    1.26   -1.19    1.89    0.98   -0.22    2.76    3.72   -0.64    4.04
  18   -4.03    0.48   -1.2    -0.79   -4.16    1.42    3.38    2.9    -1.16   -0.86
```

FIGURE 4.15   An example output from the *10_hedge_funds.dat* file

More formally, the sample covariance of n observations of k variables is the k-by-k matrix with entries given by:

$$\Sigma_{jk} = \frac{1}{n-1} \sum_{i=1}^{n} \left(X_{ij} - \bar{x}_j\right) \left(X_{ik} - \bar{x}_k\right) \tag{4.18}$$

For the covariance and correlation calculations we require a multi-asset (e.g. FoHF) portfolio of monthly returns such as that in *10_hedge_funds.dat*. For this portfolio, we have assumed equal investment across all fund types. Figure 4.15 shows an example output of the data after it has been imported using the `Import` class. Source 4.7 shows the `Cov()` member function and method implementation.

SOURCE 4.7:   THE Cov() MEMBER FUNCTION AND METHOD IMPLEMENTATION

```cpp
// Stats.h
#pragma once;


#include "Utils.h"


class Stats
{
public:
```

```
    Stats() {}
    virtual ~Stats() {}


    // Member function declarations
    V1DD VAI(const V2DD& v); // VAI()
    V1DD Mean(const V2DD& v); // Mean()
    V1DD StdDev(const V2DD& v, const char& c); // StdDev()
    V1DD Skew(const V2DD& v); // Skew()
    V1DD XSKurt(const V2DD& v); // XSKurt()


    V1DD Cov(const V2DD& v); // Cov()
private:
    // Member variable declarations
    Utils m_utils;
};


// Stats.cpp
// ...


// Cov()
V1DD Stats::Cov(const V2DD& v)
{
    if(v[0].size() < 3) m_utils.ErrorChk("More than one time series
    required!");


    UINT n = v.size();
    double tmp; // Declare a temporary holding variable


    V1DD mean = Mean(v); // Declare a 1D vector of doubles for the Mean
    V1DD cov; // Declare a 1D vector of doubles for the Covar.


    // Calculate Covar. using Eqn. (3.18)
        for(UINT k=0; k<mean.size(); k++)
    {
     for(UINT j=1; j<v[0].size(); j++)
     {
            tmp = 0.0;
            for(UINT i=0; i<n; i++)
            {
              tmp += ((v[i][j] - mean[j-1]) * (v[i][k+1] - mean[k]));
            }
            tmp /= (n-1);
            cov.push_back(tmp);
```

```
        }
    }

    return cov;
}


// main.cpp
// ...


// Declare vectors
V2DD data;
V1DD cov;


// Create class instances
Import fohf;
Stats stats;


// Call GetData()
data = fohf.GetData("./data/10_hedge_funds.dat");


V1DS v;
v.push_back("CTA");
v.push_back("CTA2");
v.push_back("CTA3");
v.push_back("GM1");
v.push_back("GM2");
v.push_back("LS1");
v.push_back("LS2");
v.push_back("LS3");
v.push_back("MN1");
v.push_back("MN2");


// Call Cov()
cov = stats.Cov(data);


// Output results
cout << "\n ";
cout << "Covariance matrix for a FoHF (10):\n";
Utils::PrintResult(cov, 3, v, 10); // 10 hedge funds (WIDTH)


// ...
```

```
[▣]                              Console Output                      – ☐ [×]

File:./data/10_hedge_funds.dat
Imported 720 values successfully!

Covariance matrix for a FoHF (10):

CTA     CTA2    CTA3    GM1     GM2     LS1     LS2     LS3     MN1     MN2
6.454  -0.278   0.158  -0.078  -1.836  -0.241   0.377   1.078   0.452   1.154
-0.278   2.351  -1.391   0.337   0.176  -0.225   0.523   0.033  -0.184  -0.791
0.158  -1.391  13.603   0.650  -0.084  -0.460  -1.220   0.659   1.549   0.555
-0.078   0.337   0.650  16.892   0.190   0.390  -1.484  -1.047   1.347  -0.453
-1.836   0.176  -0.084   0.190  19.425  -0.670   0.301  -1.792  -0.095  -1.745
-0.241  -0.225  -0.460   0.390  -0.670   4.517   1.369  -0.601   0.115  -0.045
0.377   0.523  -1.220  -1.484   0.301   1.369  11.185   0.959  -0.487   0.474
1.078   0.033   0.659  -1.047  -1.792  -0.601   0.959   9.572   0.682   0.774
0.452  -0.184   1.549   1.347  -0.095   0.115  -0.487   0.682   2.652  -0.141
1.154  -0.791   0.555  -0.453  -1.745  -0.045   0.474   0.774  -0.141   2.900
```

Notice that we have added an error check to ensure that there is more than one set of hedge fund data so that we can actually find the covariance between the two data sets i.e.:

```
if(v[0].size() < 3) m_utils.ErrorChk("More than one time series
required!");
```

We have included a full listing of the Stats class header file to show that we have updated the VAI(), Mean(), StdDev(), Skew() and XSKurt() methods to allow both input and output through vectors i.e. V1DD and V2DD. This allows us to calculate a set of variables for each statistic when we are using multiple data sets. Source 4.8 shows the updated member functions and an example implementation of Mean() for using *10_hedge_funds.dat*.

SOURCE 4.8:   THE UPDATED VAI(), Mean(), StdDev(), Skew() AND XSKurt() METHODS

```cpp
// Stats.cpp
// ...

V1DD Stats::VAI(const V2DD& v)
{
    UINT n = v.size();
    double tmp; // Declare a temporary holding variable
```

```
    V1DD vai; // Define a 1D vector of doubles for the VAI

    // Calculate VAI using Equation (3.1)
    for(UINT j=1; j<v[0].size(); j++)
    {
     tmp = 1000.0; // Initialise to $1,000
     for(UINT i=0; i<n; i++)
     {
     tmp *= (1 + v[i][j] / 100);
     }
     vai.push_back(tmp);
    }

    return vai;
}


// Mean()
V1DD Stats::Mean(const V2DD& v)
{
    UINT n = v.size();
    double tmp; // Declare a temporary holding variable

    V1DD mean; // Declare a 1D vector of doubles for the Mean

    // Calculate mean using Eqn. (3.10)
    for(UINT j=1; j<v[0].size(); j++)
    {
     tmp = 0.0;
     for(UINT i=0; i<n; i++)
     {
             tmp += v[i][j];
     }
     tmp /= n;
     //std::cout << " j: " << j << " " << " tmp: " << tmp << "\n";
     mean.push_back(tmp);
    }

return mean;
}


// StdDev() - Sample (s), Population (p)
V1DD Stats::StdDev(const V2DD& v, const char& c)
{
    if((c != 's') && (c != 'p')) m_utils.ErrorChk("Type must be 's'
```

```
(sample) or 'p' (population)!");

    UINT n = v.size();
    double tmp; // Declare a temporary holding variable

    V1DD mean = Mean(v); // Declare a 1D vector of doubles for the Mean
    V1DD std; // Declare a 1D vector of doubles for the St. Dev.

    // Calculate St. Dev. using Eqn. (3.12) or (3.13)
    for(UINT j=1; j<v[0].size(); j++)
    {
      tmp = 0.0;
      for(UINT i=0; i<n; i++)
      {
            tmp += pow((v[i][j] - mean[j-1]), 2);
      }
      if (c == 's')
            tmp /= (n-1);
      else
            tmp /= n;
      std.push_back(sqrt(tmp));
    }

    return std;
}

// Skew() - Sample Only
V1DD Stats::Skew(const V2DD& v)
{
    UINT n = v.size();
    DBL tmp; // Declare a temporary holding variable

    V1DD skew; // Declare a 1D vector of doubles for the Skew
    V1DD mean = Mean(v); // Declare a 1D vector of doubles for the Mean
    V1DD std = StdDev(v, 's'); // Declare a 1D vector of doubles
    for the St. Dev.

    // Calculate Skew using Eqn. (3.14)
    for(UINT j=1; j<v[0].size(); j++)
    {
      tmp = 0.0;
      for (UINT i=0; i<n; i++)
      {
            tmp += pow(((v[i][j] - mean[j-1]) / std[j-1]), 3);
```

```
        }
        tmp *= (DBL)n/((n-1)*(n-2));
        skew.push_back(tmp);
    }


    return skew;
}


// XSKurt() - Sample Only
V1DD Stats::XSKurt(const V2DD& v)
{
    UINT n = v.size();
    DBL tmp; // Declare a temporary holding variable


    V1DD xskurt;
    V1DD avg = Mean(v);
    V1DD std = StdDev(v, 's');


    // Calculate XS Kurt. using Eqn. (3.15)
    for(UINT j=1; j<v[0].size(); j++)
    {
     tmp = 0.0;
     for (UINT i=0; i<v.size(); i++)
     {
            tmp += pow(((v[i][j] - avg[j-1]) / std[j-1]), 4);
     }
    }
    tmp *= (DBL)n * (n+1) / ((n-1) * (n-2) * (n-3));
    tmp -= 3 * pow((DBL)(n-1), 2) / ((n-2) * (n-3));
    xskurt.push_back(tmp);


    return xskurt;
}


// main.cpp
// ...

// Declare vectors
V2DD data;
V1DD mean;

// Create class instances
Import fohf;
```

```
Stats stats;

// Call GetData()
data = fohf.GetData("./data/10_hedge_funds.dat");

V1DS v;
v.push_back("CTA");
v.push_back("CTA2");
v.push_back("CTA3");
v.push_back("GM1");
v.push_back("GM2");
v.push_back("LS1");
v.push_back("LS2");
v.push_back("LS3");
v.push_back("MN1");
v.push_back("MN2");

// Call updated Mean()
mean = stats.Mean(data);

// Output results
cout << "\n ";
cout << "Mean:\n";
Utils::PrintResult(mean, 3, v, 1); // 10 hedge funds (WIDTH)

// ...
```

```
File:./data/10_hedge_funds.dat
Imported 720 values successfully!

Mean:
  CTA    CTA2   CTA3   GM1    GM2    LS1    LS2    LS3    MN1    MN2
12.835  6.860 14.203 11.803  5.525  9.835  9.572  6.913  4.653  3.322
```

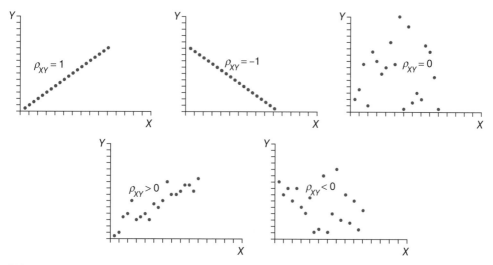

FIGURE 4.16   Some typical correlation plots

To obtain a more direct indication of how two random variables co-vary; a *correlation* measure can be used. The correlation is simply a scaled version of the covariance with relation to the standard deviations of the two sets of random variables. There are several measures for the correlation, often denoted ρ (for a population) or r (for a sample), that indicate the degree of variation between two random sets of variables. The most common of these is the *Pearson*[13] product-moment correlation coefficient, which is relevant only to linear relationships between two sets of random variables. The correlation is +1.0 in the case of a perfectly positive (increasing) linear relationship, −1.0 for a perfectly negative linear relationship and a value between −1.0 and 1.0 in all other cases (see Figure 4.16). Note that if the elements of X and Y are independent then the correlation is zero, although this does not indicate a lack of variation between X and Y only that there is no linear relationship between them. However, there may be some other form of relationship between X and Y, such as a *curvilinear*[14] one.

Given any pair of random variables, X_i and X_j, the correlation ρ_{ij} is defined as:

$$\rho_{ij} = \frac{\text{cov}(X_i, X_j)}{\sigma_i \sigma_j} \tag{4.19}$$

---

[13] Karl Pearson (1857–1936) was an extremely influential English mathematician who has been most cited for the establishment of the field of mathematical statistics.
[14] A *curvilinear* relationship indicates that the relationship between the two sets of random variables may be curved.

where σ_i and σ_j are the standard deviations of X_i and X_j, respectively. The correlation is defined only if σ_i and σ_j are finite and nonzero. As with covariance, ρ_{ij} is more often seen in the form of a correlation matrix[15] ρ, that is:

$$
\rho = \begin{pmatrix}
1 & \rho_{12} & \rho_{13} & \cdot & \cdot & \rho_{1n} \\
\rho_{21} & 1 & \rho_{23} & \cdot & \cdot & \cdot \\
\rho_{31} & \rho_{32} & 1 & \cdot & \cdot & \cdot \\
\cdot & \cdot & \cdot & \cdot & \cdot & \cdot \\
\cdot & \cdot & \cdot & \cdot & \cdot & \cdot \\
\rho_{n1} & \cdot & \cdot & \cdot & \cdot & 1
\end{pmatrix}
\tag{4.20}
$$

Clearly, correlation inherits the symmetric property of covariance i.e. $\rho_{ij} = \rho_{ji}$ and $\rho_{ii} = 1.0$ for $i = j$. Since correlation measures the relative strength of variability between two sets of random numbers, it is a very useful tool for determining the degree of diversification within a portfolio of hedge funds i.e. a FoHF. Moreover, the correlation matrix representing a portfolio of hedge funds should ideally have relatively low values indicating a well-diversified portfolio of funds. Source 4.9 shows the Corr() member function and method implementation for the FoHF monthly returns in *10_hedge_funds.dat*. The correlation values range between -0.303 and 0.266 with the majority closer to zero indicating a small degree of positive and negative variability between these sets of hedge funds. Obviously, the correlation of a hedge fund with itself is one.

SOURCE 4.9: THE Corr() MEMBER FUNCTION AND METHOD IMPLEMENTATION

```
// Stats.h
// ...


V1DD Corr(const V2DD& v); // Corr()


// ...


// Stats.cpp
// ...


// Corr()
```

---

[15] As with covariance, correlation matrices must also be positive definite.

```
V1DD Stats::Corr(const V2DD& v)
{
    if(v[0].size() < 3) m_utils.ErrorChk("More than one time series
    required!");

    UINT n = v.size();
    DBL tmp; // Declare a temporary holding variable

    V1DD mean = Mean(v); // Declare a 1D vector of dou-
bles for the Mean
    V1DD std = StdDev(v, 's'); // Declare a 1D vector of doubles
    for the St. Dev.
    V1DD corr; // Declare a 1D vector of doubles for the Correl.

    // Calculate correlation using Eqn (3.19)
    for(UINT k=0; k<mean.size(); k++)
    {
     for(UINT j=1; j<v[0].size(); j++)
     {
            tmp = 0.0;
            for(UINT i=0; i<n; i++)
            {
                    tmp += (((v[i][j] - mean[j-1]) * (v[i][k+1]
    - mean[k])) /(std[j-1] * std[k]));
            }
            tmp /= (n-1);
            corr.push_back(tmp);
     }
    }

    return corr;
}

// main.cpp
// ...

// Call GetData()
data = fohf.GetData("./data/10_hedge_funds.dat");

// Call Corr()
corr = stats.Corr(data);
```

```
// Output results
cout << "\n ";
cout << " Correlation matrix for a FoHF (10):\n";
Utils::PrintResult(corr, 3, v, 10); // 10 hedge funds (WIDTH)

// ...
```

```
 ▪                          Console Output                      –  □   ×

  File:./data/10_hedge_funds.dat
  Imported 720 values successfully!

  Correlation matrix for a FoHF (10):

  CTA     CTA2    CTA3    GM1     GM2     LS1     LS2     LS3     MN1     MN2
  1.000  -0.071   0.017  -0.007  -0.164  -0.045   0.044   0.137   0.109   0.267
 -0.071   1.000  -0.246   0.053   0.026  -0.069   0.102   0.007  -0.074  -0.303
  0.017  -0.246   1.000   0.043  -0.005  -0.059  -0.099   0.058   0.258   0.088
 -0.007   0.053   0.043   1.000   0.010   0.045  -0.108  -0.082   0.201  -0.065
 -0.164   0.026  -0.005   0.010   1.000  -0.072   0.020  -0.131  -0.013  -0.232
 -0.045  -0.069  -0.059   0.045  -0.072   1.000   0.193  -0.091   0.033  -0.012
  0.044   0.102  -0.099  -0.108   0.020   0.193   1.000   0.093  -0.089   0.083
  0.137   0.007   0.058  -0.082  -0.131  -0.091   0.093   1.000   0.135   0.147
  0.109  -0.074   0.258   0.201  -0.013   0.033  -0.089   0.135   1.000  -0.051
  0.267  -0.303   0.088  -0.065  -0.232  -0.012   0.083   0.147  -0.051   1.000
```

Investing in hedge funds and hedge fund strategies that have low correlations with each other is an ideal way for a fund manager to maximise the potential returns of an investment under a wide range of economic and market conditions.[16] Clearly, creating a well-diversified portfolio of low correlated hedge funds is an extremely valuable process for constructing profitable FoHFs.

4.12 LINEAR REGRESSION

Since the majority of hedge fund strategies involve investments in underlying financial instruments, a hedge fund manager is heavily exposed to the risks involved in using such instruments, or to so-called *market factors*. Moreover, many hedge fund managers invest in a whole range of different financial instruments in order to effectively implement a particular strategy and incorporate a degree of diversification into their portfolios. In order to help with this process, fund managers can identify the risk

---

[16] Assuming that correlations remain stable over time, which is not always the case especially in times of market turmoil and stress.

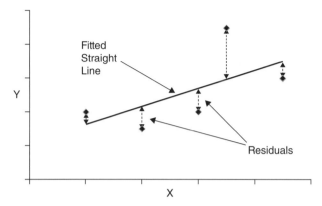

FIGURE 4.17   Simple linear regression

exposure of a given strategy by employing a combination of *correlation* and *regression* techniques. That is, for a certain hedge fund strategy (or index), a set of correlated market factors can be identified and the strength of their relationship further quantified through *regression analysis*. In this way, a relationship can be ascertained between a *dependent* variable (e.g. hedge fund strategy or index) and a set of *independent* variables (i.e. correlated market factors). Since many fund managers rely on the use of derivative instruments and varying degrees of *leverage*,[17] such analysis can only explain part of the risk exposures faced by hedge funds. In these cases, a thorough knowledge of the particular strategy and market environment allows managers to supplement these quantitative measures with qualitative estimates.

Linear regression is a *parametric* method i.e. the regression model is defined in terms of a finite number of unknown parameters estimated from a set of data. Linear regression involves using the method of *ordinary least squares* (OLS) to predict the value of a *dependent* variable Y, based on an *independent* variable X.[18] More technically, simple linear regression fits a straight line through a set of n data points such that the *sum of squared errors* i.e. the vertical distances between the data points and fitted straight line, are as small as possible (see Figure 4.17).

The linear regression equation is given by:

$$Y_i = a + bX_i + e_i \qquad (4.21)$$

where X_i are the *independent*[19] variables, Y_i are the *dependent*[20] variables, b the *slope* of the straight line, a the *intercept* and e_i are the *error terms*.[21] e_i capture all of the other

[17]The use of derivatives and leverage introduces an element of *nonlinearity* into the analysis.
[18]For each data point both X and Y are known.
[19]X_i are also known as the *regressor, exogenous, explanatory, input* or *predictor* variables.
[20]Y_i are also known as the *regressand, endogenous, response* or *measured* variables.
[21]e_i are also known as the *residual* or *noise* terms.

factors that influence the dependent variables Y_i other than the independent variable X_i. It is a necessary condition that the independent variables X_i are *linearly independent* i.e. it is not possible to express any independent variable as a linear combination of the others. Alternatively, this implies that the regression model has no *multi-collinearity* i.e. there is no strong correlation between two or more independent variables. In addition, the dependent variables Y_i should also be approximately *normally distributed*.

The intercept (a) can be calculated from the following rearrangement of the regression equation and considering mean values for X and Y:

$$a = \bar{y} - b\bar{x} \tag{4.22}$$

and the slope (b) from:

$$b = \frac{\sum_{i=1}^{n} (X_i - \bar{x})(Y_i - \bar{y})}{\sqrt{\sum_{i=1}^{n} (X_i - \bar{x})^2}} \tag{4.23}$$

where $\bar{x}$ and $\bar{y}$ are the mean values of X_i and Y_i. Source 4.10 shows the `Intercept()` and `Slope()` member functions and method implementations from the newly created `LinReg` class.

SOURCE 4.10: THE Intercept() AND Slope() member FUNCTIONS AND METHOD IMPLEMENTATIONS

```cpp
// LinReg.h
#pragma once;

#include "Maths.h"
#include "Stats.h"
#include "Utils.h"

class LinReg
{
public:
    LinReg() {}
    virtual ~LinReg() {}

    // Member function declarations
    DBL Intercept(const V2DD& v); // Intercept()
    DBL Slope(const V2DD& v); // Slope()
private:
    // Member variable declarations
    Stats m_stats; // An instance of the Stats class
```

```
      Utils m_utils; // An instance of the Utils class
      Maths m_maths; // An instance of the Maths class
};


// LinReg.cpp
#pragma once;

#include "LinReg.h"

#include <iostream>
using std::cout;

// Member function definitions
// Slope()
DBL LinReg::Slope(const V2DD& v)
{
    if(v[0].size() < 3) m_utils.ErrorChk("More than one time series required!")

    UINT n = v.size();
    DBL xy, xx; // xy = (x-xbar)*(y-ybar), xx = (x-xbar)^2

    V1DD avg = m_stats.Mean(v); // Calculate Means using the Stats class

    // Calculate Slope using Eqn. (3.23)
    for(UINT j=1; j<v[0].size(); j++)
    {
     xy = 0.0, xx = 0.0;
     for(UINT i=0; i<n; i++)
     {
            xy += (v[i][j-1] - avg[j-2]) * (v[i][j] - avg[j-1]);
            xx += (pow(v[i][j-1] - avg[j-2], 2));
     }
    }

    return (xy / xx);
}


// Intercept()
DBL LinReg::Intercept(const V2DD& v)
{
    if(v[0].size() < 3) m_utils.ErrorChk("More than one time series required!");

    UINT n = v.size();

    V1DD avg = m_stats.Mean(v); // Calculate Means using the Stats class
```

```cpp
    // Calculate Intercept using Eqn. (3.22)
    return (avg[1] - Slope(v) * avg[0]);
}


// main.cpp
#include "Import.h"
#include "LinReg.h"
#include "Utils.h"
#include <windows.h>
#include <iostream>
#include <iomanip>
using std::cin;
using std::cout;
using std::setprecision;
using std::fixed;

int main()
{
    SetConsoleTitle(L"Console Output");

    // Declare vectors
    V2DD data;

    DBL slope, icept;

    // Create class instances
    Import lssp;
    LinReg linreg;

    // Call GetData()
    data = lssp.GetData("./data/long_short_sp.dat");

    // Call Slope() & Intercept()
    slope = linreg.Slope(data);
    icept = linreg.Intercept(data);

    // Output results
    cout << fixed << setprecision(4); // Set number precision
    cout << "\n Slope:\t\t" << slope;
    cout << "\n Intecept:\t" << icept;
    cout << "\n Reg. Eq.:\t" << "y = " << slope << "x" << " + " << icept;

    cin.get();
    return 0;
}
```

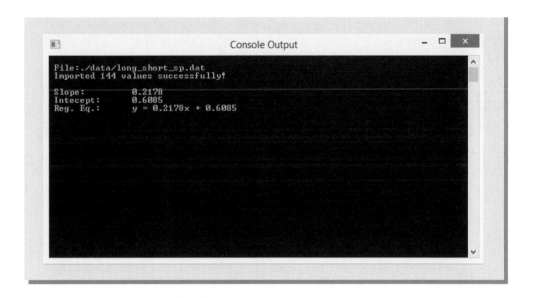

The `Maths` class contains a number of mathematical functions that we will find useful throughout the book and will discuss in more detail as and when we make more extensive use of its member functions.

4.12.1 Coefficient of Determination

The *strength* of the relationship between the dependent and independent variables can be determined by calculating the *coefficient of determination* (R^2). R^2 can be interpreted as the proportion of the variance in the dependent variable that is *predicted* (or *explained*) by the independent variable. R^2 ranges between zero and one, zero indicating that the dependent variable cannot be predicted from the independent variable and one indicating that there is no error in the relationship between the dependent and independent variable. For example, a R^2 of 0.40 means that 40% of the variance in the dependent variable Y is predicted by the independent variable X. A related measure to the coefficient of determination is the *standard error* in the regression line (see Box 4.3). The standard error of the estimate is a measure of the accuracy of predictions made by the regression line. The higher R^2, the lower the standard error, and the more accurate any predictions based on the regression model will be.

$$R^2 = \left(\frac{\sum_{i=1}^{n} (X_i - \bar{x})(Y_i - \bar{y})}{\sqrt{\sum_{i=1}^{n} (X_i - \bar{x})^2 \sum_{i=1}^{n} (Y_i - \bar{y})^2}} \right)^2 \tag{4.24}$$

where $\bar{x}$ and $\bar{y}$ are the mean values of X_i and Y_i.

Source 4.11 shows the `R2()` member function and method implementations from the `LinReg` class.

SOURCE 4.11: THE R2()member FUNCTION AND METHOD IMPLEMENTATION

```cpp
// LinReg.h
// ...

DBL R2(const V2DD& v); // R2()

// ...
// ...
// LinReg.cpp

// R2()
DBL LinReg::R2(const V2DD& v)
{
    if(v[0].size() < 3) m_utils.ErrorChk("More than one time series required!");

    UINT n = v.size();
    DBL xy, xx, yy; // xy = (x-xbar)*(y-ybar), xx = (x-xbar)^2, yy = (y-ybar)^2

    V1DD avg = m_stats.Mean(v); // Calculate Means using the Stats class

    // Calculate R-Squared using Eqn. (3.24)
    for(UINT j=1; j<v[0].size(); j++)
    {
     xy = 0.0, xx = 0.0, yy = 0.0;
     for(UINT i=0; i<n; i++)
     {
            xy += (v[i][j-1] - avg[j-2]) * (v[i][j] - avg[j-1]);
            xx += (pow(v[i][j-1] - avg[j-2], 2));
            yy += (pow(v[i][j] - avg[j-1], 2));

     }
    }

    return (pow(xy / sqrt(xx * yy), 2));
}

// main.cpp
// ...

// Call R2()
r2 = linreg.R2(data);
```

```
// Output results
cout << fixed << setprecision(4); // Set number precision
cout << "\n R-Squared:\t" << r2;

// ...
```

```
File:./data/long_short_sp.dat
Imported 144 values successfully!

R-Squared:      0.1611
```

In general, R^2 tends to *overestimate* the strength of the relationship between the dependent and independent variable, especially when there is more than one independent variable. In our case, a relatively high 16.09% of the variance in the Long-Short index is predicted (or explained) by that in the S&P 500 benchmark. Such a result is likely since the hedge fund strategy is highly equity related, and they will react similarly to the effect of a variety market factors, in particular those that directly affect the equity markets.

BOX 4.3: STATISTICAL SIGNIFICANCE

The *standard error* (*se*) about the regression line is a measure of the average amount that the regression equation *over-* or *under*-predicts the model. The *se* is a measure of the standard deviation of the coefficient in the regression model.

$$se = \sqrt{\frac{(1 - R^2) \sum_{i=1}^{n} (Y_i - \bar{y})^2}{n - 2}}$$

The *se* is used for calculating the *t-statistic* used in statistical tests of significance. The *t*-statistic is compared with the value from the *Student's t distribution* so as to determine a *p*-value. The *se* for the intercept (*a*) is given by:

$$se_a = se\sqrt{\frac{\sum_{i=1}^{n} X_i^2}{n \sum_{i=1}^{n} (X_i - \bar{x})^2}}$$

And for the slope (*b*) by:

$$se_b = \sqrt{\frac{se}{\sum_{i=1}^{n} (X_i - \bar{x})^2}}$$

The subsequent *t*-statistic for the intercept (*a*) is given by:

$$t_a = \frac{a}{se_a}$$

And for the slope (*b*) by:

$$t_b = \frac{b}{se_b}$$

The Student's *t*-distribution is generally defined as the probability distribution of a set of random variables that best fit the data without knowing the population standard deviation. The particular form of the *t*-distribution depends on the number of degrees of freedom i.e. the number of independent observations in a set of data. The higher the degrees of freedom, the closer the *t*-distribution to the standard normal distribution. The *t*-distribution is very similar in shape to the normal distribution but has fatter tails resulting in more values being further away from the mean value as shown in Figure 4.18.

The *t*-distribution plays a central role in the associated *t*-test for assessing the statistical significance of the difference between two sample means, the development of confidence intervals to determine the difference between two population means, and in linear regression analysis.

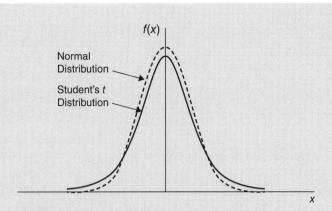

FIGURE 4.18 *t*-distribution vs. normal distribution

The *p*-value is the probability of obtaining a test statistic (e.g. *t*-statistic) at least as extreme as the one that was actually observed, assuming that the NULL hypothesis is true. It is often necessary to reject the NULL hypothesis when the *p*-value is less than 0.05 i.e. a 5% chance of rejecting the NULL hypothesis when it is true. When the NULL hypothesis is rejected, the result is said to be statistically significant. That is, if 95% of the *t*-distribution is closer to the mean than the *t*-statistic for the coefficient of the regression, this relates to a *p*-value of 5%. With such a value there is only a 5% chance that the results of the regression analysis would have occurred in a random distribution, or, there is a 95% probability that the coefficient is having some effect on the regression model. It is important to note that the size of the *p*-value for a coefficient indicates nothing about the effect the coefficient is having on the regression model i.e. it is possible to have a coefficient with a very low *p*-value which has only a minimal effect on the model.

4.12.2 Residual Plots

The error term in the linear regression model must possess the following properties:

1. The errors in the regression model must be random variables and have a mean of zero
2. The variance of the errors must be constant i.e. *homoscedastic*.[22]

---

[22]If this condition is violated the errors are said to *heteroscedastic*.

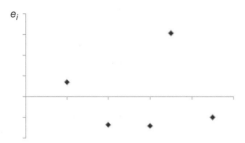

FIGURE 4.19   A residual plot

Once a regression model has been fitted to a set of data, a further investigation of the error terms allows another test of the validity of the linearity assumption. The error terms are determined from the difference between the observed values and those predicted from the linear regression model, that is:

$$e_i = Y_i - \hat{Y}_i \tag{4.25}$$

where $\hat{Y}_i = a + bX_i$. A *residual plot* as shown in Figure 4.19 can reveal the possibility of any fundamental *nonlinear* relationship between the two variables as well as the presence of *outliers*. Such outliers may represent erroneous data, or indicate a poorly fitting regression model. If the residual plot shows a random scatter of data points, as in Figure 4.20, then this is consistent with the model being linear.

The S&P 500 was used to compare the returns for a Long-Short hedge fund index to that of the equity market. The analysis involved regressing monthly returns for the Long-Short Index (dependent variable) against those of the benchmark S&P 500 (independent variable). Figure 4.20 shows the plot of the monthly returns for the Long-Short Index and S&P 500 as well as the equation of the fitted regression line and R^2 value.

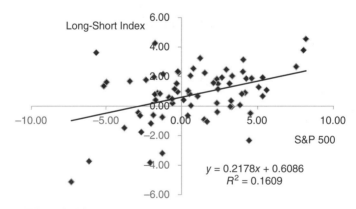

FIGURE 4.20   The linear regression plot for the Long-Short Index vs. S&P 500

In order to check the validity of a regression model it is often necessary to investigate the *statistical significance* of the estimated coefficients *a* and *b* to give us more confidence in results (see Box 4.3).

Source 4.12 shows the remaining member functions and method implementations for the LinReg class.

SOURCE 4.12   THE REMAINING MEMBER FUNCTIONS AND METHOD IMPLEMENTATIONS

```
// ...
// LinReg.h
// ...

DBL StdErrY(const V2DD& v); // StdErrY()
DBL StdErr(const V2DD& v, const char& s); // StdErr()
DBL TStat(const V2DD& v, const char& c); // TStat()
DBL PValue(const V2DD& v, const int& n, const char& c); // PValue()


// ...
// ...
// LinReg.cpp
// ...


// StdErr()
DBL LinReg::StdErr(const V2DD& v, const char& c)
{
    if(v[0].size() < 3) m_utils.ErrorChk("More than one time series required!");

    if((c != 's') && (c != 'i')) m_utils.ErrorChk("Type must be 's' (slope) or 'i'
    (intercept)!");

    UINT n = v.size();
    DBL xx, x2; // xy = (x-xbar)*(y-ybar), x2 = x^2

    V1DD avg = m_stats.Mean(v); // Calculate Means using the Stats class

    for(UINT j=1; j<v[0].size(); j++)
    {
      xx = 0.0, x2 = 0.0;
      for(UINT i=0; i<n; i++)
      {
          xx += (pow(v[i][j-1] - avg[j-2], 2));
          x2 += (pow(v[i][j-1], 2));
      }
    }
```

```
// Calculate St. Err. (see Box 4.3)
if(c == 's')
{
    return (StdErrY(v) / sqrt(xx));
}
else
    return (StdErrY(v) * sqrt(x2 / ((DBL)n * xx)));
}


// TStat()
double LinReg::TStat(const V2DD& v, const char& c)
{
    if(v[0].size() < 3) m_utils.ErrorChk("More than one time series required!");

    if((c != 's') && (c != 'i')) m_utils.ErrorChk("Type must be 's' (slope) or 'i'
    (intercept)!");

    // Calculate t-Statistic (see Box 4.3)
    if(c == 's')
    {
        return (Slope(v) / StdErr(v, 's'));
    }
    else
        return (Intercept(v) / StdErr(v, 'i'));
}


// PValue()
DBL LinReg::PValue(const V2DD& v, const int& nu, const char& c)
{
    if(v[0].size() < 3) m_utils.ErrorChk("More than one time series required!");

    if(nu <= 1) m_utils.ErrorChk("# degrees of freedom <= 1!");

    // Calculate p-value (see Box 4.3)
    return m_maths.BetaI(0.5 * nu, 0.5, (nu / (nu + (TStat(v, c) * TStat(v, c)))));
}
```

If there is a significant relationship between the dependent and independent variable (i.e. Long-Short Index and S&P 500, respectively), the slope (b) will not equal zero. In this case, the NULL hypothesis states that the slope is equal to zero. A complete listing of the statistics from the regression analysis using the LinReg class is shown in Figure 4.21. We see that the t-statistic for the slope is calculated as 3.6642 giving a p-value of around 0.0005. The p-value is the probability that a t-statistic having 70 degrees of freedom is more extreme than 3.6642. Since the p-value is less than the significance level of 5% (0.05) the NULL hypothesis must be rejected. Further

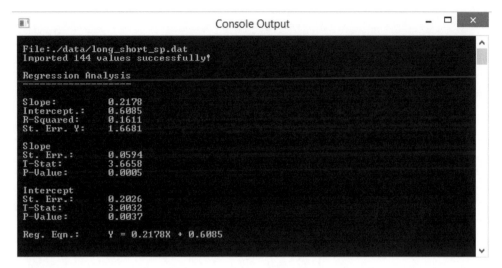

```
■       Console Output                          —  □   ×

File:./data/long_short_sp.dat
Imported 144 values successfully!

Regression Analysis
━━━━━━━━━━━━━━━━━━━━━━━━━━━━━━━━━━━

Slope:          0.2178
Intercept.:     0.6085
R-Squared:      0.1611
St. Err. Y:     1.6681

Slope
St. Err.:       0.0594
T-Stat:         3.6658
P-Value:        0.0005

Intercept
St. Err.:       0.2026
T-Stat:         3.0032
P-Value:        0.0037

Reg. Eqn.:      Y = 0.2178X + 0.6085
```

FIGURE 4.21   Summary of the statistics from the regression analysis

details of the implementation of the calculation for the *p*-value can be found in the Maths class.

In this chapter we have covered the main statistical and quantitative techniques for analysing periodic time series of hedge fund returns. We have noted that such hedge fund returns tend to show departures from the normal distribution and can possess an amount of skewness and kurtosis in their distribution. We also know that hedge fund managers are heavily exposed to the risks involved when using various underlying instruments in their investment strategies. In this case, for a certain hedge fund strategy or index, a set of correlated market factors can be identified and the strength of their relationship quantified using regression analysis. Indeed, along with a thorough knowledge of the particular strategy and market environment, hedge fund managers can further supplement these quantitative measures with qualitative estimates. A statistical analysis of a particular hedge fund (or set of hedge funds) is only the first step in making informed investment decisions. The following chapters will take these techniques further and begin to develop a more robust and informative quantitative toolkit.

CHAPTER 5

Performance Measurement

Hedge fund managers and CTAs can use leverage and take short positions (as opposed to traditional managers who cannot), and since their returns over time will be a direct function of leverage and their long-short portfolio mix, so the manager's performance should be measured on a cash basis (unleveraged) 'relative' to the 'portfolio risk' in order to offset the effects of leverage. The risk proxy measure used is generally based on the second moment of the distribution of returns e.g. the 'volatility' or some other measurable statistical estimate of the variation of the spread of returns associated with the manager. This chapter will look at the various performance measurements which can be used to analyse hedge fund returns in a risk-adjusted sense using the most common metrics applied in industry and academia.

5.1 THE PMetrics CLASS

In order to implement the performance measurements described in this chapter we will be developing another class `PMetrics` in much the same way as we did for the `Stats` class in the previous chapter. Source 5.1 shows the basic skeleton of the `PMetrics` class which we will again add to as and when required.

SOURCE 5.1: SKELETON OF THE PMetrics CLASS

```
// PMetrics.h
#pragma once;

#include "Utils.h"
#include "Stats.h"

class PMetrics: public Stats
{
```

```
public:
    PMetrics() {}
    virtual ~PMetrics() {}

    // Member function declarations
private:
    // Member variable declarations
    Utils m_utils; // An instance of the Utils class
};

// PMetrics.cpp
#include "PMetrics.h"
```

Again, the default constructor and destructor have been declared and defined in the header file by removing the semi-colon (;) and adding the opening and closing braces ({}). We have instantiated the Utils class and included the Utils.h header file as we did in the Stats class so we can perform relevant error checking and print output to the console window. Here, we have made the PMetrics class inherit from the Stats class since we will be making use of several methods available to us in the Stats class. Note that we must include the Stats.h file in the PMetrics header to allow such inheritance.

5.2 THE INTUITION BEHIND RISK-ADJUSTED RETURNS

Consider two CTAs; Manager A (MgrA) and Manager B (MgrB) and assume:

- both managers are operating in near enough the same style (e.g. diversified managed futures) and
- they both use similar underlying instruments for investment and trading purposes.

Also assume that *notional funding*[1] is available for an investor who has $5 million to collateralise a managed account with their FCM of choice and is hoping one CTA will manage all or part of their capital through a *Power of Attorney* (POA)[2] at 2%

---

[1] *Notional funding* can be used to maximise investment capital efficiency since with a margined account, only a certain amount of collateral is required for the margin (M). Usually the investor adds a cushion (C) of capital for future potential drawdowns. If the managed account has a minimum acceptable size of P, then actual funds committed are $A = M + C$, and the notional funding amount is $N = P - A$. It follows that the leverage G obtained by the investment as a function of notional funding for a fixed minimum account size is given by $G = P/A$ to one.

[2] The PoA is an official document signed by the CTA, the investor and the FCM which legally authorises the CTA to manage the client's account at the FCM and receive payment for their management services.

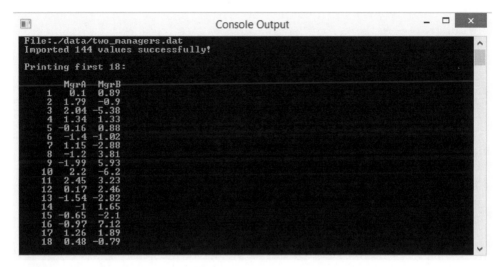

FIGURE 5.1 The first 18 values of the data file two_managers.dat

management fee and 20% incentive fee.[3] Figure 5.1 shows the first 18 values of the data file *two_managers.dat* which represent MgrA and MgrB.

Neglecting higher moments, the annualised first two moments; return (M1) and volatility[4] (M2) allow us to calculate a very simple risk-adjusted return ratio, namely M1/M2. Source 5.2 shows the M1M2() member function and method implementation.

SOURCE 5.2: THE M1M2() MEMBER FUNCTION AND METHOD IMPLEMENTATION

```
// PMetrics.h
// ...

V1DD M1M2(const V2DD& v, const char& c, const int& f); // M1M2()

// ...

// PMetrics.cpp
// ...

// M1M2()
V1DD PMetrics::M1M2(const V2DD& v, const char& c, const int& f)
```

---

[3] 2% of AuM and 20% of net new profits is the industry standard fee structure for CTAs.

[4] Strictly speaking the second moment of a normal distribution is the *variance*.

```
{
    UINT n = v.size();
    DBL tmp; // Declare a temporary holding variable

    V1DD m1m2; // Declare a 1D vector of doubles for the Skew
    V1DD mean = Mean(v, f); // Inherit Mean from the Stats class
    V1DD std = StdDev(v, c, f); // Inherit St. Dev. from the Stats class

    // Calculate M1M2
    for(UINT j=1; j<v[0].size(); j++)
    {
        tmp = 0.0;
        for (UINT i=0; i<n; i++)
        {
                tmp = mean[j-1] / std[j-1];
        }
        m1m2.push_back(tmp);
    }

    return m1m2;
}

// ...
// main.cpp
// ...

V1DS s;
s.push_back("MgrA");
s.push_back("MgrB");

// Call Mean() and StdDev() member functions of the Stats class
mean = stats.Mean(data, 12);
std = stats.StdDev(data, 'p', 12); // Population (p)

// Call M1M2() member function of the PMetrics class
m1m2 = pmetrics.M1M2(data, 'p', 12);

// Output results
// Call SortPrint() member function of the PMetrics class
cout << "\n Mean:\n";
pmetrics.SortPrint(mean, s);
cout << "\n St. Dev.:\n";
pmetrics.SortPrint(std, s);
cout << "\n M1/M2:\n";
```

```
pmetrics.SortPrint(m1m2, s);
// ...
```

You will notice the new `SortPrint()` function which is a member function of the `PMetrics`[5] class. Source 5.3 shows the `SortPrint()` member declaration and definition.

SOURCE 5.3: THE `SortPrint()` MEMBER DECLARATION AND DEFINITION

```cpp
// PMetrics.h
#pragma once;

#include "Utils.h"
#include "Stats.h"

#include <iostream>
#include <string>
#include <map>
using std::string;
using std::map;
```

---

[5] We could have made this a member of the `Utils` class but we thought it better placed in the `PMetrics` class in this case.

```cpp
class PMetrics: public Stats
{
public:
    PMetrics() {}
    virtual ~PMetrics() {}

    V1DD M1M2(const V2DD& v, const char& c, const int& f); // M1M2()
    void SortPrint(const V1DD& v, const V1DS& s); // SortPrint()

    map<string, int>::iterator PMetrics::GetName(map<string, int>& names, int n);
protected:
private:
    // Member variable declarations
    Utils m_utils; // An instance of the Utils class
};


// PMetrics.cpp
#include "PMetrics.h"
#include <algorithm>
#include <iomanip>
using std::make_pair;
using std::setw;
using std::cout;
using std::fixed;
using std::setprecision;


// GetIdx()
class GetIdx
{
public:
    GetIdx(const V1DD& target): m_target(target) {}
    virtual ~GetIdx() {}

    inline bool operator()(DBL a, DBL b) const { return m_target[a] > m_target[b];}
protected:
private:
    const V1DD& m_target;
};


map<string, int>::iterator PMetrics::GetName(map<string, int>& names, int n)
{
    // Iterate through all elements in the map and get index value
map<string, int>::iterator it = names.begin();
    while(it != names.end())
    {
        if(it->second == n)
        return it;
        it++;
```

```
        }
    }


    void PMetrics::SortPrint(const V1DD& v, const V1DS& s)
    {
        // Declare a map for the names
        map<std::string, int> names;
        for (UINT i=0; i<s.size(); i++)
        {
            // Insert names into map
            names.insert(make_pair(s[i], i+1));
        }


        V1DI y; // Declare 1D vector of integers for indexes

        // Initialise indexes
        for(size_t i = 0; i < v.size(); ++i)
            y.push_back(i);

        // Sort and store index
        sort(y.begin(), y.end(), GetIdx(v));

        cout << "\n";
        cout << fixed << setprecision(2);
        for(UINT i=0; i<y.size(); i++)
        {
            // Find and match name to index
            map<string, int>::iterator it = GetName(names, y[i]+1);
            if(it != names.end())
                    cout << " " << it->first << "\t" << v[y[i]] << "\n";
        }
    }
```

In Source 5.3 we are making use of new container class known as a *map*, for example:

```
map<string, int>::iterator PMetrics::GetName(map<string, int>& names, int n);
```

Maps are associative containers that store elements formed by a combination of a *key value* and a *mapped value*, following a specific order. The `iterator` simply allows us to access the sequence of elements in the map. Basically, we are using the map to store each hedge fund name (`string`) with a unique identifier number (`int`) i.e. 1, 2, 3, 4, etc. Then, when we call `GetName()` it will simply iterate through the list of names and return the matched name that corresponds to the index from the `GetIdx()` member function of the `GetIdx` class. All of this takes place in the

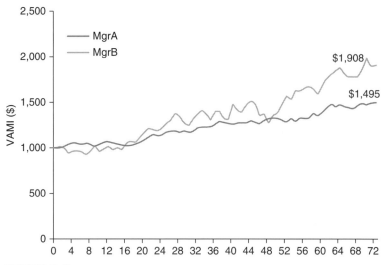

FIGURE 5.2 The VAMI for MgrA and MgrB

`SortPrint()` member function allowing us to output the results or our calculations in order of highest to lowest.

Figure 5.2 shows the monthly VAI for the two managers. At first glance, a naive investor who had to choose between MgrA and MgrB (i.e. an *all-or-nothing* investment choice) would choose MgrB, since they obviously have a historical record of providing higher returns for their investors. However, due to the possibility of notional funding commonly found in the world of managed account investing[6] with CTAs, a sophisticated investor would notice that they could fund each account at a range of funding levels so that it would be up to the CTA to decide at what actual level of funds they would calibrate their limits for trading and investing. As a result, a range of returns could be sought for each CTA regardless of their annualised return performance record i.e. notional funding can be used to set an investment return target, regardless of the CTA's historical annualised returns and future expectations (see Example 5.1).

EXAMPLE 5.1: NOTIONAL FUNDING IN PRACTICE

Consider the data for CTA managers A and B above which we will use for this example and assume the results shown in Source 5.2 are net after fees and that the risk-free rate is 0.0% for simplification purposes. You are a young savvy

---

[6] Note that notional funding is usually associated with investing in managed accounts i.e. hedge funds usually have pre-prescribed risk and return parameters in which it is difficult to leverage up or down.

investor with an appetite for high returns and have carried out all your research and due diligence and particularly like two CTAs – CTA A and CTA B – with whom you have decided to allocate your money. Since you are also rather busy you don't want to go to the hassle of filling out all the paperwork and forms necessary to set up two managed accounts, and instead want to invest all your capital with one CTA with whom you wish to develop a long-term relationship. In particular, you want to earn around 30.0% per annum on your capital of $5m (each manager accepts minimum account sizes of $1m). Since CTA A has the highest risk-adjusted return ratio you have decided to choose them as your only manager. From their track record, you know that on average you have an expectation that they can produce annualised net returns of 6.86% with an estimated volatility of 5.27% on the minimum account sizes of $1m. Considering you want to earn around 30.0% per annum and not just 6.86%, and the manager accepts notional funding, this means you need to leverage (or gear up) the managed account by a factor $G = 30.0/6.86 = 4.37$ times. That is, the investor and the CTA should agree to set up an account which is leveraged 4.37 times using notional funding. From Footnote 2, $G = P/A$ and since $G = 4.37$ and $A = \$5m$, $P = \$21.85m$. Since $N = P - A$, $N = \$16m$. Therefore, the investor should agree with the CTA to design an account which should be traded as if it were AuM representing $21.85m, of which $5m are the actual funds and the rest are notional funds of $16.85m. With this gearing, the investor will expect a net return per annum of 30.0% on their $5m through the CTA. They will, however, also expect an associated higher volatility of G times the CTA volatility i.e. $4.37 \times 5.27\% = 23.0\%$ since the risk-adjusted ratio of the CTA remains constant under gearing and if the returns (numerator) are increased by a gearing factor G, the volatility (denominator) must also be increased by a factor G for the risk-adjusted return ratio to remain constant.

Since the investor is young and $5m represents only about 10% of their net worth, they are happy to accept such a level of volatility for an expected annual return of 30.0% on the invested amount of $5m. Analysis of the manager's disclosure document shows that it is statistically acceptable to use notional funding since the manager claims to have an average *margin-to-equity* (M/E)[7] of 5.0%. With an account size of $21.85m, this will translate into an operational daily requirement of margin equal to 5.0% of $21.85m $= \$1.09m (= M)$. Since the investor is investing $5m in actual funds ($A$), the cushion $C = A - M = 5.0 - 1.09 = \$3.91m$. Statistically this cushion should be enough to prevent any future margin calls with a low probability of having to inject further collateral into the account in the event of a margin call which could happen due to the manager's

---

[7] M/E is usually defined as the average amount of margin required by the FCM (M) divided by the un-notionalised management account size of the CTA (P), thus, average $M/E\% = (M \times 100)/P$.

poor future performance or an increase in margin levels as set by the futures exchanges or both. The notional funding level is defined as

$$NF = (N \times 100)/P = (16.85 \times 100)/21.85 \approx 77\%.$$

Note the situation if the investor had been uninformed as to the virtues of risk-adjusted investing through CTAs. If they had erroneously chosen CTA B (at first glance perhaps because CTA B had higher returns) to create their 30% return expectation account using notional funding, their volatility expectation would have been higher at 35.9% (30.0/11.81 × 14.14). This example demonstrates that by using risk-adjusted returns to measure the manager's relative performance and by correctly choosing CTA A to invest in, their expected volatility for reaching an annual return of 30.0% would be around 23.0% for CTA A versus 35.9% for CTA B – a significant difference of 12.9%.

This example shows why in the world of capital-efficient leveraged investing using collateralised margining (something inherent with futures markets), the manager with the highest risk-adjusted return should be in hot demand and why as a consequence, many CTAs and hedge fund managers use the Sharpe ratio as their long-term performance objective function.

5.2.1 Risk-Adjusted Returns

Due to the notional funding argument discussed in the previous section, it can be seen that it is not just the returns that are important for maximising capital efficiency (as well as performance) of an investment. Assuming for now that only the first two moments are important for investment appraisal, the logical way to proceed for investment analysis is to create a Cartesian[8] diagram in these two dimensions. The concept of investment analysis in risk-adjusted return, mu-sigma or mean-variance space was pioneered by Harry Markowitz (1952).[9] The two-dimensional Cartesian points for each CTA are shown in Figure 5.3.

This visualisation method for looking at unique points per manager in two-dimensional space is one way to allow the investor to visualise their investment. The major drawback is of course that it assumes that only the first two moments of the return distribution are important. However, whilst being close to the truth in reality, it is not quite correct since hedge funds also suffer from higher moment risks as shown by Favre and Ranaldo (2005). For now, though, we assume that the investor is only

---

[8] Descartes (1596–1650) was a French mathematician and philosopher who developed the Cartesian coordinate system.
[9] Nowadays, Markowitz's work is considered to be the foundation of Modern Portfolio Theory (MPT).

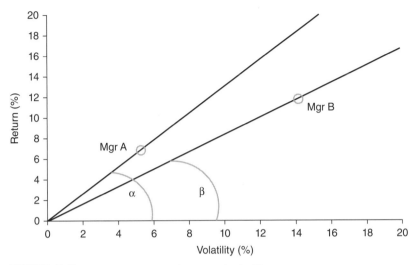

FIGURE 5.3 MgrA and MgrB in return/volatility space

interested in the returns and the riskiness of those returns as measured by volatility. Assuming the investor faces an all-or-nothing choice, which manager would be preferable? Since we know due to notional funding that an investor can in theory leverage up their investment, the objective function for the investor is simply that of a rational investor. For a certain fixed return expectation, they want to arrive at their target wealth expectation with the minimum of risk borne in the process. Since we are measuring risk at this stage solely by volatility, it therefore follows that if we were to draw two straight lines from the origin of Figure 5.3 through the unique location point of each manager, and measure the angle of each line from the x-axis, e.g. α and β angles, the manager of preference in the risk-adjusted sense would be the manager who has the largest angle. In this case, it is clear that $\alpha > \beta$, so CTA A is preferred over CTA B in the risk-adjusted sense (since it 'dominates' in mu-sigma space it is said to be the more 'efficient' of the two portfolios). As can be seen from Figure 5.2, each angle is directly proportional to the gradient[10] and it follows that:

$$\frac{R_A}{\sigma_A} > \frac{R_B}{\sigma_B} \tag{5.1}$$

The investor's risk-adjusted investment objective is usually therefore to maximise future risk-adjusted returns:

$$\theta = \left[\frac{E(R_p)}{\sigma_p}\right]_{max} \tag{5.2}$$

---

[10] A *gradient* is measured as the ratio of vertical distance to the origin over the horizontal distance to the origin for a point in two-dimensional space.

where $E(R_p)$ is the expected future returns of the investment and σ_p the expected volatility of returns. It can be seen that the gradient is indeed the same measure as the Sharpe ratio if we neglect the risk-free rate leading to the common industry approach of optimising a portfolio or hedge fund based on its Sharpe ratio as an objective function.

As can be seen from the output of Source 5.2, for the ratio M1/M2, MgrA is the obvious winner with a value of 1.301 and so MgrA is preferred over MgrB in the risk-adjusted sense. Example 5.1 demonstrates how important these concepts are in reality for the investor authorised to use notional funding.

5.3   ABSOLUTE RISK-ADJUSTED RETURN METRICS

In this section, we will describe the group of absolute metrics currently used within the industry and use an example to show how each can be calculated for 10 hypothetical hedge funds (see Box 5.1) and to present a conclusion on the final results and the differences between methods.

BOX 5.1: 10 HYPOTHETICAL HEDGE FUNDS

Figure 5.4 shows 10 hypothetical hedge fund monthly returns (first 18 only) classified as follows:

```
■                              Console Output                    -  □  ×
File:./data/10_hedge_funds.dat
Imported 720 values successfully!

Printing first 18:

      CTA1   CTA2   CTA3   GM1    GM2    LS1    LS2    LS3    MN1    MN2
 1    4.68   0.1   -2.69   0.89  -6.66   0.37   5.8   2.36  -3.09   2.81
 2   -0.18   1.79   3.61  -0.9    2.93  -1.06   4.27   0.32  -0.87  -3.51
 3    0.66   2.04  -0.28  -5.38   6.68   0.62  -3.11  -0.44   0.19  -1.56
 4   -1.45   1.34   2.95   1.33   2.26  -0.62  -4.67   4.89   0.56  -0.07
 5    3.11  -0.16  -4.83   0.88   2.21  -1.4    4.12  -1.54  -0.82   0.38
 6    1.1   -1.4    5.01  -1.02  -6.26   1.36  -0.31   1.02   0.97  -0.07
 7   -5.11   1.15   8.03  -2.88   6.66   2.02   6.87   1.12   1.5   -2.85
 8    4.91  -1.2    3.25   3.81  -0.72   0.74   0.31   4.32   2.41   0.62
 9   -0.7   -1.99  -1.96   5.93   0.38   0.54  -6.94  -0.1    2.23  -0.46
10    1.33   2.2   -0.75  -6.2    1.3    1.77   1.97  -6.56   0.51  -0.33
11   -0.52   2.45  -3.79   3.23  -2.85   1.64  -1.8   -0.55   0.93  -0.91
12    6.15   0.17   2.19   2.46   4.05  -1.42  -3.75   2.79   2.18  -0.97
13   -1.36  -1.54   2.4   -2.82  -1.01   2.16  -0.45  -0.81   1.63  -1.24
14    2.07  -1      6.18   1.65  -4.85   0.23   0.77   1.67  -1.52   0.52
15   -2.32  -0.65  -0.72  -2.1   14.91  -0.8    7.5   -0.25   2.86  -0.58
16    4.88  -0.97   3.82   7.12  -4.03   2.24  -4.34  -0.57   2.27   0.89
17    2.96   1.26  -1.19   1.89   0.98  -0.22   2.76   3.72  -0.64   4.04
18   -4.03   0.48  -1.2   -0.79  -4.16   1.42   3.38   2.9   -1.16  -0.86
```

FIGURE 5.4   10 hypothetical hedge fund monthly returns (first 18 only)

- Commodity Trading Advisors: CTA1, CTA2 and CTA3
- Global Macro funds: GM1 and GM2
- Long Short funds: LS1, LS2 and LS3
- Market Neutral funds: MN1 and MN2.

Figure 5.5 shows the sorted (or *ranked*) annualised mean and standard deviation for each of the 10 hedge funds.

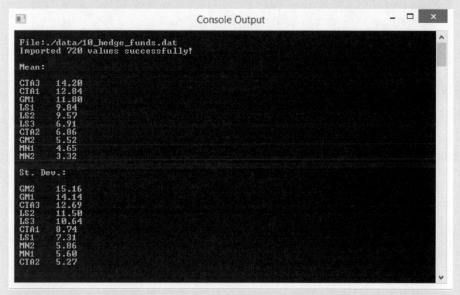

FIGURE 5.5 Annualised mean and standard deviation for each of the 10 hedge funds

Clearly, CTA3 is seen to be the best performer in terms of the mean with a return of 14.20%, closely followed by CTA1 at 12.84%. The clear poorest performer based on mean return is MN2 with a value of 3.32%. However, when considering the standard deviation of returns there is an obvious shift in the rankings, with the GM2 fund showing the highest volatility of returns and very low mean return. For comparison, Figure 5.6 shows the 10 hedge funds ranked according to the M1/M2 performance metric.

The 10 hedge fund returns will be used for the remainder of the chapter in order to demonstrate how the various metrics can be used to investigate hedge fund performance. The results will also highlight the key differences to each approach since each technique can produce different hedge fund rankings.

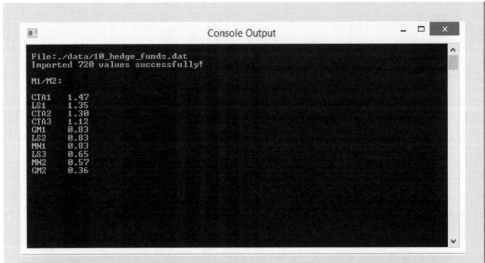

FIGURE 5.6 The M1/M2 performance metric for each of the 10 hedge funds

For completeness, Figure 5.7 shows the VAMI for each of the 10 hedge funds.

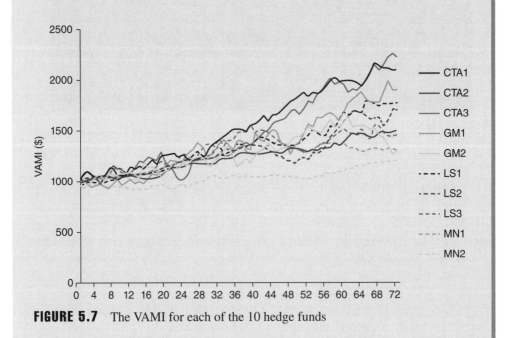

FIGURE 5.7 The VAMI for each of the 10 hedge funds

Most risk-adjusted return metrics may be generalised using the following formulation:

$$\text{Risk-Adjusted Return Metric} = (\text{Return proxy})/(\text{Risk proxy}) \qquad (5.3)$$

Usually the return proxy is the estimated ex-post annualised return for the hedge fund less the annualised risk-free rate or some minimum acceptable rate. The most widely used risk proxy is usually the volatility of returns since many investors are comfortable with viewing a manager in mu-sigma space. However, it has drawbacks due to its simplicity, for example higher moments such as kurtosis are neglected, the distribution could be asymmetrical (skewed) and drawdowns could turn out to be much worse than assumed. That is, volatility is essentially a measure of normal or Gaussian risk in an abnormal non-Gaussian real world of risk. As a result, the risk measure shown in the denominator in (5.3) has been changed and re-defined by various researchers over the years to encompass more complex and meaningful measures as demanded by sophisticated investors. These metrics will be described and modelled in the following sub-sections.

5.4 THE SHARPE RATIO

The *Sharpe ratio* (SR) aims to measure the desirability of a risky investment strategy or instrument by dividing the average period return in excess of the *risk-free rate* by the standard deviation of the periodic returns. SR is defined by Sharpe[11] (1994) as follows:

$$Sharpe = \frac{R_P - R_F}{\sigma_P} \qquad (5.4)$$

where R_P is the annualised return, R_F is the annualised risk-free rate (e.g. using the T-bill as a proxy) and σ_P is the volatility of the returns. The SR introduces the concept of a benchmark to the numerator. In other words, the investor wants to earn at least the risk-free rate and since they want the highest SR, this will start penalising hedge funds whose returns are low. Also, any fund with annualised return less than the risk-free rate will have a *negative* SR regardless of the fund volatility.

The SR undoubtedly has some value as a measure of strategy 'quality', but it also has a few limitations. The SR does not distinguish between *upside* and *downside volatility* (see Figure 5.8). In fact, high outlier returns have the effect of increasing the value of the denominator (i.e. standard deviation) more than the value of the numerator, thereby lowering the value of the ratio. For a positively skewed return distribution

---

[11]William Sharpe (1934–) is mostly known for the development of the *Capital Asset Pricing Model* (CAPM). See also (1963), (1964), and (1992).

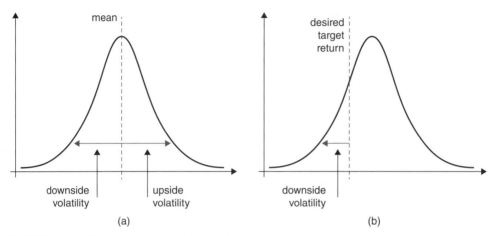

FIGURE 5.8   Upside and downside volatility

such as that of a typical trend following CTA strategy, the SR can be increased by removing the largest positive returns. This is nonsensical since investors generally welcome large positive returns.

To the extent that the distribution of returns is non-normal, the SR falls short. It is a particularly poor performance metric when comparing positively skewed strategies like trend following to negatively skewed strategies like option selling (see Figure 5.9). In fact, for positively skewed return distributions, performance is actually achieved with less risk than the SR suggests. Conversely, standard deviation understates risk for negatively skewed return distributions, i.e. the strategy is actually riskier than the SR suggests.

Source 5.4 shows the `Sharpe()` member declaration and definition.

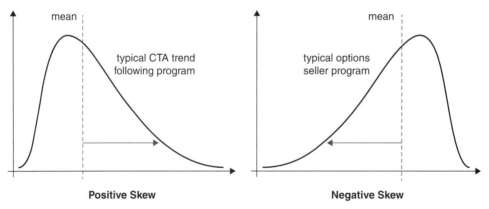

FIGURE 5.9   Upside and downside volatility

SOURCE 5.4: THE `Sharpe()` MEMBER DECLARATION AND DEFINITION

```cpp
// ...
// PMetrics.h
// ...

V1DD Sharpe(const V2DD& v, const DBL& r); // Sharpe()

// ...

// ...
// PMetrics.cpp
// ...

// Sharpe()
V1DD PMetrics::Sharpe(const V2DD& v, const DBL& r)
{
    UINT n = v.size();
    DBL tmp; // Declare a temporary holding variable

    V1DD sharpe; // Declare a 1D vector of doubles for the Sharpe ratio
    V1DD mean = Mean(v, 12); // Inherit Mean from the Stats class
    V1DD std = StdDev(v, 'p', 12); // Inherit St. Dev. from the Stats class

    // Calculate Sharpe ratio using Eqn. (5.4)
    for(UINT j=1; j<v[0].size(); j++)
    {
      tmp = 0.0;
      for (UINT i=0; i<n; i++)
      {
            tmp = (mean[j-1] - r) / std[j-1];
      }
      sharpe.push_back(tmp);
    }

    return sharpe;
}

// ...
// main.cpp
// ...

// Create class instances
Import thfs;
PMetrics pmetrics;
```

```
// Declare and call GetData()
V2DD data = thfs.GetData("./data/10_hedge_funds.dat");

V1DS s; // Declare and initialsie a 1D vector of strings
s.push_back("CTA1");
s.push_back("CTA2");
s.push_back("CTA3");
s.push_back("GM1");
s.push_back("GM2");
s.push_back("LS1");
s.push_back("LS2");
s.push_back("LS3");
s.push_back("MN1");
s.push_back("MN2");

// Declare and call the Sharpe() member function
// Assume risk-free rate = 3.0%
V1DD shrp = pmetrics.Sharpe(data, 3.0);

// Output results
cout << "\n Sharpe Ratio (Rf = 3.0%):\n";
pmetrics.SortPrint(shrp, s);

// ...
```

```
─────────────────────────────────────────────────────────
 ▪                     Console Output              ─  ▢  ✕
─────────────────────────────────────────────────────────
 File:./data/10_funds_mkt.dat
 Imported 792 values successfully!

 Sharpe Ratio (Rf = 3.0%):

 CTA1   1.13
 LS1    0.93
 CTA3   0.88
 CTA2   0.73
 GM1    0.62
 LS2    0.57
 LS3    0.37
 MN1    0.30
 GM2    0.17
 MN2    0.05
─────────────────────────────────────────────────────────
```

You will notice that we are now declaring and calling our member functions in the same statement for compactness. We have also assumed that from now on we are using the population standard deviation and annualising all values so that we no longer have to explicitly state this in our member functions parameter declarations.

As can be seen, the SR produces a ranked list which captures very well in one metric the concept of the risk-adjusted return (or return per unit risk). This metric is already a vast improvement on using just the annualised returns for performance ranking since the hedge fund manager can use leverage (as opposed to traditional fund managers who cannot use leverage), and so they need to be ranked relative to their 'peers' in a risk-adjusted sense. As mentioned earlier, a poor manager can simply use leverage to gain superior results but when measured against the SR performance metric, their results would not seem superior. It is for this primary reason that the SR is a very commonly used metric in the world of hedge funds – enabling a manager or investor to get a quick picture of whether a strategy or fund is worth pursuing. In general, the SR is the first port of call for any hedge fund analysis, and, if SR is high, further analysis is required to assess other statistical characteristics of the fund.

The disadvantage of the SR is that it is absolute in the sense that it does not measure the manager meaningfully against a market benchmark (i.e. only the risk-free rate). However, other measures will be described in the following sections which are relative versus a market benchmark for ranking purposes. Other disadvantages are that the SR is based exclusively on mean-variance, and so higher moments are neglected and are assumed to be zero. The SR therefore assumes that the returns are Gaussian which is not always the case for hedge funds, especially the more exotic relative value strategies as highlighted by Lhabitant (2007).

5.5 MARKET MODELS

In this section, we will consider performance metrics based around the *Market Model* (MM). The MM differs from the *Capital Asset Pricing Model* (CAPM) in that it is based around a regression of excess returns of individual assets on the excess returns of some reference *market benchmark* (or *aggregate index*). MM can be written as:

$$R_i = \alpha_i + R_F + \beta_i(R_M - R_F) + \varepsilon_i \tag{5.5}$$

or in terms of risk preferences, as:

$$R_i - R_F = \alpha_i + R_F + \beta_i(R_M - R_F) + \varepsilon_i \tag{5.6}$$

According to the CAPM all fairly priced assets with respect to publicly known information should fall on the *Security Market Line* (SML) as shown in Figure 5.10.

In Figure 5.10 Hedge Fund B exhibits greater than expected performance (i.e. +ve alpha) whereas Hedge Fund A exhibits less than expected performance (i.e. −ve alpha), both with respect to the market benchmark. From the CAPM we can estimate this measure of a hedge fund's added value since:

$$\alpha_P = R_P - E^{CAPM}(R_M) \tag{5.7}$$

$$\therefore \alpha_p = (R_P - R_F) - \beta_P(R_M - R_F) \tag{5.8}$$

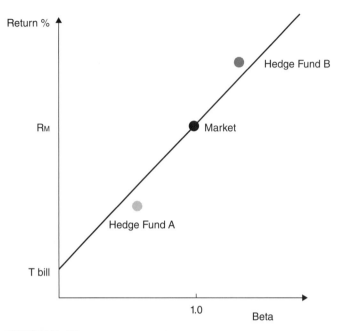

FIGURE 5.10 The SML for two hedge funds A and B

where $E^{CAPM}(R_M)$ is the *'unconditional expectation operator'* i.e. the expected return on the market (not conditioned on anything else occurring) applied to the benchmark (or market index).[12] Equation (5.8) allows the calculation of a manager's added value relative to some beta controlled quantity of systematic market return premium; (5.8) is commonly referred to as *Jensen's alpha* i.e.

$$\alpha_J = (R_P - R_F) - \beta_P(R_M - R_F) \tag{5.9}$$

5.5.1 The Information Ratio

The *information ratio* (IR) as described by Goodwin (1998) is similar to the Sharpe ratio in that it is based on a fund's return and volatility. However, where the Sharpe ratio uses a risk-free rate as a benchmark for the numerator, the information ratio goes one step further and uses a *market reference benchmark*. If R_{Pt} is the return on a fund in period t and R_{Bt} is the return on a benchmark portfolio in period t then Δ_t the excess return can be written as:

$$\Delta_t = R_{Pt} - R_{Bt} \tag{5.10}$$

---

[12]See CAIA Level 1 Study Handbook (2009).

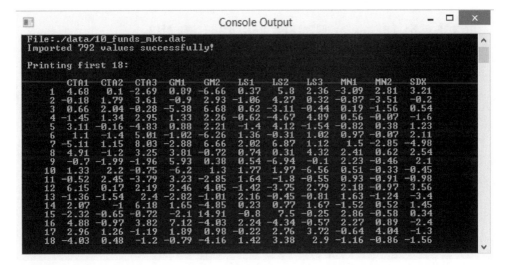

FIGURE 5.11 Monthly returns for 10 hedge funds including the new global equity benchmark (SDX)

$\bar{\Delta}$ is the mean excess returns from $t = 1$ to T i.e.

$$\bar{\Delta} = \frac{1}{T} \sum_{t=1}^{T} \Delta_t \tag{5.11}$$

where σ_Δ is the standard deviation of the excess returns from the benchmark (aka *tracking error*) written as:

$$\sigma_\Delta = \sqrt{\frac{1}{T} \sum_{t=1}^{T} (\Delta_t - \bar{\Delta})^2} \tag{5.12}$$

then, the IR is given by:

$$IR = \frac{\bar{\Delta}}{\sigma_\Delta} \tag{5.13}$$

Since we are now using a market reference we must import the *10_funds_mkt.dat* file which includes the monthly returns for a global equity benchmark (SDX). Figure 5.11 shows the same 10 hypothetical hedge funds along with the new benchmark data (first 18 only). Source 5.5 shows the IR() member declaration and definition.

SOURCE 5.5: THE `IR()` MEMBER DECLARATION AND DEFINITION

```
// ...
// PMetrics.h
// ...


V1DD IR(const V2DD& v); // IR()


// ...


// ...
// PMetrics.cpp
// ...


// IR()
V1DD PMetrics::IR(const V2DD& v)
{
    UINT n = v.size();
    DBL tmp; // Declare a temporary holding variable

    V1DD vtmp; // Declare a temporary holding 1D vector
    V2DD vadj; // Decare a 2D vector for adjusted returns
    V1DI::iterator ROW; // Declare a 1D vector iterator for the ROWS
    V1DI::iterator COL; // Declare a 1D vector iterator for the COLS
    UINT i = 0; // Declare and initialise counter to zero

    for(auto ROW = v.begin(); ROW != v.end(); ++ROW)
    {
      i = 0; // Reset counter
      vtmp.clear(); // Reset 1D vector
      for(auto COL = ROW->begin(); COL != ROW->end()-1; ++COL, ++i)
      {
            // Subtract market benchmark
            vtmp.push_back(*COL - COL[(v[0].size()-1) - i]);
      }
      vadj.push_back(vtmp); // Fill 2D vector with adjusted values
    }

    V1DD ir; // Declare a 1D vector of doubles for the Information ratio
    V1DD mean = Mean(vadj, 12); // Inherit Mean from the Stats class
    V1DD std = StdDev(vadj, 'p', 12); // Inherit St. Dev. from the Stats class

    // Calculate Information ratio using Eqn. (5.13)
    for(UINT j=0; j<vadj[0].size()-1; j++)
```

```
    {
      tmp = 0.0;
      for (UINT i=0; i<n; i++)
      {
              tmp = mean[j] / std[j];
      }
      ir.push_back(tmp);
    }


    return ir;
}


// ...
// main.cpp
// ...


// Create class instances
Import tfmkt;
PMetrics pmetrics;


// Declare and call GetData()
V2DD data = tfmkt.GetData("./data/10_funds_mkt.dat");


V1DS s; // Declare and initialsie a 1D vector of strings
s.push_back("CTA1");
s.push_back("CTA2");
s.push_back("CTA3");
s.push_back("GM1");
s.push_back("GM2");
s.push_back("LS1");
s.push_back("LS2");
s.push_back("LS3");
s.push_back("MN1");
s.push_back("MN2");
s.push_back("SDX");


// Declare and call the IR() member function
V1DD ir = pmetrics.IR(data);


// Output results
cout << "\n Information Ratio:\n";
pmetrics.SortPrint(ir, s);


// ...
```

```
Console Output                              − □ ×

File:./data/10_funds_mkt.dat
Imported 792 values successfully!

Information Ratio:

CTA1    0.59
CTA3    0.46
GM1     0.38
LS1     0.37
LS2     0.28
CTA2    0.13
LS3     0.10
GM2     0.01
MN1    -0.06
MN2    -0.15
```

You will see from Source 5.5 that we have introduced some new syntax and made use of the STL library discussed in Chapter 1. For example, we are now making use of explicit iterators, i.e.

```
V2DI::iterator ROW;
V1DI::iterator COL;
```

These allow us to walk through the vector v using ROW and COL iterators and point (*) to each element as we go and subsequently modify each element if necessary. In our case subtracting the market benchmark (SDX) from each of the 10 hedge fund returns. Since C++11, the keyword auto can be used to avoid having to specify the very long, complicated type name of the iterator. Note that we are also walking through the vector using begin() and end() member functions of the vector class. begin() returns an iterator pointing to the first element in the vector v. end(), on the other hand, returns an iterator referring to the *past-the-end* element in the vector container. The *past-the-end* element is the theoretical element that would follow the last element in the vector. Since the ranges used by functions of the STL library do not include the element pointed to by their closing iterator, this function is often used in combination with begin() to specify a range including all the elements in the container.

The address of a variable can be obtained by preceding the name of a variable with an ampersand sign (&), known as *address-of operator*. For example:

```
a = &var;
```

This would assign the address of variable var to a; by preceding the name of the variable var with the *address-of operator* (&), we are no longer assigning the content of the variable itself to a, but its address. A variable that stores the address of another variable is called a *pointer*. Pointers are said to '*point to*' the variable whose address they store. An interesting property of pointers is that they can be used to access the variable they point to directly. This is done by preceding the pointer name with the *dereference operator* (*). The operator itself can be read as '*value pointed to by*'. Unfortunately, a full discussion of *pointers* is beyond the scope this book so we have only briefly introduced them here for completeness.

The results for the IR show that the rankings have changed somewhat now that we have introduced a reference market benchmark. CTA1 is still the highest ranked and MN2 still the lowest ranked. However, CTA3 is in second place with GM1 in third. In other words, some funds are starting to look better than before in the presence of a benchmark and some are starting to slip down the rankings.

5.5.2 The Treynor Ratio

The *Treynor ratio* as (TR) introduced by Treynor (1962) is again of the same form as the generalised risk-adjusted return given by (5.3). However, this time risk is defined as the beta of the fund relative to a benchmark, such that:

$$TR = \frac{\alpha_P}{\beta_P} = \frac{R_P - R_F}{\beta_P} \qquad (5.14)$$

The beta of the portfolio β_P can be calculated in two ways. The first method has already been discussed in Chapter 4. Box 5.2 shows a detailed explanation of an alternative method of estimating beta.

BOX 5.2: ESTIMATING BETA AND ITS RELATIONSHIP TO CORRELATION

Beta is a very common measure for estimating the extent to which the hedge fund excess returns are influenced by that of the benchmark or market excess returns. The beta of the portfolio is the gradient (m) of the OLS regression line where the market excess returns are plotted on the x-axis and the hedge fund excess returns on the y-axis (see Chapter 4). The fund's beta can be visualised as a measure of its relative directional exposure to the benchmark i.e. a kind of relative elasticity as shown in Figure 5.12.

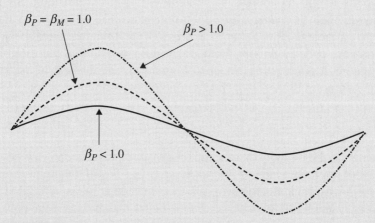

$\beta_P = \beta_M = 1.0$

$\beta_P > 1.0$

$\beta_P < 1.0$

FIGURE 5.12 Relative directional exposure to a benchmark

When the hedge fund's beta is greater than 1.0, it has a tendency to exhibit greater moves in its returns (both positive and negative) than those of the benchmark. When the fund's beta is equal to 1.0, the fund is the market held long (if the market gains 1%, the fund gains 1% and for all intents and purposes the fund is exactly matched to the market i.e. it is the market). When the fund's beta is between zero and 1.0, the fund's returns are less than those of the market (this is the region of beta usually occupied by long-short funds). If the fund's beta is zero, the fund is technically market neutral and so whatever the benchmark does it has no impact on the returns of the fund. If the fund's beta is between zero and −1.0, then the fund's returns have a tendency to be opposite to those of the fund, but in a less volatile fashion. If the fund's beta is −1.0, the fund is the benchmark held short and as such the fund models the benchmark exactly but in the opposite way (if the benchmark gains 1%, the fund loses 1% and vice versa).

Depending on your objectives, you may have different groups of betas to analyse. For example, if you are analysing a group of market neutral managers versus a market benchmark you may well have a statistical distribution of beta values around zero. However, if you are a fund of funds manager analysing the betas of various hedge funds within a diversified fund of hedge funds portfolio, you will have a group of betas distributed around one. Either way, the beta is the *sensitivity* of the fund or asset relative to some systematic factor such as the market or collective index as seen in Merton (1990) in the following form:

$$\beta_i = \frac{\sigma_{iM}}{\sigma_M^2} \qquad (5.15)$$

$$\alpha_i = \beta_i(R_M - R_F) \qquad (5.16)$$

Beta is however directly proportional to leverage which opens up a new set of problems for risk-adjusted return analysis when using beta since any equation with beta in it will be leverage dependent – a case which is usually undesirable if the manager is to be measured for his skill and not leverage. The beta, however, can be re-scaled to create an unleveraged cash equivalent *correlation coefficient*:

$$\rho_i = \frac{\sigma_M}{\sigma_P}\beta_i \tag{5.17}$$

So, in the world of hedge funds we see the emergence of the correlation coefficient as representing the sensitivity of a fund to a certain factor which has been risk-adjusted. The correlation coefficient value if multiplied by 100 will then show the percentage of the dependent variable accounted for by the source of returns or premium for the factor in question e.g. the systematic returns associated with the market portfolio if the CAPM is used. The correlation squared or *r*-squared when multiplied by 100 measures the proportion of variance captured in the dependent variable by the factor returns.

Source 5.6 shows the TR() member declaration and definition.

SOURCE 5.6: THE TR() MEMBER DECLARATION AND DEFINITION

```
// ...
// PMetrics.h
// ...


V1DD TR(V2DD& v, const DBL& r); // TR()


// ...


V1DD GetSlope(V2DD& v);
protected:
private:
// Member variable declarations
      Utils m_utils;   // An instance of the Utils class
    LinReg m_linreg;   // An instance of the LinReg class
};
```

```cpp
// ...
// PMetrics.cpp
// ...


V1DD PMetrics::GetSlope(V2DD& v)
{
    V2DD tmpv; // Declare a temporary 2D vector to hold regression data
    tmpv.resize(v.size()); // Resize temporary vector to size of v
    DBL tmp; // Declare a temporary holding variable
    V1DD slope; // Declare a 1D vector for the Slope

    for(UINT j=0; j<v[0].size()-2; j++)
    {
      for (UINT i = 0; i < tmpv.size(); ++i)
      {
              tmpv[i].resize(3); // Regression data only has 3 columns
              if(j == 0)
              {
                // Copy relevant columns for regression analysis
                // Only need first (1,2,3...) and last (SDX) columns  on
                    first iteration
                copy(v[i].begin(), v[i].begin() + 2, tmpv[i].begin());
                copy(v[i].end() - 1, v[i].end(), tmpv[i].begin() + 2);
              }
              else
              {
                // Insert relevant column into temporary vector for
                regression analysis
                copy(v[i].begin() + (j + 1), v[i].begin() + (j + 2),
                tmpv[i].begin() + 1);
              }
      }
    }
    // Swap columns for correct regression order
  for_each(tmpv.begin(), tmpv.end(), [](V1DD &tmpv) {swap(tmpv[2],
  tmpv[1]); });
    tmp = m_linreg.Slope(tmpv); // Calculate Slope
    slope.push_back(tmp);
    // Swap columns back for next iteration
  for_each(tmpv.begin(), tmpv.end(), [](V1DD &tmpv) {swap(tmpv[1],
  tmpv[2]); });
  }
```

```
        return slope;
}


// TR()
V1DD PMetrics::TR(V2DD& v, const DBL& r)
{
    UINT n = v.size();
    DBL tmp; // Declare a temporary holding variable
    V1DD tr; // Declare a 1D vector for the Treynor ratio


    V1DD mean = Mean(v, 12);  // Inherit Mean from the Stats class
    V1DD slope = GetSlope(v); // Call GetSlope() member function


    // Calculate Treynor ratio using Eqn. (5.14)
    for(UINT j=1; j<v[0].size()-1; j++)
    {
      tmp = 0.0;
      for (UINT i=0; i<n; i++)
      {
            tmp = (mean[j - 1] -  r) / slope[j - 1];
      }
      tr.push_back(tmp);
    }


    return tr;
}


// ...
// main.cpp
// ...


// Declare and call the TR() member function
// Assume risk-free rate = 3.0%
V1DD tr = pmetrics.TR(data, 3.0);


// Output results
cout << "\n Treynor Ratio (Rf = 3.0%):\n";
pmetrics.SortPrint(tr, s);


// ...
```

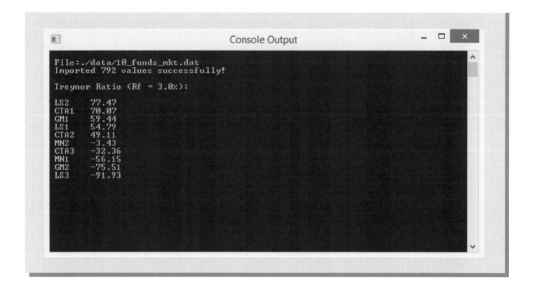

```
File:./data/10_funds_mkt.dat
Imported 792 values successfully!

Treynor Ratio (Rf = 3.0%):

LS2      77.47
CTA1     70.07
GM1      59.44
LS1      54.79
CTA2     49.11
MN2      -3.43
CTA3    -32.36
MN1     -56.15
GM2     -75.51
LS3     -91.93
```

Notice that we longer pass v by constant reference but only by reference since we are making changes to v within the member function to calculate the slope for each hedge fund based on their individual regression against the market benchmark (SDX). We have also added a handle to the LinReg class through the member variable m_linreg so that we can call LinReg member functions (e.g. Slope()) when we invoke TR(). Remember we must include the LinReg class header file in Pmetrics.h to allow access to the LinReg functions.

The TR is a metric more commonly used for active equity portfolios (much like the IR). This is due to the fact that if we are to use a benchmark for relative performance measurement, then the benchmark must be relevant. Since we are using a global equity market benchmark, it follows that CTAs (i.e. CTA1, CTA2, CTA3) and global macro funds (i.e. GM1, GM2) have little or no intuitive exposure to the benchmark, so to use it for any of the risk-adjusted metrics above would be practically meaningless. However, since most equity markets are highly correlated, the global benchmark would be efficient at capturing the returns associated with a passive investment style. As such, it may be a suitable metric for the equity hedge funds LS1, LS2, LS3 and the market neutral hedge funds MN1 and MN2 all of which are assumed to be global equity hedge funds.

From the results we can see that LS2 is now ranked the highest and LS3 the bottom ranked hedge fund. This is primarily because LS2 has a beta of 0.08 and LS3 has a beta of –0.04. In fact, the results can be highly misleading, since both betas may be no different from zero which can be tested using hypothesis testing (see Chapter 4). Note that, in such a market neutral case, the TR approaches infinity. The higher the maxima and minima of the ranks of the TR, therefore, the more market neutral the fund is and so the manager's returns are subsequently less influenced by the market which is a sign of outperformance with respect to the market. In general, the TR is difficult to interpret and clearly unsuitable for analysing non-equity hedge funds.

5.5.3 Jensen's Alpha

One of the key goals of quantitative manager selection is the determination of *alpha*. Alpha is the residual return left over once all known factors and risk adjustments have been accounted for and deducted from a fund's excess net return. As such, alpha is technically meant to measure the manager's absolute skill at using their *information set* to predict future price states in the various financial instruments employed in their fund. Hedge fund managers are meant to be only active position takers since they are not paid to hold passive positions unless those positions are uniquely available to them alone. It would be too easy for them to do this; and managers should not be remunerated for something you could easily do yourself.

Jensen's alpha (JA) is given as in (5.9) above:

$$\alpha_J = (R_P - R_F) - \beta_P(R_M - R_F)$$

Although a basic measure, it is widely used in the world of traditional investing and is nevertheless a way to begin attacking the problem of alpha and beta separation (Jensen 1968). The separation process helps break down the three components of return usually found within hedge funds i.e. alpha (skill), the beta continuum as alluded to by Anson (2008) (skill to no skill) and the risk-free rate (no skill). Since managers of hedge funds usually charge high fees for their services (e.g. 2 and 20), it is of concern to investors that they have a good idea of what it is they are paying for. Source 5.7 shows the JA() member declaration and definition.

SOURCE 5.7: THE JA() MEMBER DECLARATION AND DEFINITION

```
// ...
// PMetrics.h
// ...

V1DD JA(V2DD& v, const DBL& r); // JA()

// ...
// ...
// PMetrics.cpp
// ...

// JA()
V1DD PMetrics::JA(V2DD& v, const DBL& r)
{
    UINT n = v.size();
    DBL tmp; // Declare a temporary holding variable
    V1DD ja; // Declare a 1D vector for Jensen's alpha

    V1DD mean = Mean(v, 12);   // Inherit Mean from the Stats class
```

```cpp
    V1DD slope = GetSlope(v); // Call GetSlope() member function

    // Calculate Jensen's alpha using Eqn. (5.9)
    for(UINT j=1; j<v[0].size()-1; j++)
    {
      tmp = 0.0;
      for (UINT i=0; i<n; i++)
      {
              tmp = mean[j - 1] -  (r + slope[j - 1] * (mean[v[0]
              .size() - 2] - r));
      }
      ja.push_back(tmp);
    }

    return ja;
}

// ...
// main.cpp
// ...

// Declare and call the TR() member function
// Assume risk-free rate = 3.0%
V1DD ja = pmetrics.JA(data, 3.0);

// Output results
cout << "\n Jensen's Alpha:\n";
pmetrics.SortPrint(ja, s);

// ...
```

```
┌──────────────────────────────────────────────────────────┐
│ ▣                    Console Output              ─  □  ✕   │
├──────────────────────────────────────────────────────────┤
│ File:./data/10_funds_mkt.dat                              │
│ Imported 792 values successfully!                         │
│                                                           │
│ Jensen's Alpha (Rf = 3.0%):                               │
│                                                           │
│ CTA3    12.02                                             │
│ CTA1     9.50                                             │
│ GM1      8.45                                             │
│ LS1      6.54                                             │
│ LS2      6.37                                             │
│ LS3      4.01                                             │
│ CTA2     3.67                                             │
│ GM2      2.60                                             │
│ MN1      1.72                                             │
│ MN2      0.54                                             │
│                                                           │
└──────────────────────────────────────────────────────────┘
```

Interestingly, CTA1 has been toppled from its premier position in the rankings by CTA3. In other words, CTA1 has been found guilty of *free-riding* on the market to a certain extent in order to produce a percentage of their returns. This is generally something frowned upon in the industry since a manager should not get paid for taking passive risk on an easily replicable asset class as the same exposure can usually be obtained cheaply using ETFs or futures positions held long and rolled as necessary. CTA3, which was third as ranked by the SR, is now in first place with a JA of 12.02%. While CTA1 is still in second place, GM1 keeps its place in third with a similar ranking to the TR, but LS1 has been demoted to fourth place having been second in the SR rankings. MN2 is still however the bottom ranked fund.

5.5.4 M-Squared

The *M-squared* (MM) metric was developed by Modigliani and Modigliani[13] as a risk-adjusted measure which could be more easily interpreted by the average investor once the various hedge funds had been volatility adjusted for their average returns and then ranked. The intuition is that by using a benchmark with an estimated volatility the fund is either *leveraged* or *de-leveraged* so that its volatility matches that of the benchmark. The leveraged or de-leveraged return of the fund is then reported and ranked. As such, the fund's return can be interpreted as the return that would have been produced had the fund's volatility been equivalent to that of the market benchmark. When various funds are processed in this way and ranked, it is easier for the less sophisticated investor to see how they outperform the benchmark to which they have had their risk profile matched. In our case, the market benchmark (SDX) has an annualised return of 5.36% and a volatility of 10.90% for matching purposes. MM is given by:

$$MM = \frac{\sigma_M}{\sigma_P}(R_P - R_F) - R_F \qquad (5.18)$$

Source 5.8 shows the MM() member declaration and definition.

SOURCE 5.8: THE MM() MEMBER DECLARATION AND DEFINITION

```
// ...
// PMetrics.h
// ...


V1DD MM(V2DD& v, const DBL& r); // MM()
```

---

[13] See Modigliani (1997) and Modigliani and Modigliani (1997).

```cpp
// ...

// ...
// PMetrics.cpp
// ...


// MM()
V1DD PMetrics::MM(V2DD& v, const DBL& r)
{
    UINT n = v.size();
    DBL tmp; // Declare a temporary holding variable
    V1DD mm; // Declare a 1D vector for Jensen's alpha

    V1DD mean = Mean(v, 12);  // Inherit Mean from the Stats class
    V1DD std = StdDev(v, 'p', 12);  // Inherit St. Dev. from the Stats class

    // Calculate M-Squared using Eqn. (5.19)
    for(UINT j=1; j<v[0].size()-1; j++)
    {
      tmp = 0.0;
      for (UINT i=0; i<n; i++)
      {
            tmp = (std[v[0].size() - 2] / std[j - 1]) * (mean[j - 1]
            - r) - r;
      }
      mm.push_back(tmp);
    }

    return mm;
}


// ...
// main.cpp
// ...


// Declare and call the TR() member function
// Assume risk-free rate = 3.0%
V1DD mm = pmetrics.MM(data, 3.0);

// Output results
cout << "\n M-Squared (Rf = 3.0%):\n";
pmetrics.SortPrint(mm, s);

// ...
```

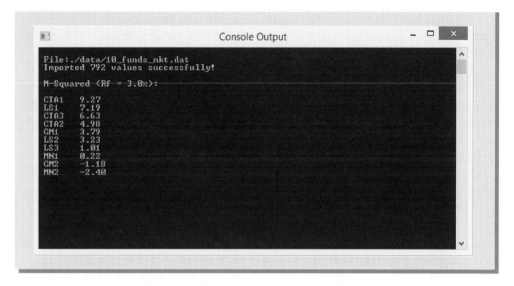

```
File:./data/10_funds_mkt.dat
Imported 792 values successfully!

M-Squared (Rf = 3.0%):

CTA1     9.27
LS1      7.19
CTA3     6.63
CTA2     4.98
GM1      3.79
LS2      3.23
LS3      1.01
MN1      0.22
GM2     -1.18
MN2     -2.40
```

From the results we see that the rankings are identical to those of the Sharpe ratio. However, the main point of the MM metric is that it is easy to interpret the rankings since they represent returns corresponding to volatilities that have been matched to that of the benchmark. Since the benchmark return is 5.36%, it follows that any fund with a return higher than 5.36% outperforms the market in a risk-adjusted sense i.e. CTA1, LS1 and CTA3 (which is not instantly obvious from the SR rankings). Also, it is comforting for investors to know by how many percentage points their returns would be greater or less than the market for volatility matched hedge funds.

5.6 THE MINIMUM ACCEPTABLE RETURN

These last two metrics are based around the concept of separating out upside 'good volatility' and downside 'bad volatility'. The variance and the standard deviation are two-sided measures of the degree of the spread in an asset's returns. However, often it is desirable to be able to specify a *Minimum Acceptable Return* (MAR) threshold for a certain statistic in order to define some kind of minimum acceptable loss threshold.

5.6.1 The Sortino Ratio

The *Sortino*[14] ratio (STR) is defined as:

$$
Sortino = \frac{R_P - MAR}{\sqrt{\dfrac{1}{T} \sum_{\substack{t=0 \\ R_P < MAR}}^{T} (R_{P,t} - MAR)^2}}
\tag{5.19}
$$

---

[14]Initially defined by Brian M. Rom in 1986 but later developed by Frank Sortino (1994).

The STR is another enhanced variant of the SR. The problem with the SR is that it uses volatility as a measure of risk for the entire time series of returns. As a result, both large *upswings* and large *downswings* in value are penalised as they translate into higher volatility and a lower SR. In many ways, the STR is a better choice, especially when measuring and comparing the performance of managers whose programs exhibit skew in their return distributions. The STR is a modification of the SR but uses *downside deviation* rather than standard deviation as the measure of risk i.e. only those returns falling below a user-specified target (see Figure 5.7) or required rate of return are considered risky.

From (5.19) we see that the denominator uses the concept of the MAR to set a reference point for the measurement of returns. Basically the MAR is a fixed point, e.g. 3.0%, which sets a minimum rate of return agreed by the investor thereby splitting the returns into two categories i.e. those greater than or equal to MAR (i.e. the *upside semi-deviation*) and those less than MAR (i.e. the *downside semi-deviation*). Since the idea of risk-adjusted returns is to try to have the least risk possible, a typical investor will not want their upside risk to penalised. To account for this, the STR uses a measure of standard deviation in the denominator which only uses the downside returns. Thus, the higher the STR, the better the manager is at controlling downside returns while not being penalised for upside returns. As such it is a good metric for assessing the risk-management capabilities of a hedge fund manager. Source 5.9 shows the STR() member declaration and definition.

SOURCE 5.9: THE STR() MEMBER DECLARATION AND DEFINITION

```
// ...
// PMetrics.h
// ...

V1DD STR(V2DD& v, const DBL& mar); // STR()

// ...

// ...
// PMetrics.cpp
// ...

// STR()
V1DD PMetrics::STR(V2DD& v, const DBL& mar)
{
    UINT n = v.size();
    DBL tmp;  // Declare a temporary holding variable
```

```
      V1DD str; // Declare a 1D vector for the Sortino ratio
      V1DD avg; // Declare a 1D vector for Averages

      // Inherit Mean from the Stats class
      V1DD mean = Mean(v, 12);
      DBL m = mean.size();
      DBL sum, pmean;

      // Calculate Portfolio (10 hedge fund) Mean
      for(UINT i=0; i<m; i++)
      {
        sum += mean[i];
      }
      pmean = sum/m;

      // Calculate Averages
      for(UINT j=1; j<v[0].size(); j++)
      {
        tmp = 0.0;
        for(UINT i=0; i<n; i++)
        {
                tmp += pow(min(0.0, v[i][j] - mar), 2);
        }
      tmp /= n;
      avg.push_back(tmp);
      }

      // Calculate Sortino ratio using Eqn. (5.19)
      for(UINT j=1; j<v[0].size(); j++)
      {
        tmp = 0.0;
        for (UINT i=0; i<n; i++)
        {
                tmp = (pmean - mar) / sqrt(avg[j - 1]);
        }
        str.push_back(tmp);
      }

      return str;
}

// ...
// main.cpp
// ..
```

```
// Create class instances
Import thfs;
PMetrics pmetrics;

// Declare and call GetData()
V2DD data = thfs.GetData("./data/10_hedge_funds.dat");

V1DS s; // Declare and initialsie a 1D vector of strings
s.push_back("CTA1");
s.push_back("CTA2");
s.push_back("CTA3");
s.push_back("GM1");
s.push_back("GM2");
s.push_back("LS1");
s.push_back("LS2");
s.push_back("LS3");
s.push_back("MN1");
s.push_back("MN2");

 // Declare and call the TR() member function
// Assume MAR = 3.0%
V1DD str = pmetrics.STR(data, 3.0);

// Output results
cout << "\n Sortino ratio (MAR = 3.0%):\n";
pmetrics.SortPrint(str, s);

// ...
```

```
File:./data/10_hedge_funds.dat
Imported 720 values successfully!

Sortino ratio (MAR = 3.0%):

CTA2    1.94
LS1     1.90
CTA1    1.83
MN1     1.81
MN2     1.74
LS3     1.48
LS2     1.47
CTA3    1.45
GM1     1.33
GM2     1.18
```

Notice we have gone back to the original *10_hedge_funds.dat* file since we no longer need the market benchmark data. The results show that there seems to be a clear leader emerging from the risk-adjusted rankings, namely CTA1, i.e. it has been the top ranked for several of the performance metrics. CTA3 is also favoured over LS1 due to the MSR result i.e. showing that the high kurtosis of CTA3 must be associated with good kurtosis i.e. high returns in the upside semi-deviation. Whilst having a negative skew, the returns in the downside semi-deviation below the MAR are milder than those associated with the downside semi-deviation in LS1 on a risk-adjusted basis. As we go down the STR rankings, we also notice that GM1 is to be preferred over CTA2. In a nutshell, it shows how the population estimates of skewness and kurtosis can be misleading since CTA2 has a higher skewness (CTA2: 0.351 vs. GM1: −0.023) and a lower kurtosis (CTA2: −0.848 vs. GM1: −0.114); meanwhile the STR ranks GM1 higher than CTA2.

5.6.2 The Omega Ratio

The Omega ratio as defined by Keating and Shadwick (2002) is a non-parametric method i.e. it does not rely upon calculating the moments of a distribution of returns for determining the ranking of each hedge fund versus a threshold level. Developed in the early 2000s it has gained popularity with practitioners due to its inclusiveness of the full distribution of the returns in describing the relative ranking of a fund. As such, it incorporates all first moments (and theoretically beyond). As mentioned earlier, investors like high odd moments and low even moments and the risks borne of holding an asset prone to fourth moment risk especially are non-negligible. Its popularity also stems from the fact that it inherently describes the risk-reward properties of the return distribution and so can be easily interpreted. The ratio considers returns below and above a specific loss *threshold* return level. In doing so, it places a threshold return on the distribution of returns (i.e. the return PDF with an area of one underneath) which have been accumulated by summing (i.e. taking the integral) from the left hand side to form the CDF, $F(x)$. Instead of using the positive and negative infinity signs to signify the limits on either side of the integral, we use a for the downside limit and b for the upside limit. The Omega ratio is written as:

$$\Omega(L) = \frac{\int_{L}^{b} (1 - F(x)dx}{\int_{a}^{L} F(x)dx} \qquad (5.20)$$

The returns below a certain threshold are considered as losses, and the returns above are considered profits. It follows from (5.20) that a higher value of Omega for a given threshold is preferred over a lower value for a rational investor. As such when the Omega ratio takes a value of one, this represents the mean of the portfolio since it is the balancing point in terms of moments. The Omega ratio can therefore be used to create rankings based on various return thresholds. The rankings may change as a function of a perceived loss threshold which will vary from investor to investor depending on their appetite for risk which is interpreted here as the magnitude of return threshold. The Omega ratio is non-parametric and reflects all moments of the distribution so a fund with a high excess kurtosis will be ranked lower than one with no excess kurtosis assuming both funds have the same return, volatility and skewness.

The risk-adjusted return metrics described in this chapter are the ones most commonly used within the hedge fund industry. There are others which have emerged in recent times, for example the *Stutzer index* (Stutzer 2000), the *Sharpe-Omega ratio* (Gupta, Kazemi and Schneeweiss 2003), *AIRAP* (Sharma 2004) and *Kappa* (Kaplan and Knowles 2004). Lo (2002) also reports a modified risk-adjusted ratio method adjusted for autocorrelation.

This chapter nonetheless gives a broad introduction to the subject of risk-adjusted returns and demonstrates that when appraising hedge fund performance, returns must be risk-adjusted to be meaningful.

Mean-Variance Optimisation

H edge fund analysis primarily involves ascertaining relevant statistical properties of the hedge fund returns distribution in order to make informed decisions about the characteristics and performance of a hedge fund. We have already looked in detail at the two prominent statistical parameters most often cited: the mean and standard deviation. In 1953, H.M. Markowitz introduced the topic of modern portfolio theory which opened up the possibility of being able to optimise a portfolio of assets so as to minimise the portfolio risk for an acceptable level of portfolio return. Clearly, such a technique is extremely valuable to hedge fund managers, especially when dealing with asset allocation and the efficient distribution of wealth across a portfolio.

Chapter 6 introduces the main ideas behind mean-variance optimisation and implements the method of Lagrange multipliers to find the set of optimal investment weights for a 10-hedge-fund portfolio.

6.1 THE OPTIMISE CLASS

As in the previous chapters we will be developing another class Optimise in much the same way as we did for the other classes. Source 6.1 shows the basic skeleton of the Optimise class which will we again add to as we develop through the chapter.

SOURCE 6.1: SKELETON OF THE Optimise CLASS

```
// Optimise.h
#pragma once;

#include "Stats.h"

class Optimise: public Stats
```

```
{
    public:
    Optimise() {}
    virtual ~Optimise() {}

    // Member function declarations
private:
    // Member variable declarations
};

// RMetrics.cpp
#include "Optimise.h"
```

In Source 6.1, the default constructor and destructor have again been declared and defined in the header file by removing the semi-colon (;) and adding the opening and closing braces ({}). Also, as with the PMetrics class, we have made Optimise inherit from the Stats class since we will be making use of several methods available to us in the Stats class.

6.2 MEAN-VARIANCE ANALYSIS

6.2.1 Portfolio Return and Variance

All hedge fund managers would like to achieve the highest possible return from their investment portfolios; however, this has to be weighed up against the amount of risk they are willing to accept. Figure 6.1 shows the risk-return scatter plot for the 10 hypothetical hedge funds with monthly returns (*10_hedge_funds.dat*). Figure 6.1 shows the results from Chapter 5 for the mean and standard deviation of the 10 hedge funds which are subsequently plotted in Figure 6.2.

It is not unknown that assets with higher returns generally correlate with higher risk. However, a hedge fund manager can reduce their overall exposure to the risk from individual assets by investing in a well-diversified portfolio of uncorrelated assets. For example, it is generally accepted that equity markets move independently of the bond market and so a combination of both assets in a portfolio can lead to an overall lower level of risk. Indeed, diversification can lead to a reduction in risk even if asset returns are not negatively correlated. By holding a combination of assets that are not perfectly correlated (i.e. $-1 \leq \rho_{ij} < 1$) one can effectively achieve the same expected portfolio return but with a much lower level of portfolio risk (as measured by the portfolio variance). H.M. Markowitz[1] (1952) was one of the first to look at the correlation between

---

[1] Harry Markowitz (1927–) is an American economist best known for his pioneering work in *modern portfolio theory* (MPT), studying the effects of asset risk, return, correlation and diversification on portfolio returns.

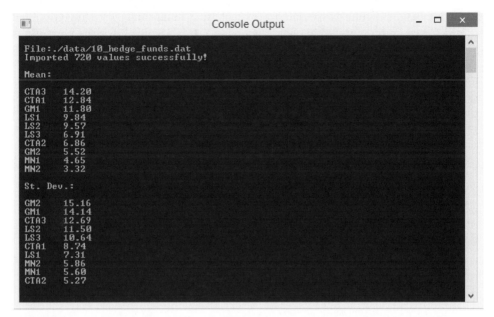

FIGURE 6.1 Annualised mean and standard deviation for each of the 10 hedge funds

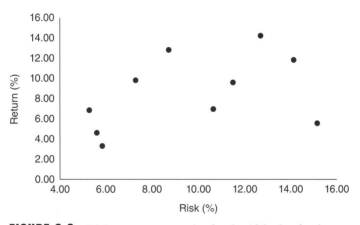

FIGURE 6.2 Risk-return scatter plot for the 10 hedge funds

various assets in order to obtain a mean portfolio return and subsequent reduction in the overall risk through diversification.[2] More technically, for a portfolio made up of N (≥ 2) risky assets, $i = 1,...., N$, the expected *portfolio return* r_p is given by:

$$r_p = \sum_{i=1}^{N} w_i \bar{r}_i \qquad (6.1)$$

---

[2] Under the assumption that asset returns are normally distributed, investors are rational and markets are efficient.

where $\bar{r}_i$ are the mean return associated with each risky asset i and w_i are the individual holdings (or weights) invested in each risky asset i. It is assumed that the portfolio is fully invested so that the total holdings in each asset always add up to 100% i.e. the following condition on the weights must hold:

$$\sum_{i=1}^{N} w_i = 1 \tag{6.2}$$

The *portfolio variance* σ_p^2 is given by:

$$\sigma_p^2 = \sum_{i=1}^{N} \sum_{j=1}^{N} w_i w_j \sigma_i \sigma_j \rho_{ij} \tag{6.3}$$

where w_i and w_j are the weights, σ_i and σ_j are the standard deviations, and ρ_{ij} is the correlation between the returns of assets i and j. Note that for any pair of random variables, X_i and X_j, the correlation ρ_{ij} can be written as:

$$\rho_{ij} = \frac{\sigma_{ij}}{\sigma_i \sigma_j} \tag{6.4}$$

where $\sigma_{ij} = \text{cov}(X_i, X_j)$.

The portfolio variance can therefore be written as:

$$\sigma_p^2 = \sum_{i=1}^{N} \sum_{j=1}^{N} w_i w_j \sigma_{ij} \tag{6.5}$$

where, more formally, $\sigma_{ij} = \text{cov}(\bar{r}_i, \bar{r}_j)$ and $\sigma_i^2 = \text{cov}(\bar{r}_i, \bar{r}_i)$.

Both the mean portfolio return and variance can also be transformed into a compact matrix notation. That is, we can write the *portfolio return*:

$$r_p = \sum_{i=1}^{N} w_i \bar{r}_i = \mathbf{w}^T \mathbf{R} \tag{6.6}$$

where $\mathbf{w}^T$ is the matrix *transpose* of $\mathbf{w}$ which contains all the individual asset weights, w_i and $\mathbf{R}$ is the vector of mean returns for assets i. $\mathbf{w}$, $\mathbf{w}^T$ and $\mathbf{R}$ are given by:

$$\mathbf{w} = \begin{pmatrix} w_1 \\ w_2 \\ w_3 \\ \cdot \\ \cdot \\ w_N \end{pmatrix} \tag{6.7}$$

$$\mathbf{w}^T = (\, w_1 \quad w_2 \quad w_3 \quad . \quad . \quad w_N \,) \tag{6.8}$$

$$\mathbf{R} = \begin{pmatrix} \bar{r}_1 \\ \bar{r}_2 \\ \bar{r}_3 \\ . \\ . \\ \bar{r}_N \end{pmatrix} \tag{6.9}$$

Although $\mathbf{w}$, $\mathbf{w}^T$ and $\mathbf{R}$ are vectors, they can also be thought of as $(n \times 1)$ or $(1 \times n)$ matrices. The *portfolio variance* in matrix form can thus be written as:

$$\sigma_p^2 = \sum_{i=1}^{N} \sum_{j=1}^{N} w_i w_j \sigma_{ij} = \mathbf{w}^T \Sigma \mathbf{w} \tag{6.10}$$

where Σ is the *variance-covariance* matrix[3] for the individual assets i and j given by:[4]

$$\Sigma = \begin{pmatrix} \sigma_1^2 & \text{cov}_{12} & \text{cov}_{13} & . & . & \text{cov}_{1n} \\ \text{cov}_{21} & \sigma_2^2 & \text{cov}_{23} & . & . & . \\ \text{cov}_{31} & \text{cov}_{32} & \sigma_3^2 & . & . & . \\ . & . & . & . & . & . \\ . & . & . & . & . & . \\ \text{cov}_{n1} & . & . & . & . & \sigma_N^2 \end{pmatrix} \tag{6.11}$$

Source 6.2 shows the `PRet()` and `PVar()` member functions and method implementations.

SOURCE 6.2:   THE PRet() AND PVar() MEMBER FUNCTION AND METHOD IMPLEMENTATIONS

```
// Optimise.h
#pragma once;


#include "Matrix.h"
#include "Stats.h"
```

---

[3] Practitioners usually refer to Σ as the VCV matrix.

[4] As with all covariance matrices, Σ must be *positive definite* i.e. a symmetric $n \times n$ real matrix is said to be positive definite if the scalar $\mathbf{w}^T \Sigma \mathbf{w}$ is positive for every non-zero column vector $\mathbf{w}$ of n real numbers.

```
class Optimise: public Stats
{
   public:
   Optimise() {}
   virtual ~Optimise() {}

   // Member function declarations
   Matrix PRet(const V2DD& v); // PRet()
   Matrix PVar(const V2DD& v); // PVar()
   private:
   // Member variable declarations
   Matrix m_matrix;     // An instance of the Matrix class
};


// Optimise.cpp
#include "Optimise.h"

Matrix Optimise::PRet(const V2DD& v)
{
    UINT n = v[0].size()-1;

      // Declare wT and R matrices
    Matrix wT = Matrix(1, n);
    Matrix R = Matrix(n, 1);

    // Transpose weights
    for (UINT i=1; i<=n; i++)
      wT(1, i) = 1 / (DBL)n; // Equal weights

    // Mean returns
    V1DD r = Mean(v, 12);

    // R matrix
    for (UINT i=1; i<=n; i++)
        R(i, 1) = r[i-1];

    return wT * R;
}

Matrix Optimise::PVar(const V2DD& v)
{
    UINT n = v[0].size()-1;

    // Declare w, wT and VCV matrices
```

```
    Matrix w = Matrix(n, 1);
    Matrix wT = Matrix(1, n);
    Matrix VCV = Matrix(n, n);

    // Initialise portfolio weights
    for (UINT i=1; i<=n; i++)
      w(i, 1) = 1 / (DBL)n; // Equal weights

    // Transpose weights
    for (UINT i=1; i<=n; i++)
      wT(1, i) = 1 / (DBL)n; // Equal weights

    // Covariance matrix
    V1DD cov = Cov(v);

    // VCV matrix
    int k = 0; // Covariance offset
    for (UINT i=1; i<=n; i++)
    {
      for (UINT j=1; j<=n; j++)
      {
        VCV(i, j) = cov[j+k-1];
      if(i == j)
              VCV(i, j) *= 12; // Annualise variance
      }
      k+=10;
    }

    return wT * VCV * w;
}

// ...
// main.cpp
// ...

// Create class instances
Import thfs;
Optimise optimise;

// Declare and call GetData()
V2DD data = thfs.GetData("./data/10_hedge_funds.dat");

// Declare and call PRet() and PVar() member function
Matrix pret = optimise.PRet(data);
Matrix pvar = optimise.PVar(data);
```

```
// Output results
cout << "\n Port. Ret. (%) = ";
pret.Print();
cout << " Port. Var. (%) = ";
pvar.Print();

// ...
```

```
File:./data/10_hedge_funds.dat
Imported 720 values successfully!

Port. Ret. (%) = 8.552
Port. Var. (%) = 10.725
```

Source 6.2 shows that the annual portfolio return and variance for the 10-hedge-fund portfolio are 8.552% and 10.725%, respectively. In Source 6.2 we have assumed in the first instance an equally weighted portfolio i.e. `1/(DBL)n;`, where we have cast n from `UINT` to `DBL` (see Figure 6.3).

Notice that we have multiplied the variance for each hedge fund along the main diagonal of the VCV matrix by 12 to annualise i.e. `VCV(i, j) *= 12;` (see Figure 6.4).

In Source 6.2 we have included a new `Matrix` class to handle all of the necessary matrix calculations. Source 6.3 shows the `Matrix.h` and `Matrix.cpp` files of the `Matrix` class.

SOURCE 6.3:   THE Matrix.h AND Matrix.cpp FILES OF THE Matrix CLASS

```
// Matrix.h
#pragma once
```

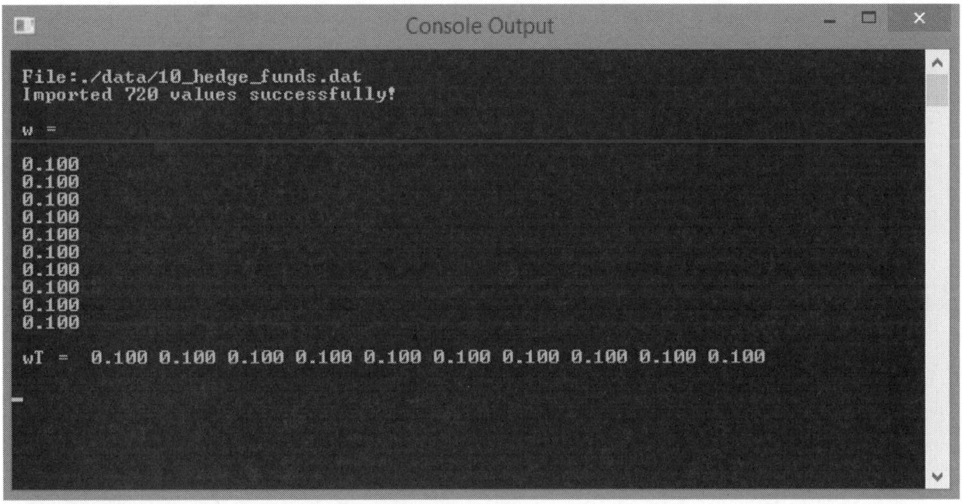

FIGURE 6.3 Equal weights for W and W^{T}

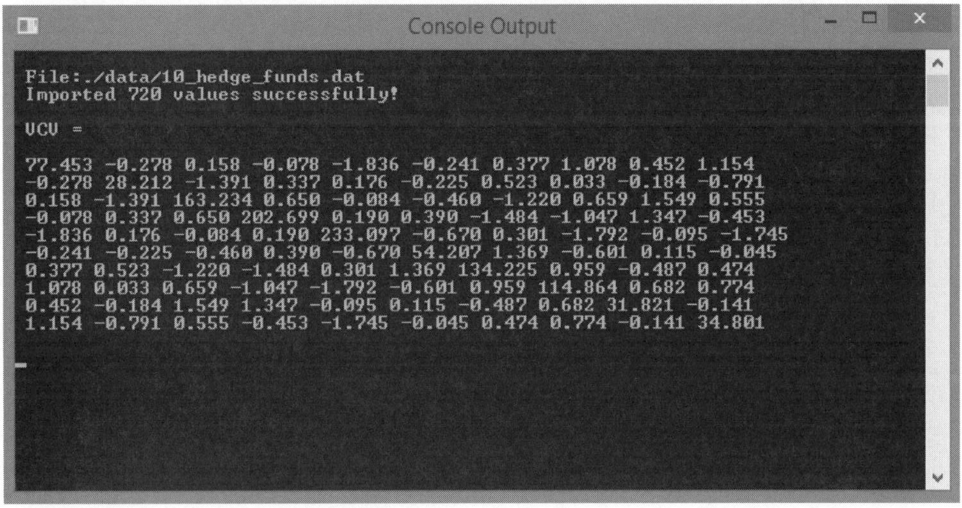

FIGURE 6.4 The annualised VCV matrix

```cpp
#include "Utils.h"

#include <cstdlib>
#include <cstdio>
#include <math.h>

class Matrix
{
```

```cpp
public:
  Matrix(); // Default constructor
  Matrix(const int row_count, const int column_count); // Constructor
  ~Matrix(); // Destructor

  DBL& operator()(const int r, const int c);                // Overloaded
  operator ()

  void Print() const; // Print matrix

  friend Matrix operator* (const Matrix& a, const Matrix& b);
  // Multiply Matrix by Matrix (*)
  friend Matrix operator*(const Matrix& a, const DBL b);    // Multiply
  Matrix with double (*)
  friend Matrix operator*(const DBL b, const Matrix& a);    // Multiply
  double with Matrix (*)

  Matrix(const Matrix& a);                 // Copy constructor
  Matrix& operator=(const Matrix& a); // Assignment operator
private:
  int rows;          // Matrix rows
  int cols;          // Matrix columns
  DBL** p;           // Double pointer to a Matrix of doubles
};

// Matrix.cpp
#include "Matrix.h"

#include <iostream>
using std::cout;

// Default constructor
// Creates a NULL (empty) Matrix object
Matrix::Matrix() : p(NULL), rows(0), cols(0)
{
}

// Constructor
// Creates a NULL (empty) Matrix object with specific rows and columns
Matrix::Matrix(const int row_count, const int column_count)
{
    p = NULL; // Empty pointer

    if (row_count > 0 && column_count > 0)
    {
      rows = row_count;
      cols = column_count;
```

```
        p = new DBL*[rows];

        for (UINT r=0; r<rows; r++)
        {
        p[r] = new DBL[cols];

                // Initially fill with zeros
                for (UINT c=0; c<cols; c++)
                {
                        p[r][c] = 0;
                }
            }
        }
}

// Destructor
Matrix::~Matrix()
{
    // Delete all allocated memory on the heap
    for (UINT r=0; r<rows; r++)
    {
     delete p[r];
    }
    delete p;
    p = NULL; // Empty pointer
}

// Copy constructor
Matrix::Matrix(const Matrix& a)
{
    rows = a.rows;
    cols = a.cols;

    p = new DBL*[a.rows];

    for (int r = 0; r < a.rows; r++)
    {
     p[r] = new DBL[a.cols];

        // Copy values from Matrix a
        for (UINT c=0; c<a.cols; c++)
        {
        p[r][c] = a.p[r][c];
        }
    }
}

// Assignment operator
```

```
Matrix& Matrix::operator=(const Matrix& a)
{
    rows = a.rows;
    cols = a.cols;
    p = new DBL*[a.rows];

    for (UINT r=0; r<a.rows; r++)
    {
     p[r] = new DBL[a.cols];

     // Copy values from Matrix a
     for (UINT c=0; c<a.cols; c++)
     {
     p[r][c] = a.p[r][c];
     }
    }

    return *this;
}

// Overloaded operator ()
// Note: indices are one-based, not zero-based
double& Matrix::operator()(const int r, const int c)
{
    if (p != NULL && r > 0 && r <= rows && c > 0 && c <= cols)
    {
     return p[r-1][c-1];
    }
    else
    {
     cout << "\nSubscript out of range!\n";
    }
}

// Overloaded operator *
Matrix operator*(const Matrix& a, const Matrix& b)
{
    // Check if dimensions match
    if (a.cols == b.rows)
    {
     Matrix res(a.rows, b.cols);

     for (UINT r=0; r<a.rows; r++)
     {
             for (UINT c_res=0; c_res<b.cols; c_res++)
             {
                     for (UINT c=0; c<a.cols; c++)
                     {
```

```
                    res.p[r][c_res] += a.p[r][c] * b.p[c][c_res];
                }
            }
        }
     return res;
     }
     else
     {
      cout << "\nMatrix dimensions does not match! \n";
     }
     // Return an empty matrix
     // (Should never happen but just for safety)
     return Matrix();
}


// Multiply Matrix by a double (*)
Matrix operator*(const Matrix& a, const DBL b)
{
    Matrix res = a;
    res.Multiply(b);
    return res;
}


// Multiply double by a Matrix (*)
Matrix operator*(const DBL b, const Matrix& a)
{
    Matrix res = a;
    res.Multiply(b);
    return res;
}


 // Print Matrix
void Matrix::Print() const
{
    if (p != NULL)
    {
    printf(" ");
    for (UINT r=0; r<rows; r++)
    {
    if (r > 0)
    {
            printf(" ");
    }
    for (UINT c=0; c<cols-1; c++)
    {
            printf("%.3f ", p[r][c]);
    }
    if (r < rows-1)
```

```
        {
              printf("%.3f\n", p[r][cols-1]);
        }
        else
        {
              printf("%.3f\n", p[r][cols-1]);
        }
        }
    }
    else
    {
    // Matrix is empty
    printf("[ ]\n");
    }
}
```

We have made use of *pointers* in the `Matrix` class and we briefly discuss their implementation here but please note that a full explanation of pointers is beyond the scope of this book.

A *pointer* is an object; whose value refers to (or '*points to*') another value stored elsewhere in memory using its *address*. A pointer *references* a location in memory, and obtaining the value stored at that location is known as *dereferencing* the pointer. Pointers to data significantly improve performance for repetitive operations such as traversing matrices. In particular, it is often much cheaper in time to copy and dereference pointers than it is to copy and access the data to which the pointers point. Whenever a program needs to *dynamically allocate memory*, C++ provides the operators `new` and `delete`. Dynamic memory is allocated using the `new` operator and returns a pointer to the beginning of the new block of memory allocated, for example:

```
double* ptr; or
ptr = new double[5];
```

In the second case, the system dynamically allocates space for five elements of type `double` and returns a pointer to the first element of the sequence, which is assigned to `ptr` (a pointer). Therefore, `ptr` now points to a valid block of memory with space for five elements of type `double`. In Source 6.3, we have declared a pointer `ptr` as follows:

```
DBL** p;
```

This is in fact a *double* pointer. We have used a double pointer since we are dealing with dynamic 2D arrays. In essence we are saying; `DBL**` is a pointer to `DBL*` and

`DBL*` is a pointer to `DBL` i.e. the number of `*` tell us how many pointers deep we are going. So, we can access the rows of an array, for example, by:

```
p = new DBL*[rows];
```

and the columns with:

```
p[r] = new double[cols];
```

The dynamic memory requested by a program is allocated by the system from the memory *heap*. However, computer memory is a limited resource, and it can be exhausted. Therefore, there are no guarantees that all requests to allocate memory using operator `new` are going to be granted by the system. In most cases, memory allocated dynamically is only needed during specific periods of time within a program; once it is no longer needed, it can be freed so that the memory becomes available again for other requests to dynamic memory. This is the purpose of operator `delete`, for example:

```
delete ptr; or
delete[] ptr;
```

The first statement releases the memory of a single element allocated using `new`, and the second one releases the memory allocated for arrays of elements using `new` and a size in brackets (`[]`). In Source 6.3 we explicitly delete all allocated memory in the destructor.

You will notice in Source 6.3 that we have introduced for the first time the *copy constructor* and *assignment operator*. A *copy constructor* is a special constructor for a class that is used to make a copy of an existing instance. In Source 6.3 we declare a copy constructor as follows:

```
Matrix(const Matrix& a);
```

Note that if you do not explicitly declare a copy constructor, the compiler gives you one implicitly. The implicit copy constructor does a member-wise copy of the source object. The compiler-provided copy constructor is exactly equivalent to:

```
AClass::AClass(const AClass& other) :
        a( other.a ), b( other.b ), c( other.c ) {}
```

In many cases, this is sufficient. However, there are certain circumstances where the member-wise copy version is not good enough. By far, the most common reason the default copy constructor is not sufficient is because the object contains raw pointers and you need to take a '*deep*' copy of the pointer. That is, you do not wish to copy the pointer itself; instead you want to copy what the pointer *points to*. Why do you need to take deep copies? This is typically because the instance owns the pointer; that is, the instance is responsible for calling *delete* on the pointer at some point (generally through the destructor). If two objects end up calling delete on the same non-NULL pointer, *heap corruption* results.

The *assignment operator* allows us to use (=) to assign one instance to another. For example:

```
AClass m1, m2;
m1 = m2; // Assigns m2 to m1
```

In Source 6.3 we declare an assignment operator as follows:

```
Matrix& operator=(const Matrix& a);
```

As with the copy constructor, if you do not explicitly declare an assignment operator, the compiler gives you one implicitly. The implicit assignment operator does member-wise assignment of each data member from the source object. For example, the compiler-provided assignment operator is exactly equivalent to:

```
AClass& AClass::operator=( const AClass& other )
{
        a = other.a;
        b = other.b;
        c = other.c;
        return *this;
}
```

In general, any time you create your own custom copy constructor, you also need to write a custom assignment operator. Note that the return type for the assignment operator is a pointer to `this`, that is:

```
return *this;
```

In this case we are just returning a reference to the object i.e. this is a pointer and we are simply dereferencing it. If you try to use `return *this;` on a function whose return type is `Type` and not `Type&`, the compiler will try to make a copy of the object and then immediately call the destructor, usually not the intended behaviour. So the return type should be a reference (`&`) as in Source 6.3.

In Source 6.3 we have introduced several `friend` of the `Matrix` class so that we can perform the relevant matrix operations (`*`) i.e. matrix by matrix and pre and post multiplication of a matrix by a scalar. That is:

```
friend Matrix operator*(const Matrix& a, const Matrix& b);
friend Matrix operator*(const Matrix& a, const DBL b);
friend Matrix operator*(const DBL b, const Matrix& a);
```

We briefly encountered a `friend` in Chapter 1; a `friend` can access the `private` and `protected` members of the class in which it is declared as a `friend`. Friendship may allow a class to be better encapsulated by granting per-class access to parts of its implementation that would otherwise have to be public. This increased encapsulation comes at the cost of tighter coupling between classes.

6.2.2 The Mean-Variance Optimisation Problem

Markowitz's work ultimately led to the development of *mean-variance* portfolio optimisation[5] as a method of achieving a desired level of portfolio expected return for a degree of portfolio risk i.e. variance. Given a target expected return r^*, the mean-variance optimisation problem can be stated as follows:

$$\min \frac{1}{2} \mathbf{w}^T \Sigma \mathbf{w}$$

subject to the constraints:

$$\mathbf{w}^T \mathbf{R} = r^*$$
$$\sum_{i=1}^{N} w_i = 1$$

Such an optimisation problem can be solved *analytically* (as opposed to *numerically*) by using the *method of Lagrange multipliers*.

6.2.2.1 The Method of Lagrange Multipliers

A portfolio is a *frontier portfolio* if it minimises the variance for a given expected return i.e. a frontier portfolio solves the following optimisation problem:

$$\min \frac{1}{2} \mathbf{w}^T \Sigma \mathbf{w}$$

subject to the constraints:

$$\mathbf{w}^T \mathbf{R} = r^*$$
$$\mathbf{w}^T \mathbf{1} = 1$$

---

[5] Such a technique is known as a *quadratic programming* (QP) problem involving the optimisation (either *minimising* or *maximising*) of a quadratic function of several variables subject to a set of linear constraints on these variables. In this case, portfolio variance is a quadratic function of the weights w_i.

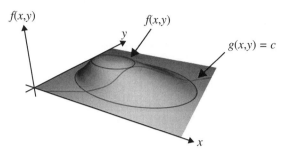

FIGURE 6.5   Find x and y to maximise f(x, y) subject to a constraint g(x, y) = c

The set of all frontier portfolios is called the *minimum variance frontier*. Any minimum variance portfolio can be solved by setting up the *Lagrangian*[6] corresponding to the optimisation problem. The method of Lagrange multipliers is a strategy for finding the local maxima and minima of a function subject to *equality constraints*. For example, consider the optimisation problem (see Figure 6.5):

$$\max f(x, y)$$

subject to the constraint:

$$g(x, y) = 0$$

Firstly, we require both f and g to have continuous first order *partial derivatives*. We introduce a new variable (λ) called a *Lagrange multiplier* defined by:

$$L(x, y, \lambda) = f(x, y) - \lambda \cdot g(x, y) \tag{6.12}$$

where the λ term may be either added or subtracted. If $f(x_0, y_0)$ is a maximum of $f(x, y)$ for the original constrained problem, then there exists λ_0 such that (x_0, y_0, λ_0) is a *stationary point* for the Lagrange function (stationary points are those points where the partial derivatives of L are zero). However, not all stationary points yield a solution of the original problem. Thus, the method of Lagrange multipliers yields a necessary condition for optimality in constrained problems. Sufficient conditions for a minimum or maximum also exist.

For our optimisation problem, the solution involves the application of differential calculus to the equation for portfolio variance ($\mathbf{w}^T \Sigma \mathbf{w}$), subject to the constraints that

---

[6] Joseph-Louis Lagrange (1736–1813) was an Italian mathematician and astronomer who made significant contributions to the fields of analysis, number theory and both classical and celestial mechanics.

the weights must sum to one and that the portfolio must achieve some expected return (r^*). Note that the following assumes an outright investment of capital i.e. the size of the positions in each hedge fund are based upon some amount of capital allocated to the portfolio e.g. capital equals one. Taking into account our optimisation problem, the Lagrangian can be written as:

$$L(\mathbf{w}, \lambda_1, \lambda_2 | \mathbf{R}, \Sigma) = \mathbf{w}^T \mathbf{V} \mathbf{w} - \lambda_1 (r^* - \mathbf{w}^T \mathbf{R}) - \lambda_2 (1 - \mathbf{w}^T \mathbf{1}) \qquad (6.13)$$

where λ_1 and λ_2 are Lagrange multipliers. Differentiating (6.13) gives:

$$\frac{\partial L}{\partial \mathbf{w}} = \mathbf{w}^T \mathbf{V} - \lambda_1 \mathbf{R}^T - \lambda_2 \mathbf{1}^T = 0$$

$$\frac{\partial L}{\partial \lambda_1} = r^* - \mathbf{w}^T \mathbf{R} = 0$$

$$\frac{\partial L}{\partial \lambda_2} = 1 - \mathbf{w}^T \mathbf{1} = 0$$

Rearranging leads to:

$$\mathbf{w}^T = \lambda_1 \mathbf{R}^T V^{-1} - \lambda_2 \mathbf{1}^T \mathbf{V}^{-1} = 0 \qquad (6.14)$$

$$\mathbf{w}^T \mathbf{1} = 1 \qquad (6.15)$$

$$\mathbf{w}^T \mathbf{R} = r^* \qquad (6.16)$$

Post-multiplying equation (6.14) with $\mathbf{R}$ and recognising the expression for r^* in (6.15) gives:

$$\mathbf{w}^T \mathbf{R} = r^* = \lambda_1 \mathbf{R}^T V^{-1} \mathbf{R} + \lambda_2 \mathbf{1}^T \mathbf{V}^{-1} \mathbf{R} \qquad (6.17)$$

Similarly, post-multiplying equation (6.14) with $\mathbf{1}$ and recognising the expression for 1 in (6.16) gives:

$$\mathbf{w}^T \mathbf{1} = 1 = \lambda_1 \mathbf{R}^T \mathbf{V}^{-1} \mathbf{1} + \lambda_2 \mathbf{1}^T \mathbf{V}^{-1} \mathbf{1} \qquad (6.18)$$

Noting that:

$$A = \mathbf{1}^T \mathbf{V}^{-1} \mathbf{R}$$
$$B = \mathbf{R}^T \mathbf{V}^{-1} \mathbf{R}$$
$$C = \mathbf{1}^T \mathbf{V}^{-1} \mathbf{1}$$
$$D = BC - A^2$$

leads to the following system of equations:

$$r^* = \lambda_1 B - \lambda_2 A$$
$$1 = \lambda_1 A - \lambda_2 C$$

Solving for λ_1 and λ_2, gives:

$$\lambda_1 = \frac{B - Ar^*}{D}$$
$$\lambda_2 = \frac{Cr^* - A}{D}$$

Substituting λ_1 and λ_2 into (6.14) gives:

$$\mathbf{w}^T = \frac{1}{D}(B\mathbf{1}^T - A\mathbf{R}^T)\mathbf{V}^{-1} + \frac{1}{D}(C\mathbf{R}^T - A\mathbf{1}^T)\mathbf{V}^{-1}r^* = g + hr^* \qquad (6.19)$$

where:

$$g = \frac{1}{D}(B\mathbf{1}^T - A\mathbf{R}^T)\mathbf{V}^{-1}$$
$$h = \frac{1}{D}(C\mathbf{R}^T - A\mathbf{1}^T)\mathbf{V}^{-1}$$

Source 6.4 shows the additional member functions required in the `Matrix` class to perform the relevant matrix operations to implement the method of Lagrange multipliers.

SOURCE 6.4: ADDITIONAL MEMBER FUNCTIONS IN THE Matrix CLASS

```
// ...
// Matrix.h
// ...


Matrix& Add(const DBL v);     // Add a double
Matrix& Subtract(const DBL v); // Subtract a double
Matrix& Divide(const DBL v);  // Divide a double

Matrix Minor(const int row, const int col) const; // Matrix minor
Matrix Diag(const int n);       // Matrix diagonal (overloaded)
Matrix Diag(const Matrix& v);  // Matrix diagonal (overloaded)
DBL Det(const Matrix& a);       // Matrix determinant
Matrix Inv(const Matrix& a);  // Matrix inverse
```

```cpp
friend Matrix operator+(const Matrix& a, const Matrix& b); // Add a Matrix
    to a Matrix (+)
friend Matrix operator+ (const Matrix& a, const DBL b); // Add a Matrix to
    a double (+)
friend Matrix operator+ (const DBL b, const Matrix& a); // Add a double
    to a Matrix (+)
friend Matrix operator-(const Matrix& a, const Matrix& b); // Subtract
    a Matrix from a Matrix (-)
friend Matrix operator- (const Matrix& a, const DBL b); // Subtract
    Matrix by double (-)
friend Matrix operator-(const DBL b, const Matrix& a); // Subtract
    double by Matrix (-)
friend Matrix operator-(const Matrix& a); // Unary operator (-)
friend Matrix operator/(const Matrix& a, const Matrix& b);   // Division
    of Matrix by Matrix (/)
friend Matrix operator/(const Matrix& a, const DBL b); // Division of
    Matrix by double (/)
friend Matrix operator/(const DBL b, const Matrix& a); // Division of
    DBL by Matrix (/)

int GetRows() const;
int GetCols() const;
DBL Get(const int r, const int c) const;

// ...

// ...
// Matrix.cpp
// ...

// Add a double value (elements wise)
Matrix& Matrix::Add(const DBL v)
{
    for (UINT r=0; r<rows; r++)
    {
    for (UINT c=0; c<cols; c++)
    {
        p[r][c] += v;
    }
    }

    return *this;
}

// Subtract a double value (elements wise)
Matrix& Matrix::Subtract(const DBL v)
```

```cpp
{
    return Add(-v);
}


// Divide by a double (elements wise)
Matrix& Matrix::Divide(const double v)
{
    return Multiply(1/v);
}


// Add a Matrix to a Matrix (+)
Matrix operator+(const Matrix& a, const Matrix& b)
{
    // Check if dimensions match
    if (a.rows == b.rows && a.cols == b.cols)
    {
      Matrix res(a.rows, a.cols);

      for (UINT r=0; r<a.rows; r++)
      {
          for (UINT c=0; c<a.cols; c++)
          {
              res.p[r][c] = a.p[r][c] + b.p[r][c];
          }
      }
      return res;
    }
    else
    {
      cout << "\n Dimensions does not match!\n";
    }
    // Return empty matrix
    return Matrix();
}


// Add a Matrix to a double (+)
Matrix operator+(const Matrix& a, const DBL b)
{
    Matrix res = a;
    res.Add(b);
    return res;
}


// Add a double to a Matrix (+)
Matrix operator+(const DBL b, const Matrix& a)
{
```

```
    Matrix res = a;
    res.Add(b);
    return res;
}


// Subtract a Matrix from a Matrix (-)
Matrix operator-(const Matrix& a, const Matrix& b)
{
    // Check if dimensions match
    if (a.rows == b.rows && a.cols == b.cols)
    {
     Matrix res(a.rows, a.cols);

     for (UINT r=0; r<a.rows; r++)
     {
            for (UINT c=0; c<a.cols; c++)
            {
                    res.p[r][c] = a.p[r][c] - b.p[r][c];
            }
     }
     return res;
    }
    else
    {
     cout << "\n Dimensions does not match\n";
    }
    // Return empty matrix
    return Matrix();
}


// Subtract Matrix by double (-)
Matrix operator-(const Matrix& a, const DBL b)
{
    Matrix res = a;
    res.Subtract(b);
    return res;
}


// Subtract double by Matrix (-)
Matrix operator-(const DBL b, const Matrix& a)
{
    Matrix res = -a;
    res.Add(b);
    return res;
}
```

```cpp
// Unary operator (-)
Matrix operator-(const Matrix& a)
{
    Matrix res(a.rows, a.cols);

    for (UINT r=0; r<a.rows; r++)
    {
     for (UINT c=0; c<a.cols; c++)
     {
     res.p[r][c] = -a.p[r][c];
     }
    }

    return res;
}

// Division of Matrix by double (/)
Matrix operator/(const Matrix& a, const DBL b)
{
    Matrix res = a;
    res.Divide(b);
    return res;
}

// Division of double by Matrix (/)
Matrix operator/(const DBL b, const Matrix& a)
{
    Matrix b_matrix(1, 1);
    b_matrix(1,1) = b;

    Matrix res = b_matrix / a;
    return res;
}

// Matrix minor
Matrix Matrix::Minor(const int row, const int col) const
{
    Matrix res;

    if (row > 0 && row <= rows && col > 0 && col <= cols)
    {
     res = Matrix(rows - 1, cols - 1);

     // copy the content of the matrix to the minor, except the selected
     for (UINT r=1; r<=(rows - (row >= rows)); r++)
     {
```

```
      for (UINT c=1; c<=(cols - (col >= cols)); c++)
      {
              res(r - (r > row), c - (c > col)) = p[r-1][c-1];
      }
      }
    }
    else
    {
    cout << "\n Index for minor out of range\n";
    }

return res;
}


// Matrix diagonal
Matrix Matrix::Diag(const int n)
{
  Matrix res = Matrix(n, n);

  for (int i = 1; i <= n; i++)
  {
    res(i, i) = 1;
  }
  return res;
}


// Matrix diagonal
Matrix Matrix::Diag(const Matrix& v)
{
  Matrix res;

  if (v.GetCols() == 1)
  {
    // the given matrix is a vector n x 1
    int rows = v.GetRows();

    res = Matrix(rows, rows);

    // Copy values of vector to Matrix
    for (UINT r=1; r <= rows; r++)
    {
      res(r, r) = v.Get(r, 1);
    }
  }
  else if (v.GetRows() == 1)
  {
```

```
    // Matrix is a vector 1 x n
    int cols = v.GetCols();
    res = Matrix(cols, cols);

    // Copy values of vector to Matrix
    for (int c=1; c <= cols; c++)
    {
    res(c, c) = v.Get(1, c);
    }
  }
  else
  {
    cout << "\n Parameter for diagonal must be a vector\n";
  }
  return res;
}


// Matrix determinant
DBL Matrix::Det(const Matrix& a)
{
  DBL d = 0;     // Value of the determinant
  int rows = a.GetRows();
  int cols = a.GetRows();

  if (rows == cols)
  {
    // A square matrix
    if (rows == 1)
    {
      // A 1 x 1 matrix
      d = a.Get(1, 1);
    }
    else if (rows == 2)
    {
      // A 2 x 2 matrix
      // Determinant of [a11,a12;a21,a22] is det = a11*a22-a21*a12
      d = a.Get(1, 1) * a.Get(2, 2) - a.Get(2, 1) * a.Get(1, 2);
    }
    else
    {
      // A 3 x 3 matrix or larger
      for (int c = 1; c <= cols; c++)
      {
        Matrix M = a.Minor(1, c);
        //d += pow(-1, 1+c) * a(1, c) * Det(M);
        d += (c%2 + c%2 - 1) * a.Get(1, c) * Det(M); // Faster than pow()
```

```
        }
      }
    }
    else
    {
      cout << "\n Matrix must be square!\n";
    }
    return d;
}

// Matrix inverse
Matrix Matrix::Inv(const Matrix& a)
{
    Matrix res;
    double d = 0;    // Value of the determinant
    int rows = a.GetRows();
    int cols = a.GetRows();

    d = Det(a);
    if (rows == cols && d != 0)
    {
      // A square matrix
      if (rows == 1)
      {
        // A 1 x 1 matrix
        res = Matrix(rows, cols);
        res(1, 1) = 1 / a.Get(1, 1);
      }
      else if (rows == 2)
      {
        // A 2 x 2 matrix
        res = Matrix(rows, cols);
        res(1, 1) = a.Get(2, 2);
        res(1, 2) = -a.Get(1, 2);
        res(2, 1) = -a.Get(2, 1);
        res(2, 2) = a.Get(1, 1);
        res = (1/d) * res;
      }
      else
      {
        // A matrix of 3 x 3 or larger
        // Calculate inverse using Gauss-Jordan elimination
        res = Diag(rows);    // A diagonal Matrix
        Matrix ai = a;    // Make a copy of Matrix a

        for (int c = 1; c <= cols; c++)
        {
```

```
              // Element (c, c) should be non-zero.
// If not, swap content of lower rows
      int r;
      for (r=c; r<=rows && ai(r, c) == 0; r++)
      {
      }
      if (r != c)
      {
          // Swap rows
          for (UINT s=1; s<=cols; s++)
          {
            Swap(ai(c, s), ai(r, s));
            Swap(res(c, s), res(r, s));
          }
      }

      // Eliminate non-zero values on the other rows at column c
      for (UINT r=1; r<=rows; r++)
      {
        if(r != c)
        {
        // eleminate value at column c and row r
        if (ai(r, c) != 0)
        {
          double f = - ai(r, c) / ai(c, c);

          // Add (f * row c) to row r to eleminate the value at column c
          for (UINT s=1; s<=cols; s++)
          {
            ai(r, s) += f * ai(c, s);
            res(r, s) += f * res(c, s);
          }
        }
      }
      else
      {
        // Make value at (c, c) one,
        // Divide each value on row r with the value at ai(c,c)
        double f = ai(c, c);
        for (UINT s=1; s<=cols; s++)
        {
          ai(r, s) /= f;
          res(r, s) /= f;
        }
      }
    }
```

```
          }
        }
      }
    else
    {
        if (rows == cols)
        {
        cout << "\n Matrix must be square!\n";
        }
        else
        {
        cout << "\n Determinant of matrix is zero\n";
        }
    }

    return res;
}

// # rows
int Matrix::GetRows() const
{
    return rows;
}

// # columns
int Matrix::GetCols() const
{
    return cols;
}

// Get index
DBL Matrix::Get(const int r, const int c) const
{
    if (p != NULL && r > 0 && r <= rows && c > 0 && c <= cols)
    {
    return p[r-1][c-1];
    }
    else
    {
    cout << "\n Subscript out of range\n";
    }
}
```

Source 6.5 shows the implementation of the method of Lagrange multipliers to find the optimised set of weights for a target portfolio return of 9.0% in our 10-hedge-fund portfolio.

SOURCE 6.5: IMPLEMENTATION OF THE METHOD OF Lagrange MULTIPLIERS

```cpp
// ...
// Optimise.h
//...

Matrix MLM(const V2DD& v, const DBL rtar); // MLM()

//...

//...
// Optimise.cpp
//...

Matrix Optimise::MLM(const V2DD& v, const DBL rtar)
{
   UINT n = v[0].size()-1;

   Matrix o = Matrix(n, 1);    // Matrix of ones
   Matrix oT = Matrix(1, n);   // Ones transposed
   Matrix R = Matrix(n, 1);    // R Matrix
   Matrix RT = Matrix(1, n);   // R transposed
   Matrix V = Matrix(n, n);    // VCV Matrix
   Matrix Vi = Matrix(n, n);   // VCV inverse

   // o Matrix
   for (UINT i=1; i<=n; i++)
     o(i, 1) = 1.0;

   // o transpose
   for (UINT i=1; i<=n; i++)
     oT(1, i) = 1.0;

   // Mean returns
   V1DD r = Mean(v, 12);

   // R matrix
   for (UINT i=1; i<=n; i++)
      R(i, 1) = r[i-1];

   // R transpose
   for (UINT i=1; i<=n; i++)
     RT(1, i) = R(i, 1);
```

```cpp
    // Covariance matrix
    V1DD cov = Cov(v);

    // VCV matrix
    UINT k = 0; // Covariance offset
    for (UINT i=1; i<=n; i++)
    {
      for (UINT j=1; j<=n; j++)
      {
        V(i, j) = cov[j+k-1];
     if(i == j)
            V(i, j) *= 12; // Annualise variance
      }
      k+=10;
    }

    // V inverse
    Vi = Vi.Inv(V);

    Matrix A = oT * Vi * R;
    DBL a = A.Get(1,1);

    Matrix B = RT * Vi * R;
    DBL b = B.Get(1,1);

    Matrix C = oT * Vi * o;
    DBL c = C.Get(1,1);

    DBL d = b * c - a * a;

    Matrix Vio = Vi * o;
    Matrix ViR = Vi * R;

    Matrix g = (Vio * b - ViR * a) * (1.0 / d);
    Matrix h = (ViR * c - Vio * a) * (1.0 / d);
    Matrix w = g + h * (rtar / 100.0);

    return w;
}

// ...
// main.cpp
// ...
```

```
// Declare and call MLM() member function
// Target portfolio return = 9.0%
Matrix mlm = optimise.MLM(data, 9.0);

printf("\n Optimised weights = \n\n");
mlm.Print();
printf("\n");

//...
```

```
Console Output                                    —  □  ×

File:./data/10_hedge_funds.dat
Imported 720 values successfully!

Optimised weights =

-0.238
0.272
-0.148
-0.067
0.059
-0.092
-0.032
0.057
0.536
0.654
```

If we assume the hedge fund portfolio has a current value of $100m (AuM), Figure 6.6 shows the suggested investment for each fund for an expected 9.0% return based on the optimisation method. Note that for practical purposes, the existence of negative weights can be problematic, since this involves selling assets short.

6.2.3 The Global Minimum Variance Portfolio

The portfolio that minimises variance regardless of expected return is known as the *global minimum variance portfolio*. The global minimum variance portfolio has weights, $\mathbf{w}_{mvp}$ given by:

$$\mathbf{w}_{mvp}^T = (\mathbf{1}^T \mathbf{V}^{-1} \mathbf{1})^{-1} \mathbf{1}^T \mathbf{V}^{-1} = \frac{1}{C} \mathbf{1}^T \mathbf{V}^{-1} \qquad (6.20)$$

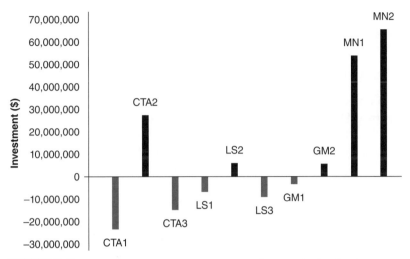

FIGURE 6.6 Amount of investment for each of the 10 hedge funds

For the global minimum variance portfolio (see Figure 6.7):

$$E[r_{mvp}] = \frac{A}{C}$$

$$\sigma[r_{mvp}] = \sqrt{\frac{1}{C}}$$

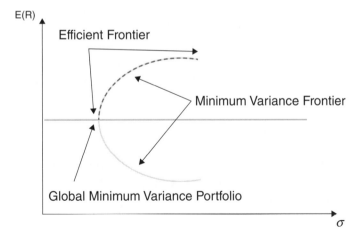

FIGURE 6.7 Efficient frontier, minimum variance frontier and global minimum variance portfolio

Indeed, portfolios on the minimum variance frontier with expected returns greater than or equal to $E[r_{mvp}]$ are called *efficient portfolios*.

6.2.4 Short Sale Constraints

The above optimisation problem assumes that *short selling* is allowed i.e. the weights can be negative. However, if no short selling is allowed, the optimisation problem can be modified by adding a further constraint. This has led to the investigation of restricted mean variance frontiers, where the weights are constrained to be non-negative. The optimisation problem can be written as:

$$\min \frac{1}{2} \mathbf{w}^T \Sigma \mathbf{w}$$

subject to the constraints:

$$\mathbf{w}^T \mathbf{R} = r^*$$

$$\sum_{i=1}^{N} w_i = 1$$

$$w_i \geq 0$$

It is also possible to impose a constraint on the maximum allowable investment limits (or *bounds*) on one or more of the assets in the portfolio i.e. $w_i \leq b$ where b is a real number. In general, a mean-variance optimisation attempts to find a constrained minimum of a scalar function ($\mathbf{w}^T \Sigma \mathbf{w}$) of several variables starting at an initial estimate. This is generally referred to as *constrained nonlinear optimisation*. However, such restricted minimum variance portfolios are much harder to deal with analytically, since they do not admit a general solution, one rather has to investigate the *Karush-Kuhn-Tucker* (KKT) conditions. KKT are first order necessary conditions for a solution in nonlinear programming to be optimal, provided that some regularity conditions are satisfied. Allowing inequality constraints, the KKT approach to nonlinear programming generalises the method of Lagrange multipliers, which allows only equality constraints.

In this chapter we have introduced the main ideas behind mean-variance optimisation and how an optimisation problem can be solved analytically using the method of Lagrange multipliers. Such techniques can prove invaluable to hedge fund managers who are often tasked with managing the risk of the fund and efficient allocation of resources across the portfolio. Indeed, many hedge fund managers develop increasingly complex optimisation problems utilising a range of performance metrics and risk measures.

Market Risk Management

We have encountered throughout the book the problems relating to the risk that the value of a hedge fund will decrease due to the impact of various market factors, for example changes in interest and foreign currency rates. Moreover, with the heightened publicity of recent financial events, hedge fund managers have come under increased pressure from investors and regulators to efficiently manage, monitor, measure and report such market risk inherent in their investment strategies. Indeed, experience has clearly shown that the measurement and management of extreme market conditions is of paramount importance for hedge funds.

Chapter 7 provides an introduction to market risk management for hedge funds and presents the fundamentals of quantitative risk measures and models used in the industry today. The chapter also covers some of the more advanced risk measures available that can more effectively manage risk in a hedge fund in light of the limitations encountered with traditional market risk measures.

7.1 THE RMetrics CLASS

As in the previous chapters we will be developing a further class RMetrics in much the same way as we did for the other classes. Source 7.1 shows the basic skeleton of the RMetrics class which will we again add to as we develop through the chapter.

SOURCE 7.1: SKELETON OF THE RMetrics CLASS

```
// RMetrics.h
#pragma once;

#include "Utils.h"
```

```
#include "Stats.h"

class RMetrics: public Stats
{
    public:
    RMetrics() {}
    virtual ~RMetrics() {}

    // Member function declarations
private:
    // Member variable declarations
    Utils m_utils;  // An instance of the Utils class};

// RMetrics.cpp
#include "RMetrics.h"
```

Again, the default constructor and destructor have been declared and defined in the header file by removing the semi-colon (;) and adding the opening and closing braces ({}). We have instantiated the Utils class and included the Utils.h header file so we can access member functions of these classes as we did before. Also, as with the PMetrics class, we have made RMetrics inherit from the Stats class since we will be making use of several methods available to us in the Stats class.

7.2 VALUE-AT-RISK

The *Value-at-Risk* (VaR)[1] for a portfolio of assets is the worst estimated loss over a given time horizon (e.g. monthly) at a specified level of confidence (e.g. 95%). That is, the riskiness of the hedge fund portfolio at a specific level of probability in the *left-tail* of the P&L distribution. VaR is often based on the assumption that asset returns follow a *normal distribution* and that the performance of the hedge fund portfolio is affected by a set of linear market factors. As discussed in Chapter 4, under such assumptions it is possible to describe the distribution of asset returns by just two statistical parameters i.e. μ and σ. That is, assuming that a distribution of monthly hedge fund P&Ls is characterised by a normal distribution, then, at a confidence $c\%$ there is an expected loss for the hedge fund of no more than z_α standard deviations (i.e. $z_\alpha\sigma$) below the mean over the next month.

For example, at a 95% confidence level (5th percentile or significance), 95% of the time the loss is expected to be no worse than 1.645σ. That is, the critical value is

---

[1] VaR is an example of a *downside risk* measure i.e. the likelihood that an investment will decline in value, or the amount of loss that could result from such a potential decline.

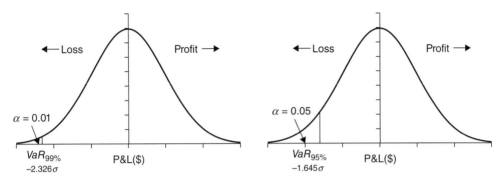

FIGURE 7.1   VaR at the 95% and 99% confidence levels

−1.645 indicating that there is a 5% probability that a particular value will be at least 1.645 standard deviations below the mean (i.e. -1.645σ) (see Figures 7.1 and 7.2). Table 7.1 shows the two most common confidence levels at 95% and 99% and their associated critical values z_α for the standard normal distribution.

For a standard normal distribution (i.e. $\mu = 0$ and $\sigma = 1$), the VaR for a hedge fund at a $100(1 - \alpha)\%$ confidence level, $VaR_{1-\alpha}$ is given by:

$$VaR_{1-\alpha} = Z_\alpha \tag{7.1}$$

Where Z_α is the critical value from the standard normal distribution at the required significance level, α. So, VaR at the $100(1 - \alpha)\%$ confidence level is defined as the

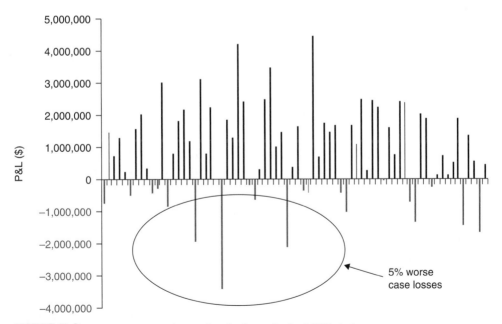

FIGURE 7.2   5% worse case losses for the hypothetical CTA index

TABLE 7.1   Critical values for 95% and 99% confidence
intervals

c	$\alpha = (1 - c)$	Critical value (z_α)
95%	5%	−1.64485363
99%	1%	−2.32634787

lower $100\alpha^{\text{th}}$ percentile of the P&L distribution (see Box 7.1). However, since μ and σ are parameters[2] of the hedge fund P&L distribution, $VaR_{1-\alpha}$ can be written more formally as:[3]

$$VaR_{1-\alpha} = \mu + Z_\alpha \sigma \qquad (7.2)$$

BOX 7.1:   QUANTILES AND PERCENTILES

Quantiles are points taken at regular intervals from a probability distribution. More formally, the quantile function for any probability distribution is the inverse of the *Cumulative Distribution Function* (CDF). Some *q*-quantiles have special names, for example:

- 4-quantiles are known as *quartiles*
- 100-quantiles are known as *percentiles*.

For an ordered set of data from smallest to largest the required percentile is a value that represents the number below which a certain percentage of the data fall e.g. the 5th percentile is the value below which 95% of all the observations fall.

Note that $VaR_{1-\alpha}$ scales with the volatility (see Box 7.2). VaR is usually reported on a monthly basis in negative dollar terms, which further emphasises that it is a measure of losses, or as an *absolute* positive dollar amount. In (7.2), since Z_α is negative, $VaR_{1-\alpha}$ will always be a negative value indicating a dollar loss. Some fund managers report VaR on a monthly basis in percentage terms so as to be consistent with the reporting of other risk measures. Note that VaR does not give any information about the amount of loss (i.e. the magnitude) expected in excess of VaR but only indicates

---

[2] Indeed, this is an example of the *parametric* method for calculating VaR.
[3] In (7.2), μ is used to centre the normal distribution, before subtracting the relevant number of σ's to get the VaR.

that $100\alpha\%$ of the time the loss to the hedge fund is estimated to be at least as bad over a certain period.

BOX 7.2: SQUARE ROOT RULE FOR VaR

If a series of hedge fund P&Ls are quoted in monthly or quarterly figures, then they can be transformed into an equivalent annualised series using a similar *square root rule* to that applied to standard deviation. To get the annualised figure, the original VaR is multiplied by the square root of the frequency representing the original time period e.g. 12 for monthly and 4 for quarterly.[4] More formally:

$$\text{annual } VaR_{1-a} = \text{monthly } VaR_{1-a} \times \sqrt{12}$$

$$\text{annual } VaR_{1-a} = \text{quarterly } VaR_{1-a} \times \sqrt{4}$$

7.3 TRADITIONAL VaR METHODS

There are generally three industry accepted methods for estimating VaR,[4] namely:

1. Historical simulation
2. Parametric method and
3. Monte-Carlo simulation.

Each has a different approach in terms of how they describe the distribution of losses. Monte-Carlo simulates data, historical simulation uses actual data, and the parametric approach utilises the data but only in order to generate the necessary parameters to characterise the distribution. All of these traditional measures of VaR have their strengths and weaknesses.

7.3.1 Historical Simulation

Of all the traditional VaR methods, the *historical simulation* (or non-parametric) method is probably the simplest to implement since only a set of historical hedge fund returns over a given time period is required. In general, the historical simulation method requires a relatively long history of returns in order to get a meaningful

---

[4] When considering daily P&Ls, practitioners generally assume there are 252 trading days in a year.

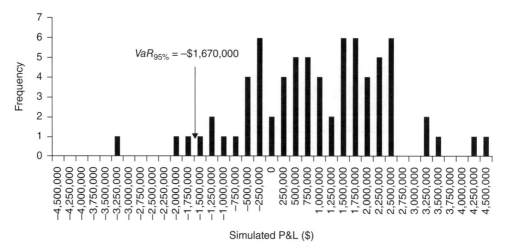

FIGURE 7.3   Histogram showing monthly VaR using historic simulation

value for VaR. That is, determining VaR for a hedge fund with only a few data points will not provide a good estimate of VaR. There are no specific assumptions about the return distribution only that the past is an accurate characterisation of the future. It is important to be careful not to draw any conclusions from the data if it is not large enough to be representative of the returns distribution in the future. In this sense, the assumption that historic monthly hedge fund returns are an accurate representation of the future is a major disadvantage of this method since there is no certainty that the past will replicate the future.

Estimating VaR by historical simulation involves calculating a series of simulated P&L values based on a set of historical hedge fund returns. A set of simulated P&Ls are generated for each hedge fund return and ordered smallest to largest using a relevant sorting algorithm. For a 95% confidence level (e.g. $\alpha = 0.05$), the $100\alpha = 5^{th}$ percentile in the sorted P&L is used to estimate VaR. That is, if we want to know the worse expected loss at 95% confidence then we look at the 5th percentile since, on an historical basis, the simulated P&L distribution tells us that 95% of the time we will not lose any more than this amount. Source 7.2 shows an implementation of the historical simulation method to estimate the monthly VaR at a 95% confidence level for the hypothetical CTA Index (i.e. *cta_index.dat*) with a value of $100m (AuM). The historical monthly VaR is estimated at $1 670 000 for a 95% confidence level i.e. over the next month there is a 5% probability that the CTA Index will lose $1 670 000 in value.[5] If required, to express VaR in percentage terms, simply divide by the current value of the hedge fund AuM (i.e. $100m). Figure 7.3 shows the

---

[5] With *historical simulation*, since *actual* monthly returns are used, the distribution is already assumed to be centred, so there is no need to subtract the relevant number of σ's from μ in order to get the VaR figure.

distribution of monthly P&L values and an indicator for the VaR at a 95% confidence level in the left-tail of the distribution at the 5th percentile. Note that there are losses in excess of the VaR value further to the left of the tail which indicates that VaR does not tell us anything about the actual magnitude of the extreme losses in the tail.

SOURCE 7.2: MONTHLY VaR AT 95% CONFIDENCE LEVEL USING HISTORICAL SIMULATION

```cpp
// ...
// RMetrics.h
// ...

DBL HistoricVaR(const V2DD& v, const int& p); // HistoricVaR()
// ...
// RMetrics.cpp
#include "RMetrics.h"

#include <algorithm> // For using sort()

DBL RMetrics::HistoricVaR(const V2DD& v, const int& p)
{
    UINT n = v.size();
    DBL tmp; // Declare a temporary holding variable
    DBL aum = 100000000.0; // Initialise to $100,000,000 (AuM)

    V1DD pnl; // Define a 1D vector of doubles for the P&L

    // Calculate Historic P&L
    for(UINT j=1; j<v[0].size(); j++)
    {
     for(UINT i=0; i<n; i++)
     {
            tmp = aum * (v[i][j] / 100.0);
            pnl.push_back(tmp);
     }
    }

    // Sort P&L in descending order
    sort(pnl.begin(), pnl.end());

    // Calculate pth percentile of ordered P&L e.g., 95th
    DBL pp =* (pnl.begin() + int(pnl.size() * (1 - p / 100.0)));
```

```
    return pp;
}

// ...
// main.cpp
// ...

// Create class instances
Import ctai;
RMetrics rmetrics;

// Declare and call GetData()
V2DD data = ctai.GetData("./data/cta_index.dat");

// Declare and call HistoricVaR() member function
DBL hvar = rmetrics.HistoricVaR(data, 95);

// Output results
cout << "\n Historic VaR = $" << fixed << setprecision(0) << hvar << '\n';
// ...
```

```
File:./data/cta_index.dat
Imported 72 values successfully!

Historic VaR = $-1670000
```

7.3.2 Parametric Method

The parametric method does not require all of the data that the historic simulation requires but may use the data to determine parameters of the hedge fund return distribution. If we generally assume the hedge fund returns are consistent with a normal distribution then we only need two parameters to characterise the distribution, namely the *mean, μ* and *standard deviation, σ*. That is, once we have determined those two parameters we no longer require all of the historical data to calculate VaR. Recall from (7.2) that the VaR can be written formally as:

$$VaR_{1-\alpha} = \mu + Z_\alpha \sigma \qquad (7.3)$$

Source 7.3 shows an implementation of this function to determine the monthly VaR at a 95% confidence level for the CTA Index with a current value of $100m AuM.

SOURCE 7.3:   MONTHLY VAR AT 95% CONFIDENCE LEVEL USING PARAMETRIC METHOD

```
// ...
// RMetrics.h
// ...


DBL ParametricVaR(const V2DD& v, const int& p); // ParametricVaR()


protected:
private:
        // Member variable declarations
    static const DBL z95;    // z-value for 95% confidence level
    static const DBL z99;    // z-value for 99% confidence level
    static const DBL e95;    // z-value for 95% confidence level (ES)
    static const DBL e99;    // z-value for 99% confidence level (ES)


// ...


// ...
// RMetrics.cpp

// Initialise static members of the RMetrics class
const DBL RMetrics::z95 = -1.64485363;
const DBL RMetrics::z99 = -2.32634787;
const DBL RMetrics::e95 = -2.06271281;
const DBL RMetrics::e99 = -2.66521422;


// ...


// ParametricVaR()
DBL RMetrics::ParametricVaR(const V2DD& v, const int& p)
{
    UINT n = v.size();
    DBL tmp; // Declare a temporary holding variable
    DBL aum = 100000000.0; // Initialise to $100,000,000 (AuM)


    V1DD pnl; // Define a 1D vector of doubles for the P&L
```

```cpp
  // Calculate historic P&L
  for(UINT j=1; j<v[0].size(); j++)
  {
    for(UINT i=0; i<n; i++)
    {
        tmp =  aum * (v[i][j] / 100.0);
        pnl.push_back(tmp);
    }
  }

  DBL mean = Mean(pnl, 1);        // Inherit Mean from the Stats class
  DBL std = StdDev(pnl, 'p', 1); // Inherit St. Dev. from the Stats class
  DBL pvar;

  // Check for correct confidence level
  if((p != 95) && (p != 99)) m_utils.ErrorChk("p must be 95 (95%) or 99 (99%)!");

  if(p == 95)
  {
   pvar = mean + std * z95;
  }
  else
  {
   pvar = mean + std * z99;
  }

  return pvar;
}

// ...
// main.cpp
// ...

// Create class instances
Import ctai;
RMetrics rmetrics;

// Declare and call GetData()
V2DD data = ctai.GetData("./data/cta_index.dat");

// Declare and call ParametricVaR() member function
DBL pvar = rmetrics.ParametricVaR(data, 95);

// Output results
cout << "\n Parametric VaR = $" << fixed << setprecision(0) << pvar << '\n';

// ...
```

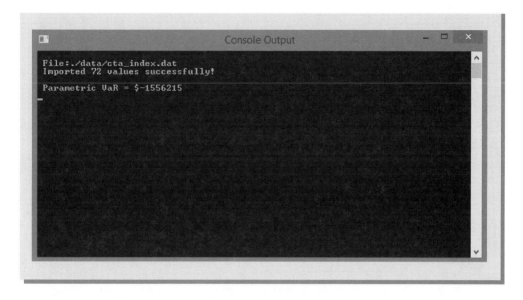

You will notice from Source 7.3 that we have used two slightly different member functions from the `Stats` class for the `Mean()` and `StDev()`. These are declared as type `DBL` and now take a `V1DD` input parameter as opposed to a `V2DD`. Source 7.4 shows how we have *overloaded* the member functions so we can use them to calculate a single value for the parametric VaR.

SOURCE 7.4: Mean() AND StDev() OVERLOADED MEMBER FUNCTIONS OF THE Stats CLASS

```cpp
// Stats.h
// ...

V1DD Mean(const V2DD& v, const int& f); // Mean()
DBL Mean(const V1DD& v, const int& f); // Mean()
V1DD StDev(const V2DD& v, const char& c, const int& f); // StDev()
DBL StDev(const V1DD& v, const char& c, const int& f); // StDev()
// ...
// ...
// Stats.cpp
// ...

// Mean()
DBL Stats::Mean(const V1DD& v, const int& f = 1)
{
    UINT n = v.size();
    double tmp; // Declare a temporary holding variable
```

```cpp
    DBL mean; // Declare a double for the Mean

    // Calculate mean using Eqn. (3.10)
     tmp = 0.0;
    for(UINT i=0; i<n; i++)
    {
       tmp += v[i];
    }
    tmp /= n;
    tmp *= (double)f; // Cast frequency (f) to double
    mean = tmp;

    return mean;
}

// ...

// StdDev() - Sample (s), Population (p)
DBL Stats::StdDev(const V1DD& v, const char& c, const int& f = 1)
{
    if((c != 's') && (c != 'p')) m_utils.ErrorChk("Type must be 's'
    (sample) or 'p' (population)!");

    UINT n = v.size();
    double tmp; // Declare a temporary holding variable

    DBL mean = Mean(v); // Declare a double for the Mean
    DBL std; // Declare a double for the St. Dev.

    // Calculate St. Dev. using Eqn. (3.12) or (3.13)
    tmp = 0.0;
    for(UINT i=0; i<n; i++)
    {
       tmp += pow((v[i] - mean), 2);
    }
    if (c == 's')
       tmp /= (n-1);
    else
     tmp /= n;
    //std.push_back(sqrt(tmp) * sqrt((double)f)); // Cast frequency (f) to
    double
    std = sqrt(tmp) * sqrt((double)f);

    return std;
}
// ...
```

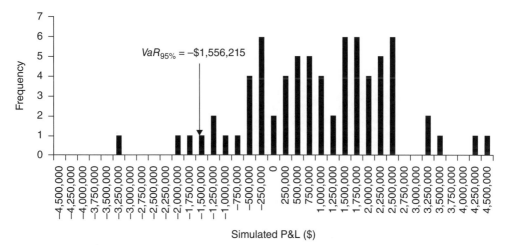

FIGURE 7.4 Histogram showing monthly VaR using the parametric method

Source 7.5 shows that the monthly VaR for a CTA Index valued at $100m (AuM) for a 95% confidence level is $1 556 215 i.e. there is only a 5% chance that the value of the CTA Index will fall by more than $1 556 215 over the next month. Figure 7.4 shows a histogram indicating the monthly VaR figure.

SOURCE 7.5: MONTHLY VaR AT 95% CONFIDENCE LEVEL USING MVaR METHOD

```
// ...
// RMetrics.h
// ...

DBL ModifiedVaR(const V2DD& v, const int& p);    // ModifiedVaR()

// ...

// ...
// RMetrics.cpp

// ModifiedVaR()
DBL RMetrics::ModifiedVaR(const V2DD& v, const int& p)
{
    UINT n = v.size();
    DBL tmp; // Declare a temporary holding variable
    DBL aum = 100000000.0; // Initialise to $100,000,000 (AuM)
```

```
    DBL z, zcf;
    DBL mvar;

    // Calculate historic P&L
    V1DD pnl;
    for(UINT j=1; j<v[0].size(); j++)
    {
     for(UINT i=0; i<n; i++)
     {
            tmp =  aum * (v[i][j] / 100.0);
            pnl.push_back(tmp);
     }
    }

    DBL mean = Mean(pnl, 1);        // Inherit Mean from the Stats class
    DBL std = StdDev(pnl, 's', 1); // Inherit St. Dev. from the Stats class
    DBL skew = Skew(pnl, 1);        // Inherit Skew from the Stats class
    DBL xskurt = XSKurt(pnl, 1);    // Inherit Excess Kurtosis from the Stats
                                       class

    // Check for correct confidence level
    if((p != 95) && (p != 99)) m_utils.ErrorChk("p must be 95 (95%) or 99 (99%)!");

    if(p == 95)
    {
      z = z95;
    }
    else
    {
      z = z99;
    }

    zcf = z+(((pow(z, 2) - 1)*skew) / 6) + (((pow(z, 3) - 3 * z) * xskurt) / 24)
    - ((((2*pow(z, 3)) - 5 * z) * pow(skew, 2) / 36)); // Cornish-Fisher variate

    mvar = mean + zcf * std;

    return mvar;
}

// ...
// main.cpp
// ...

// Create class instances
Import ctai;
RMetrics rmetrics;
```

```
// Declare and call GetData()
V2DD data = ctai.GetData("./data/cta_index.dat");

// Declare and call ModifiedVaR() member function
DBL mvar = rmetrics.ModifiedVaR(data, 95);

// Output results
cout << "\n Modified VaR = $" << fixed << setprecision(0) << mvar << '\n';

// ...
```

```
File:./data/cta_index.dat
Imported 72 values successfully!

Parametric VaR = $-1636085
```

7.3.3 Monte-Carlo Simulation

The *Monte-Carlo* (MC) method assumes that a series of hedge fund returns can be characterised by a stochastic (or probabilistic) model. MC methods are a widely used class of computational algorithms for simulating the behaviour of various physical and mathematical systems having been popularised by John von Neumann[6] and Nicholas Metropolis[7] to name but two. MC methods are distinguished from other simulation-based methods by being of a *stochastic* nature, that is the MC model includes a non-deterministic component that introduces a degree of uncertainty or randomness into the process through the use of *random number generators*.[8] The fundamental idea

---

[6] John von Neumann (1903–1957) was a Hungarian-American mathematician who made major contributions to a vast range of fields, including set theory, functional analysis, quantum mechanics, economics, game theory, computer science and numerical analysis.

[7] Nicholas Metropolis (1915–1999) was a Greek American physicist.

[8] MC simulations rely heavily on the sampling method and stability of the *random number generator* (RNG). For this reason, many financial houses spend a great deal of time, money and effort developing better and more robust RNGs.

behind the technique involves simulating 1000s of trials (or paths) that a series of hedge fund returns are likely to follow over a certain time period in the future based on a specific stochastic (or probabilistic) model. Each trial leads to a terminal value for the hedge fund P&L at the end of each simulation period. After 1000s of such runs, a simulated P&L distribution is obtained from which a VaR can be estimated at a preferred confidence level in much the same way as the historical simulation i.e. ordering the P&L and locating the relevant percentile P&L value i.e. loss. A drawback (although not a restrictive one) to the MC method is that the simulated P&L distribution relies on specific model parameters that a series of hedge fund returns are expected to be governed by in the future. Such a model is primarily driven by the mean, μ and standard deviation, σ of the hedge fund return distribution determined from historical data as well as the inclusion of a degree of subjective knowledge (i.e. market experience) into the model where necessary. The stochastic model is often the fundamental building block to many MC simulations being used extensively throughout the financial markets. For this reason, the MC method is a very powerful and much used technique for estimating VaR within the hedge fund community. Not only is the method robust and probabilistically strong, it is also an excellent way of building in *nonlinearity* into the return distribution and facilitating a better understanding of the characteristics of the use of derivatives within the portfolio with greater confidence. However, the MC method can easily become mathematically challenging and computational hungry especially when dealing with the inherent complexities of a particular hedge fund portfolio and strategy.

Table 7.2 gives a brief summary of the advantages and disadvantages of the three traditional methods of determining an estimate for VaR.

In addition to the estimation of VaR through either of the traditional methods, hedge fund managers will also carry out a variety of *stress tests* on the hedge fund

TABLE 7.2 Comparison of traditional VaR methods

Method	Advantages	Disadvantages
Historical Simulation	No assumptions about the return distributions.	Assumes data used in the simulation is representative of the future.
Parametric Method	Mathematically simple to understand and implement.	Strong assumptions about the hedge fund P&L distribution in terms of μ and σ. Less accurate for nonlinear instruments used within the hedge fund portfolio and strategy.
Monte-Carlo Method	Flexibility in terms of choosing the stochastic process and allows for the inclusion of subjective judgements into the model.	Most demanding in terms of computational resources. Can become mathematically complex and challenging.

portfolio. That is, the parameters and risk factors that affect hedge fund performance will be greatly magnified, for example raising the volatility over a particular period (e.g. by 100% or 200%) of the original value so as to cause a serious risk to the hedge fund of losing a catastrophic amount of money. This helps the fund manager understand where problems may be concentrated and allows them to be prepared for such events should they arise (however unlikely). Similarly, fund managers may run *scenario analyses* using a set of historical data and related parameters that covers a specific turbulent period in the financial markets, such as the financial crisis of 2008 or the more recent on-going European economic turmoil. This will also help the manager identify potential areas of large losses and allow them to develop strategic measures to alleviate such problems in the event of a similar financial disaster.

7.4 MODIFIED VaR

Despite the use of stress tests and scenario analysis, the most erroneous (and potentially damaging) assumption when using traditional VaR methods is that of hedge fund returns following a normal distribution. Clearly, this is invalid since it is well known that hedge fund returns generally have fatter tails and an asymmetric return distribution i.e. the presence of negative skewness and positive excess kurtosis. In order to address this issue many extensions to the traditional VaR methods have been put forward as better estimators of hedge fund market risk. Such methods either explicitly incorporate skewness and kurtosis into the model or focus primarily on the left-tails of the returns distribution where most of the extreme negative returns (i.e. large losses) occur.[9] One such extension is the *modified VaR* (MVaR). MVaR explicitly takes into account the third and fourth moments of the return distribution, namely skewness and kurtosis. That is, there is a branch of mathematics that is involved with power series expansions of quantile functions (see Box 7.1) such as those related to VaR. Indeed, the higher moments of the distribution are incorporated into the VaR measure using the celebrated *Cornish-Fisher expansion* (1937), such that the following power series can be obtained for the first few terms:

$$z_{cf} \approx z_\alpha + \frac{1}{6}\left(z_\alpha^2 - 1\right)s + \frac{1}{24}\left(z_\alpha^3 - 3z_\alpha\right)k - \frac{1}{36}\left(2z_\alpha^3 - 5z_\alpha\right)s^2 \qquad (7.4)$$

where z_{cf} is the Cornish-Fisher critical value from the normal distribution at the respective significance level, α. Note that when the return distribution is normally distributed, s and k will both be zero and therefore:

$$z_{cf} \approx z_\alpha \qquad (7.5)$$

---

[9] Many other distributions exist that offer better estimates of VaR for hedge funds e.g. Johnson distributions and simulated skewed Student's *t*-distribution.

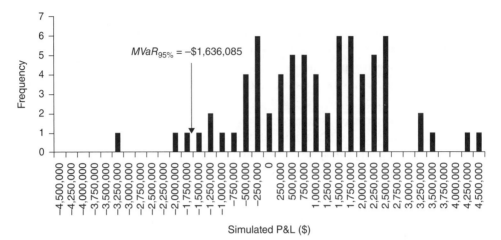

FIGURE 7.5 Histogram plot showing monthly MVaR

The MVaR at a confidence level $100 (1 - \alpha)\%$, $MVaR_{1-\alpha}$ is given by:

$$MVaR_{1-\alpha} = \mu + Z_{cf}\sigma \tag{7.6}$$

where μ is the mean of the returns, s is the sample skewness, k is the sample excess kurtosis and z_α is the critical value from the normal distribution at the required significance level, α. It turns out that using (7.6) leads to a more accurate measure of the VaR, however, there are limitations to this estimation. The higher the confidence level (e.g. 99%) the deeper we are in the left-tail of the distribution and this can lead to inaccurate results since the Cornish-Fisher expansion breaks down at these levels. MVaR is also unreliable when the returns distribution is highly skewed and fat-tailed. Source 7.5 shows that the monthly $MVaR_{95}$ is $1 636 085. Figure 7.5 shows a histogram indicating the monthly MVaR figure which is clearly higher when compared to the parametric VaR_{95} estimate of $1 556 215 for the CTA Index.

You will notice from Source 7.5 that we have similarly used two slightly different member functions from the `Stats` class for the `Skew()` and `XSKurt()`. These are again declared as type `DBL` and now take a `V1DD` input parameter as opposed to a `V2DD`. Source 7.6 shows how we have *overloaded* the member functions so we can use them to calculate a single value for MVaR.

SOURCE 7.6: Skew() AND XSKurt() OVERLOADED MEMBER FUNCTIONS OF THE Stats CLASS

```
// Stats.h
// ...
```

```cpp
V1DD Skew(const V2DD& v, const int& f); // Skew()
DBL Skew(const V1DD& v, const int& f); // Skew()
V1DD XSKurt(const V2DD& v, const int& f); // XSKurt()
DBL XSKurt(const V1DD& v, const int& f); // XSKurt()
// ...
// ...
// Stats.cpp
// ...

// Skew() - Sample Only
DBL Stats::Skew(const V1DD& v, const int& f = 1)
{
    UINT n = v.size();
    double tmp; // Declare a temporary holding variable

    DBL mean = Mean(v); // Declare a 1D vector of doubles for the Mean
    DBL std = StdDev(v, 's'); // Declare a 1D vector of doubles for the St. Dev.

    DBL skew; // Declare a 1D vector of doubles for the Skew

    // Calculate Skew using Eqn. (3.14)
    tmp = 0.0;
    for (UINT i=0; i<n; i++)
    {
     tmp += pow((((v[i] - mean) / std), 3);
    }
    tmp *= (double)n/((n-1)*(n-2));
    tmp /= sqrt((double)f); // Cast frequency (f) to double
    skew = tmp;

    return skew;
}

// XSKurt() - Sample Only
DBL Stats::XSKurt(const V1DD& v, const int& f = 1)
{
    UINT n = v.size();
    double tmp; // Declare a temporary holding variable

    DBL mean = Mean(v);
    DBL std = StdDev(v, 's');

    DBL xskurt;

    // Calculate XS Kurt. using Eqn. (3.15)
    tmp = 0.0;
    for (UINT i=0; i<v.size(); i++)
    {
```

```
    tmp += pow(((v[i] - mean) / std), 4);
    }


    tmp *= (double)n * (n+1) / ((n-1) * (n-2) * (n-3));
    tmp -= 3 * pow((double)(n-1), 2) / ((n-2) * (n-3));
    tmp /= (double)f; // Cast frequency (f) to double
    xskurt = tmp;


    return xskurt;
    }
// ...
```

Figure 7.5 shows a histogram indicating the monthly MVaR figure which is clearly higher when compared to the parametric VaR_{95} estimate of \$1 556 215 for the CTA Index.

7.5 EXPECTED SHORTFALL

Apart from the assumption that the P&L distribution is normal, VaR also fails to satisfy one of the concepts of a coherent risk measure. Artzner *et al.* (1999) have stated that a desirable measure of risk should satisfy four basic properties or axioms of risk, namely:

1. Must be monotonic i.e. if asset $X \geq 0$, VaR(X) ≤ 0 i.e. positive returns should not increase risk.
2. Must be sub-additive i.e. for assets X_1 and $X2$, VaR($X_1 + X_2$) $\leq$ VaR(X_1) + VaR(X_2) i.e. the risk of a portfolio of two assets should not be larger than the risk of the sum of the individual assets. If this were the case, then adding assets to a portfolio to reduce risk through diversification would not be possible.
3. Must possess positive homogeneity so for any positive real number, a, VaR(aX) = aVaR(X) i.e. increasing the size of the portfolio by a times should increase the risk by a multiple of a assuming all the assets within the portfolio remain the same in terms of weighting.
4. Must be translational invariant such that for any real number, a, VaR($X + a$) $\leq$ VaR(X) – a i.e. adding amount of cash (or risk-free asset) to the portfolio should result in a reduction of the risk by an amount a.

Unfortunately, VaR only satisfies three of the axioms of risk i.e. it fails to satisfy the sub-additive rule. For this reason, an alternative (and often complementary) measure of VaR was developed known as *expected shortfall* (ES)[10] which is discussed in

---

[10] Also known as Conditional VaR (CVaR), mean excess loss, beyond VaR or tail VaR.

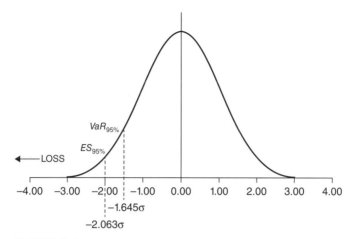

FIGURE 7.6 Comparison of ES and VaR at the 95% confidence level

detail in Rockafellar and Uryasev (2000). ES does satisfy all the axioms of risk and is considered a coherent risk measure. ES is the *conditional expectation* of loss given that the loss is beyond VaR i.e. the loss conditional on that exceeding VaR, that is:

$$ES_{1-\alpha} = E[-X \,|-X \geq VaR_{1-\alpha}] \tag{7.7}$$

where $ES_{1-\alpha}$ is the estimated ES at a $100(1-\alpha)\%$ confidence level. $E[X \,|B]$ is the conditional expectation of the random variable X given event B i.e. the average loss when VaR is exceeded. Yamai and Yoshiba (2002) show that (7.7) can be derived as:

$$ES_{1-\alpha} = E[-X \,|-X \geq VaR_{1-\alpha}] = \frac{E\left[-X \cdot I_{X \leq -VaR_{1-\alpha}}\right]}{\alpha} = -\frac{1}{\alpha \sigma_X \sqrt{2\pi}} \int_{-\infty}^{-VaR_{1-\alpha}} t \cdot e^{-\frac{t^2}{2\sigma_X^2}} dt$$

$$= -\frac{1}{\alpha \sigma_X \sqrt{2\pi}} \left[-\sigma_X^2 e^{-\frac{t^2}{2\sigma_X^2}}\right]_{-\infty}^{-VaR_{1-\alpha}} = \frac{\sigma_X}{\alpha \sqrt{2\pi}} e^{-\frac{VaR_{1-\alpha}^2}{2\sigma_X^2}} = \frac{\sigma_X}{\alpha \sqrt{2\pi}} e^{-\frac{q_\alpha^2 \sigma_X}{2\sigma_X^2}} = \frac{e^{-\frac{q_\alpha^2}{2}}}{\alpha \sqrt{2\pi}} \sigma_X$$

$$\tag{7.8}$$

where I_A is the indicator function whose value is 1 when A is true and 0 when A is false, and q_α is the $100\alpha^{th}$ percentile of the normal distribution. When the P&L distribution is normal, VaR does not have the problems pointed out by Artzner *et al.* (1999) and as such VaR does not have the issue of left-tail risk. That is, ES and VaR are simply scalar multiples of each other, because they are scalar multiples of the standard deviation, σ. For example, VaR at the 95% confidence level is -1.645σ, while ES at the same confidence level is -2.063σ as shown in Figure 7.6.

TABLE 7.3 ES critical values for 95% and 99% confidence intervals

c	$\alpha = (1 - c)$	Critical value (z_α)
95%	5%	−2.06271281
99%	1%	−2.66521422

Table 7.3 shows the two most common confidence levels at 95% and 99% and their associated critical values z_α for the ES. Note that both zES5 and zES1 have been negated in both cases to be consistent with the critical values for VaR and to indicate a loss in the left-tail of the P&L distribution.

Using the standard formula for $VaR_{1-\alpha}$ from (7.2), we have similarly:

$$ES_{1-\alpha} = \mu + Z_{ES\alpha}\sigma \tag{7.9}$$

where $Z_{ES\alpha}$ is the critical value from a normal distribution at the required significance level, α. This gives the estimate of the ES in the left-tail of the P&L distribution but of course it is only the average of the left-tail; the loss could be further along the distribution. Since ES is by definition more than VaR, ES is a more conservative estimate of VaR and thus why it is often used as a complement to traditional VaR measures. Source 7.7 shows that the monthly ES_{95} is $2 189 835.

SOURCE 7.7: MONTHLY VaR AT 95% CONFIDENCE LEVEL USING ES

```
// ...
// RMetrics.h
// ...

DBL ExShortfall(const V2DD& v, const int& p);   // ExShortfall()

// ...

// ...
// RMetrics.cpp

// ExShortfall()
DBL RMetrics::ExShortfall(const V2DD& v, const int& p)
{
    UINT n = v.size();
    DBL tmp; // Declare a temporary holding variable
    DBL aum = 100000000.0; // Initialise to $100,000,000 (AuM)
```

```
    DBL es;

    // Calculate historic P&L
    V1DD pnl;
    for(UINT j=1; j<v[0].size(); j++)
    {
     for(UINT i=0; i<n; i++)
     {
            tmp = aum * (v[i][j] / 100.0);
            pnl.push_back(tmp);
     }
}

    DBL mean = Mean(pnl, 1);        // Inherit Mean from the Stats class
    DBL std = StdDev(pnl, 's', 1); // Inherit St. Dev. from the Stats class
    DBL skew = Skew(pnl, 1);        // Inherit Skew from the Stats class
    DBL xskurt = XSKurt(pnl, 1);   // Inherit Excess Kurtosis
    from the Stats class

    // Check for correct confidence level
    if((p != 95) && (p != 99)) m_utils.ErrorChk("p must be 95 (95%) or 99 (99%)!");

    if(p == 95)
    {
     es = mean + e95 * std;
    }
    else
    {
     es = mean + e99 * std;
    }

    return es;
}

// ...
// main.cpp
// ...

// Create class instances
Import ctai;
RMetrics rmetrics;

// Declare and call GetData()
V2DD data = ctai.GetData("./data/cta_index.dat");

// Declare and call ExShortfall() member function
DBL es = rmetrics.ExShortfall(data, 95);
```

```
// Output results
cout << "\n Expected Shortfall = $" << fixed << setprecision(0) << es << '\n';

// ...
```

```
Console Output                                    – □ ✕

File:./data/cta_index.dat
Imported 72 values successfully!

Expected Shortfall = $-2189835
```

Figure 7.7 shows a histogram indicating the monthly ES figure which is clearly higher when compared to both the parametric VaR_{95} ($1 556 215) and $MVaR_{95}$ ($1 636 085). Clearly, ES is a much more conservative value than that of traditional VaR measures, offering a greater insight into the actual loss that could be faced over the next month in the value of the CTA Index.

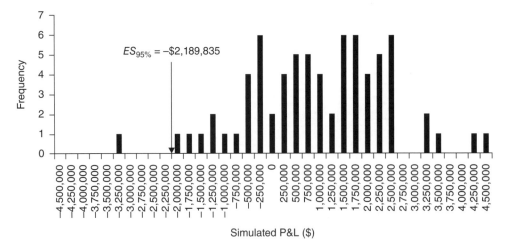

$ES_{95\%} = -\$2,189,835$

Simulated P&L ($)

FIGURE 7.7 Monthly ES at 95% confidence level

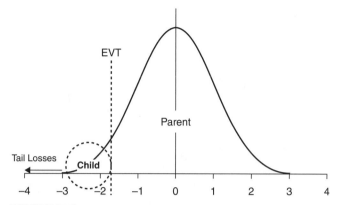

FIGURE 7.8   The 'child' and 'parent' distributions

Although ES is a more conservative and a useful indication of the estimated VaR at a particular confidence level, it is important to note that the ES figure does not give any indication of the severity of loss by which VaR is exceeded, only the expected (or average) loss. Moreover, if considering a 99% confidence in the left-tail then, for 100 P&L values, only 1% of 100 i.e. 1 value will be used to determine the average of the tail loss. In this case, it is necessary to investigate further the area of extreme losses with a deeper analysis of the left-tail of the P&L distribution.

7.6 EXTREME VALUE THEORY

We have already stated and discussed the fact that hedge fund return distributions have negative skewness and positive excess kurtosis i.e. the distribution does not adequately capture the probability where losses are severe i.e. left-tail. The thinner the tails of the normal distribution the larger will be the underestimate of the magnitude of the tail losses. This is where the branch of mathematics known as *extreme value theory*[11] (EVT) becomes a very useful tool to apply to such a problem. The theoretical foundations of EVT were first developed heuristically by Fisher and Tippett (1928) and have since been applied to insurance and finance by Embrecht *et al.* (1999). In general, EVT is the theory of modelling and measuring events which occur with very small probability. Clearly this is useful for analysing the extreme losses (i.e. left-tail) in the return (or P&L) distribution. Indeed, EVT is really the only method of extracting an accurate measure of the estimated loss given the limited data around an extreme event. Figure 7.8 shows the 'parent' distribution characterised by the first two moments (i.e. μ and σ) and a separate 'child' distribution that specifically characterises the distribution of losses in the left-tail of the parent distribution i.e. the extreme tail losses.

---

[11] Some hedge fund managers prefer to use *stress testing* and *scenario analysis* rather than EVT to estimate their exposures to tail events.

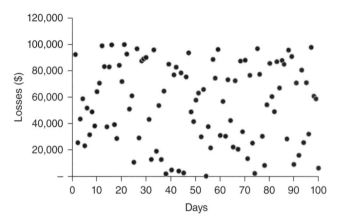

FIGURE 7.9 Hypothetical hedge fund losses over 100 days

Interpreting the main distribution in terms of the parent and then a child distribution within the parent gives us some qualitative understanding of how EVT is applied.

Consider Figure 7.9 that shows a hypothetical plot of the losses for a particular hedge fund over a 100-day period. Given such information the obvious next step is to try to characterise the losses over this period in some mathematical way. EVT offers two fundamental methods for such characterisations, namely the *block maxima* and *point over threshold* methods.[12]

7.6.1 Block Maxima

The *block maxima* (BM) method is based on subdividing the time period into a set of buckets (or blocks) of equal size. For example, Figure 7.10 reproduces the loss data given in Figure 7.9 for the hypothetical hedge fund over the 100-day period but divides the time into 10 blocks i.e. each block is a 10-day period that will contain a certain number of losses. Taking the maximum loss in each of the 10-day blocks gives us 10 local block maxima i.e. 10 data points which can be used to characterise (or fit) a probability distribution. This is often known as a *generalised extreme distribution* (GED).

Within the hedge fund arena, the block maxima method is the less preferred estimation of VaR using the EVT.

7.6.2 Peaks Over Threshold

The *peaks over threshold* (POT) method is a more modern and widely accepted method for estimating VaR although mathematically somewhat demanding. The basic

---

[12]Both methods are mathematically challenging and beyond the scope of this book and the reader is referred to cited references for more detailed explanations.

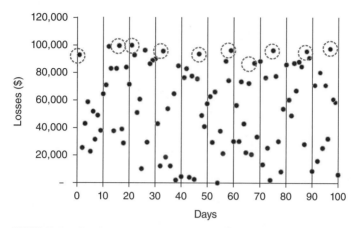

FIGURE 7.10   The largest losses in each 10-day block

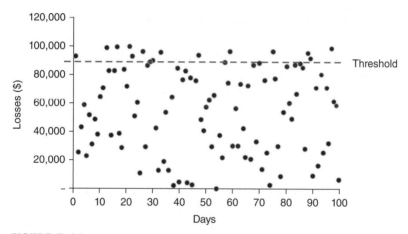

FIGURE 7.11   Losses over a threshold

idea behind the POT method is to choose a numerical threshold for which every loss over that threshold is considered an extreme loss. The number of data points over the threshold can be used to characterise (or fit) a probability distribution i.e. in this case it is known as the *generalised Pareto*[13] *distribution* (GPD). Figure 7.11 shows an example of a typical threshold in which only those losses exceeding $90 000 will be considered extreme relative to the value of the portfolio.

We have already seen in Chapter 4 how to consider a probability distribution in terms of a CDF i.e.

$$F(x) = P(X \leq x) \tag{7.10}$$

---

[13] Vilfredo Pareto (1848–1923) was an Italian engineer, sociologist, economist and philosopher. He made several important contributions to economics, particularly in the study of income distribution.

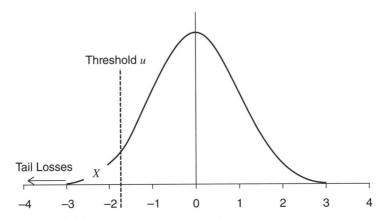

FIGURE 7.12 The random variable X and threshold u

i.e. for a given value, x, $F(x)$ is the probability that observed value of a random variable X will be at most x i.e. less than or equal to x. For EVT there is a different function to consider based on a conditional probability (in a similar way to how the conditional expectation models the ES). That is, for an excess distribution of the return variable X over a certain threshold u, the conditional probability distribution of $y = X - u$ such that $X > u$ can be written as:

$$F_u(y) = P(X - u \le y \,|\, X > u) \qquad (7.11)$$

The CDF is now the probability that $y = X - u$ i.e. the excess loss (or exceedance) over the threshold is less than or equal to y conditional on X exceeding the threshold u (Figure 7.12). One of the main theorems of EVT developed by Pickands (1975) states that for a reasonably high threshold, u, $F_u(y)$ can be approximated by the GPD which can be written as:

$$G(X) = \begin{cases} 1 - \left(1 + \dfrac{\xi y}{\beta}\right)^{-1/\xi} & \text{if } \xi \neq 0 \\[3mm] 1 - \exp\left(-\dfrac{y}{\beta}\right) & \text{if } \xi = 0 \end{cases} \qquad (7.12)$$

where $y = X - u$, $\xi = 1/\alpha$ is the shape parameter, α the tail index and β a simple scaling parameter. There are several approaches to estimating the parameters in (7.12), such as *maximum likelihood, elemental percentile method* and the *method of moments* described in the studies by Hosking and Wallis (1987), Grimshaw (1993) and Castillo and Hadi (1997).

An estimate of the VaR using the GPD approach described above can be written as:

$$VaR_{1-\alpha} = u + \frac{\beta}{\xi} \left(\left(\frac{N}{n_u} \alpha \right)^{-\xi} - 1 \right)$$ (7.13)

where N is the total number of data points, and n_u the number of data points that exceed the threshold u. Furthermore, the method can be extended so that the expected shortfall $ES_{1-\alpha}$ can be stated in terms of the $VaR_{1-\alpha}$, that is:

$$ES_{1-\alpha} = \frac{VaR_{1-\alpha}}{1-\xi} \frac{\beta - \xi u}{1-\xi}$$ (7.14)

For hedge funds, the amount of data in the tail of the returns distribution is often small and therefore leads to broad confidence intervals and weak significance estimates. Both the BM and POT method suffer from the problem of limited data although it is possible to reduce the time division in the BM method or lower the threshold for the POT technique to produce more data points to fit to the desired distribution.

In this chapter we have provided an introduction to the main quantitative risk measures from the traditional VaR approaches to some of the more advanced and challenging theoretical hedge fund market risk models. We have seen throughout the book that hedge fund returns usually have fatter tails and an asymmetric return distribution which clearly violates the assumption of a normal distribution that underlies traditional measures. In order to address such limitations many extensions to the traditional VaR methods have been developed as better estimates of hedge fund market risk. Such methods either explicitly incorporate skewness and kurtosis into the model or focus primarily on the left-tails of the return distribution where most of the large losses occur. Despite the availability of more robust and potentially accurate market risk models, it must be pointed out that the analysis here covers only one component of the risks associated with hedge funds. A more complete treatment would involve incorporating other equally important risks into the analysis. For example, the monitoring, management and reporting of credit, liquidity and operational risk should also be considered alongside market risk within a robust and effective hedge fund risk management process.

References

Amenc, N. and Martellini, L. (2003), Desperately seeking pure style indices. Working Paper, EDHEC Risk and Asset Management Research Centre.

Amenc, N., Sfeir, D. and Martellini, L. (2003), An integrated framework for style analysis and performance measurement, *Journal of Performance Measurement*, Summer, 35–41.

Anson, M. (2008), The beta continuum: from classic beta to bulk beta, *Journal of Portfolio Management*, 34(2), 11.

Artzner, P. Delbaen, F. Eber, J. M. and Heath, D. (1999), Coherent measures of risk, *Mathematical Finance*, 3(9), 203–228.

Castillo, E. and Hadi, A. (1997), Fitting the Generalised Pareto Distribution to data, *Journal of the American Statistical Association*, 92(440), 1609–1620.

Cornish, E. and Fisher, R. (1937), Moments and cumulants in the specification of distributions, *Review of the International Statistical Institute*, 5, 307–320.

Embrecht, P. Klüppelberg, C. and Mikosch, T. (1999), *Modelling Extremal Events*, Springer-Verlag, Berlin.

Favre, L. and Ranaldo, A. (2005), Hedge fund performance and higher-moment market models, *The Journal of Alternative Investments*, 8(3), 37–51.

Fisher, R.A. and Tippett, L.H.C. (1928), Limiting forms of the frequency distributions of the largest or smallest member of a sample. *Proceedings of the Cambridge Philosophical Society*, 24, 180–190.

Fung, W. and Hsieh, D.A. (2000a), Performance characteristics of hedge funds and commodity funds: Natural versus spurious biases, *Journal of Financial and Quantitative Analysis*, 35(3), 291–307.

Fung, W., and Hsieh, D.A. (2000b), The risk in hedge fund strategies: Theory and evidence from trend followers, *Review of Financial Studies*, 14, 313–341.

Fung, W. and Hsieh, D.A. (2004), Hedge fund benchmarks: A risk-based approach, *Financial Analysts Journal*, 60(5), 65–80.

Goodwin, T.H. (1998), The Information Ratio, *Financial Analysts Journal*, 54(4), 34–43.

Grimshaw, S.D. (1993), Computing maximum likelihood estimates for the Generalised Pareto Distribution, *Technometrics*, 35, 185–191.

Gupta, R.H., Kazemi, H. and Schneeweis, T. (2003), Omega as a performance measure. CISDM Research Paper, June.

Hosking, J.R.M. and Wallis, J.R. (1987), Parameter and quantile estimation for the Generalised Pareto Distribution, *Technometrics*, 29(3), 339–349.

Jensen, M.C. (1968), The performance of mutual funds in the period 1945–1964, *Journal of Finance*, 23(2), 389–416.

Kaplan, P.D. and Knowles, J.A. (2004), Kappa, a generalized downside risk-adjusted performance measure, *Journal of Performance Measurement*, 8(3), 42–54.

Keating, C. and Shadwick, W. (2002), A universal performance measure, *Journal of Performance Measurement*, 6(3), 59–84.

Kernighan, B.W. and Ritchie, D. (1978), *The C Programming Language*, Prentice Hall.

Lo, A.W. (2002), The statistics of Sharpe Ratios, *Financial Analysts Journal*, 58(4), 36–52.

Lhabitant, F.-S. (2007), *Hedge Funds – Quantitative Insights*, Wiley Finance.

Malkiel, B.G. (1995), Returns from investing in equity mutual funds 1971 to 1991, *Journal of Finance*, 50(2), 549–572.

Markowitz, H. (1952), Portfolio selection, *Journal of Finance*, 7(1), 77–91.

Merton, R.C. (1990), *Continuous-Time Finance*. Oxford, UK: Blackwell Publishing.

Modigliani, F. and Modigliani, L. (1997), Risk-adjusted performance, *Journal of Portfolio Management*, 23(2), 45–54.

Modigliani, L. (1997), Yes, you can eat risk-adjusted returns, *Morgan Stanley U.S. Investment Research*, 17 March, 1–4.

Pickands, J. (1975), Statistical inference using extreme order statistics, *Annals of Statistics*, 3(1), 119–131.

Rockafellar, R.T. and Uryasev, S. (2000), Optimisation of Conditional Value-at-Risk, *Journal of Risk*, 2(3), 21–41.

Sharma, M. (2004), A.I.R.A.P. – Alternative risk-adjusted performance measures for alternative investments, *Journal of Investment Management*, 2(4), 34–65.

Sharpe, W.F. (1963), A simplified model for portfolio analysis, *Management Science*, 9(2), 277–293.

Sharpe, W.F. (1964), Capital Asset Prices: A theory of market equilibrium under conditions of risk. *Journal of Finance*, 19(3), 425–442.

Sharpe, W.F. (1992), Asset allocation: Management style and performance measurement, *Journal of Portfolio Management*, 18(2), 7–19.

Sharpe, W.F. (1994), The Sharpe Ratio, *Journal of Portfolio Management*, Fall, 49–58.

Sortino, F.A. and Price, L.N. (1994), Performance Measurement in a downside risk framework, *Journal of Investing*, 3(3), 59–64.

Stutzer, M. (2000), Portfolio Performance Index, *Financial Analysts Journal*, 56(3), 52–61.

Treynor, J.L. (1952), Toward a theory of market value of risky assets. Unpublished manuscript printed as Chapter 2 in *Asset Pricing and Portfolio Performance*. Edited by Robert A. Korajczyk (1991), Risk Books.

Jones, A.W. (1949), Fashions in forecasting, *Fortune*, 180, 88–91.

Xu, X.E., Liu, J. and Loviscek, A.L. (2009), Hedge fund attrition, survivorship bias, and performance: Perspectives from the Global Financial Crisis. Working Paper, Seton Hall University.

Yamai, Y. and Yoshiba, T. (2002), On the validity of Value-at-Risk: Comparative analyses with expected shortfall, *Monetary and Economic Studies*, 20(1), 57.

Index

Note: Page references in *italics* refer to Figures; those in **bold** refer to Tables